# Tajikistan
# in the New Central Asia

# Tajikistan
# in the New Central Asia

Geopolitics, Great Power Rivalry and Radical Islam

LENA JONSON

I.B. TAURIS

LONDON · NEW YORK

Reprinted in 2009 by I.B.Tauris & Co Ltd
6 Salem Road, London W2 4BU
175 Fifth Avenue, New York NY 10010
www.ibtauris.com

In the United States of America and in Canada distributed by Palgrave Macmillan,
a division of St. Martin's Press, 175 Fifth Avenue, New York NY 10010

First published in 2006 by I.B.Tauris & Co Ltd
Copyright © Lena Jonson 2006

International Library of Central Asian Studies 2

ISBN 978 1 84511 293 6

A full CIP record for this book is available from the British Library
A full CIP record is available from the Library of Congress

Library of Congress Catalog Card Number: available

Printed and bound in India by Replika Press Pvt. Ltd.
Camera-ready copy edited and supplied by the author

# CONTENTS

# LIST OF MAPS AND TABLES

# ACRONYMS AND ABBREVIATIONS

| | |
|---|---|
| ASSR | Autonomous Soviet Socialist Republic |
| BISNIS | Service for Business Information on the New Independent States |
| CACO | Central Asian Cooperation Organization |
| CAEU | Central Asian Economic Union |
| CENTCOM | Central Command (US) |
| CIS | Commonwealth of Independent States |
| CNR | Comission of National Reconciliation |
| CP | Communist Party |
| CST | Collective Security Treaty (1992) |
| CSTO | Collective Security Treaty Organization |
| DP | Democratic Party |
| ECO | Organization for Economic Cooperation |
| EEC | Eurasian Economic Community |
| EU | European Union |
| EUR | euro |
| EXBS | Export Control and Border Security (programme) (US) |
| FDI | foreign direct investment |
| FSB | Federal Security Service (Federal'naya Sluzhba Bezopasnosti) (Russia) |
| FY | fiscal year (US) |
| G8 | Group of Eights industrialized countries |
| IMF | International Monetary Fund |
| IMU | Islamic Movement of Uzbekistan |
| IRP | Islamic Revival Party |
| MRD | Motorized Rifle Division |
| NATO | North Atlantic Treaty Organization |
| NGO | non-governmental organization |
| OSCE | Organization for Security and Co-operation in Europe |
| PDP | People's Democratic Party |
| PFP | Partnership for Peace |
| RAO UES | Russian Joint Stock Company Unified Energy Systems |
| RUR | Russian rouble |
| SCO | Shanghai Cooperation Organization |
| SDP | Social Democratic Party |

| | |
|---|---|
| SP | Socialist Party |
| SSR | Soviet Socialist Republic |
| TACIS | EU programme for the republics of the former Soviet Union |
| UK | United Kingdom |
| UN | United Nations |
| USAID | US Agency for International Development |
| USD | US dollar |
| UTO | United Tajik Opposition |

# Acknowledgements

The first time I visited Tajikistan was in April–May 1997. The civil war had not yet ended, and there was still almost two months to go until the General Peace Agreement was to be signed. The impact of the war was visible in the battered buildings and infrastructure, and the lawless traffic in the centre of Dushanbe. The non-civil character of daily life was reflected when, when one day after the failed attempt to assassinate the president I went by air from Dushanbe to Khujand, and 11 passengers sat with Kalashnikovs in their laps. People left the streets as soon as darkness fell. I returned to Tajikistan in January 2002 to work at the OSCE Mission at a time when the United Nations considered Tajikistan to be as dangerous as Afghanistan. As summer 2002 came closer the true character of Dushanbe appeared—a calm, friendly and beautiful little capital. The stabilization of the security situation resulted in people staying out late on the streets to enjoy the warm early summer evenings chatting with friends. Hope for a better future had awakened again. I returned for a month in summer 2004, and again in 2005, when construction work was under way everywhere. By then I knew enough people to bump into several acquaintances when strolling along Rudaki Avenue, and I had friends with whom I could discuss different aspects of the political and cultural life of Tajikistan.

I am grateful to many people who helped me to learn more about Tajikistan. The first to mention in this regard are my close friends Saodat Olimova and Muzaffar Olimov. As is obvious from the footnotes, I have been able to draw a great deal from their publications at the Sharq Independent Research Institute in Dushanbe. I also want to thank friends like Parviz, Faridun, Abdugani and Abduali, and many more people could be mentioned who generously invited me to come and listen in at seminars, conferences and round table discussions.

For constructive comments on the manuscript I want to thank colleagues and friends back home in Stockholm—Olav Knudsen, Torgny Hinnemo, Bo Utas, Gudrun Persson, Ingmar Oldberg, Gösta Lavén and Björn Hagelin. Without the support of my home institute, the Swedish Institute of International Affairs, I would not have had the opportunity to concentrate on writing this book. I have benefited greatly from the comments and knowledge of all the colleagues, too numerous to mention, to whom I have presented parts of my work at different conferences. Writing in a foreign language, I am grateful to Eve Johansson for language help. Mirja Juntunen gave generously of her time and expertise to lay out the text and prepare it for publication. I express my gratitude to all these people, but I alone am responsible for any errors that remain.

Last, but certainly not least, I want to express my gratitude for the personal encouragement and support of those closest to me.


Lena Jonson

Map 1  Tajikistan

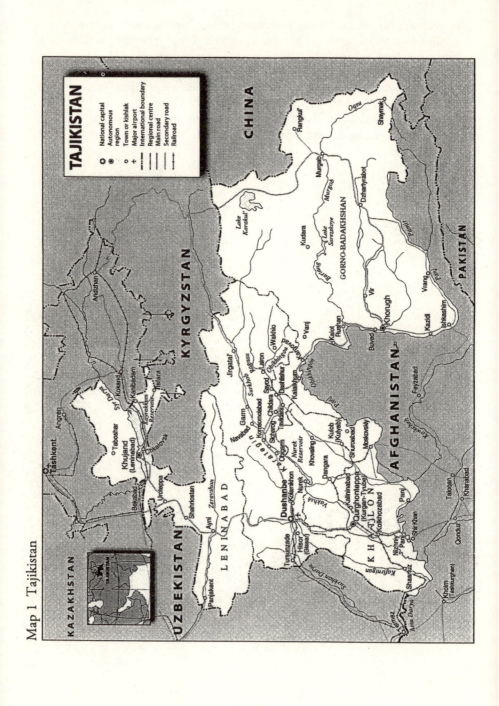

Map 2 Historical Boundaries of the Samanid Empire, the Bukhara Emirate and the Khiva Khanate, and Contemporary State Borders

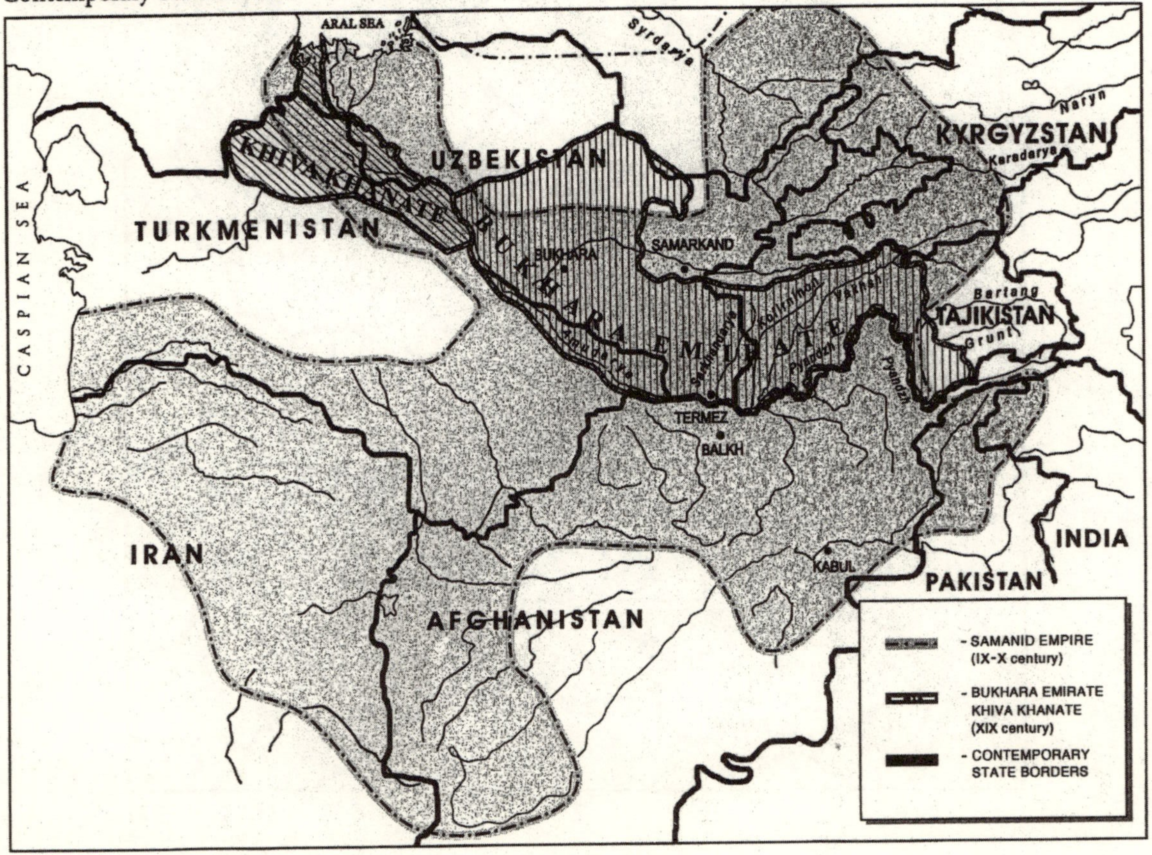

Map 3 Tajikistan: Rail and Road Exits

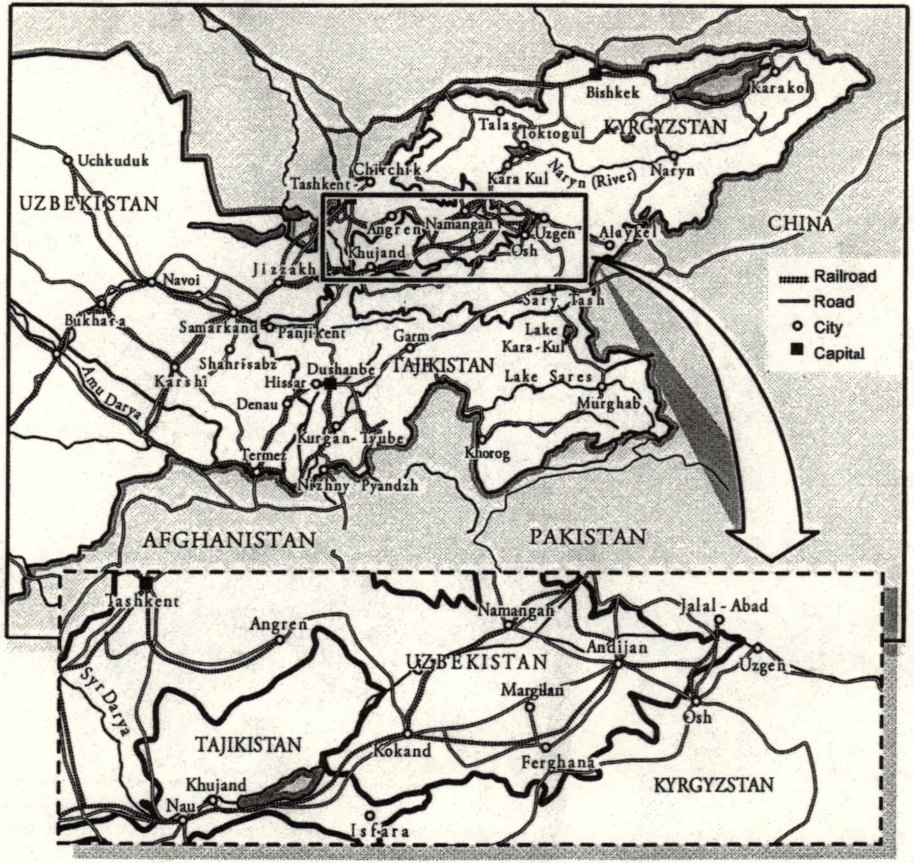

# PART I

# THE BACKGROUND

# 1

# INTRODUCTION

Most studies of Central Asia are carried out from the perspective of the policies and interests of the big powers engaging in the region, and thus focus on the competition between these states in a contemporary repetition of the so called 'Great Game'. In such analyses the region looks like a chessboard on which the individual states, and the small states in particular, are nothing but pawns to be moved around by the large powers. This study takes the opposite perspective. It raises the question: How does a small state act in a period of change as big powers direct their attention towards the region where it is located?

This book is about the foreign policy of Tajikistan during the first four years after the terrorist attacks of 11 September 2001 in New York and Washington. The attacks led the United States to engage not only in Afghanistan but also in Uzbekistan, Kyrgyzstan and Tajikistan. This is a period of increasing foreign engagement and growing concern with geopolitical change in the region. It is also a period when the Central Asian regimes were challenged from within to a degree not seen before, as demonstrated by the fall of the regime of President Askar Akaev in Kyrgyzstan in March 2005 and the riots in Andijan in the Uzbek part of the Fergana Valley in May that year.

The study deals with three sets of questions: What policy changes have there been in Tajik foreign policy? Why? And what are the possible implications of these policy changes?

## Towards an Independent Foreign Policy?

Since independence in 1991, Tajikistan's foreign policy has focused on two main tasks—surviving as a nation and securing international assistance in order to maintain national security. The Tajik civil war (1992–97) left the country and the regime highly dependent upon Russia for national and regime security. It resulted in former Soviet military troops staying in Tajikistan under the label of Russian peacekeeping troops on a Commonwealth of Independent States (CIS) mission, and an increase in the numbers of former Soviet border troops to protect the Tajik–Afghan border. These troops guaranteed not only Tajikistan's national security but also, since the late 1992, the regime of President Emomali Rakhmonov. Tajikistan supported Russia's initiatives for closer bilateral and multilateral security cooperation in the Central Asian region. Against the background of the Taliban takeover of power in Kabul in 1996 and the increasing concern of the regime in Uzbekistan about its own domestic security situation—for which it partly blamed Tajikistan— Russia's military presence was a security guarantee.

Yet the dependence on Russia had another side as well. The civil war and continued domestic turmoil reduced Tajikistan's external contacts, and the close cooperation with Russia further contributed to its international isolation. Other foreign governments stayed away. If any country in Central Asia was considered Russia's backyard, it was Tajikistan.

The terrorist attacks on the World Trade Centre in New York and the Pentagon in Washington on 11 September 2001 were events with major consequences for Central Asia. As the United States initiated the bombing of Afghanistan on 7 October 2001, its interest in the neighbouring countries, among them Tajikistan, increased. The course of events after 11 September created a completely new situation for Tajikistan, which without doubt brought new opportunities if only the Tajik government would make use of them. A 'window of opportunity' opened as the USA increased its engagement in Central Asia. During the following years Tajikistan's foreign policy was activated, its relations with Western and Asian countries expanded, and its foreign policy was diversified. Its participation in the US-led anti-terrorist coalition became an instrument for Tajikistan to reach out to the world. As a result, its partnership with Russia was reduced in relative terms. Although partnership with Russia remained important to Tajikistan, Tajikistan started to balance its policy in relation to Russia with the help of the wider cooperation with other big powers.

Tajikistan thus developed its foreign relations, although it was still bound by a framework of agreements with Russia and Russian-led security arrangements. Previous ties with Russia were kept, but a new 'balancing' foreign policy in relation to Russia was in the making.

After independence, Tajikistan's economic development remained heavily dependent on Russia's willingness to assist. The Tajik leadership therefore saw the limited Russian economic engagement and investment as a problem. It was in sharp contrast to the immense Russian military presence. To Tajikistan—in urgent need of assistance for economic development after the end of the civil war—developments after 11 September brought new prospects for economic assistance and potential partnerships with foreign governments and international organizations. The developments improved the general security situation in the region as they provided a chance to normalize relations with the two neighbouring states which had previously been considered major threats to Tajikistan's security, Afghanistan and Uzbekistan. In general, the post-11 September situation opened up new opportunities for Tajikistan to tackle its major security problems.

Not only was Tajikistan a weak power on the international scene, it was also a weak state. The regime was extremely fragile, first of all as a result of the five-year-long civil war. The post-2001 situation helped the regime to reinforce its position, but it remained fragile in the way that all the authoritarian Central Asian regimes were fragile. This was demonstrated by the March 2005 revolution in Kyrgyzstan, which sent shivers down the spines of all the Central Asian presidents. The domestic crisis in Uzbekistan, starting with the riots in Andijan in May, suggested that the upheaval in Kyrgyzstan was not to be an isolated event. Tajikistan's parliamentary elections, held at the same time as the Kyrgyz elections, in February 2005, did not reveal any comparable political discontent, but even so it becomes natural to ask how sustainable the new Tajik foreign policy is if the stability of the regime is in question.

This study will analyse the factors that may explain Tajik foreign policy during the first four years after September 2001. How important are changes in the international environment, that is, the ongoing changes in the region, for Tajik foreign policy making? What role do factors on the Tajik domestic scene play? Moreover, what changes reveal these factors and what do they suggest about future trends and prospects? Tajikistan is developing relations with Western countries, but in what direction will it orient itself in the long run? Russia, after a period of reduced influence, has reactivated its policy in Central Asia since 2002. Meanwhile Tajikistan is the only Persian-speaking country of the former Soviet Union with a long history of being included in various empires. It is a Muslim country where a religious revival is in progress. Tajikistan's present close partnership with Russia and the United States cannot be taken for granted in the long term.

But a study of Tajikistan is of interest for other reasons as well. It gives a unique chance, a kind of 'analytical keyhole', to look into processes going on in Central Asia with regard to shifts in the balance of different foreign powers engaging in the region, as well as the regional and domestic challenges the region faced and faces. At first glance Tajikistan may seem to be only one small country among several Central Asian countries, but its geographical location gives it a crucial role for the security of Central Asia as a whole. With large groups of ethnic kin in Afghanistan and Uzbekistan, as well as a large Uzbek minority of its own, Tajikistan is receptive to influences from these countries. It is also capable of influencing these states by itself.

Tajikistan's location makes it a gateway to Central Asia from Afghanistan for drugs, weapons, people and radical ideas. It is also crucial for transit in the opposite direction. From having been a transit country during the period of Taliban rule in Afghanistan for most material assistance to the anti-Taliban Northern Alliance, Tajikistan today is taking part in the post-war reconstruction of Afghanistan. Its location next to Uzbekistan makes Tajikistan not only vulnerable in relation to Uzbekistan but also a strategic ally of any other state that is concerned about the developments in Uzbekistan.

The domestic politics of Tajikistan makes the country unique on the former Soviet territory. It is the only post-Soviet state to have the experience of national reconciliation after a civil war and of integrating an Islamic political opposition. At the same time, the regime presents authoritarian characteristics, although of a 'softer' kind than some other Central Asian regimes. The international engagement in Tajikistan has created opportunities for future economic and democratic reform, but the standard of living for most of the population remains extremely low. The state of the economy is well illustrated by the fact that, out of a population of 6.2 million inhabitants, some 600,000 live in Russia as migrant labour. A potential for social unrest is thus embedded in the social and economic situation.

It remains an open question whether the government is capable of delivering reforms and a better future. Against the background of the Rose, Orange and Tulip revolutions on former Soviet territory, the Tajik regime is challenged by a secular opposition that is strengthened by the spread of transnational values of human and democratic rights. There is also fear that if the government policy fails many people will follow the siren calls of radical Islamism and its promises of a brighter future.

A study of Tajikistan thus encapsulates processes and trends of a sub-region consisting of Tajikistan, Afghanistan and Uzbekistan. The development of Tajikistan has to be studied as part of this regional sub-system. Moreover, Tajikistan is becoming an attractive partner for many Western and Asian governments, not least the US government. Although it has no large-scale resources of oil or gas, Tajikistan is rich in coal, marble, gold, silver, tungsten, lead, uranium and zinc, and has 65 per cent of Central Asia's water resources.[1] It is a strategic country on the new global political map. Around it, international and regional powers will either compete in the modern version of a 'Great Game' with an enlarged number of players, or cooperate—to the benefit of Tajikistan.

Not only has the USA cast its eyes on Tajikistan; Tajikistan is also developing relations with Iran, China and India, as well as with all the major international organizations and financial institutions. Although it is a close ally of Russia, Tajikistan's rapidly growing contacts with the outside world reflect the reconfiguring of international contact and cooperation in the region. In sum, several of the determinants for the future of Central Asia's security meet in Tajikistan.

Lastly, Tajikistan is of interest as a small state that lives in the shadow of a big power and former regional hegemon—Russia. What enables a small power to change its foreign policy course? A small power is most often regarded as a victim of circumstances and as being dependent on the goodwill of the big powers. What possible assets can a small power have? The case of Tajikistan can shed light on both the problems and the foreign policy options of a small state.

## The Foreign Policy of a Small Power

What is a small state? Tajikistan, with a population of some 6.5 million inhabitants (in 2003) and a territory of 143,000 square kilometres (km), of which only 6–7 per cent is arable land, is of course small. Yet, although small size in a literal sense may be a contributing factor, it is the relationship to a dominant power which defines the smallness. As one 'small state' scholar writes, 'It is not the size of the unit, but the kind of relationship that is of interest here. While continuing to use the term small state, it is the experience of power disparity and the manner of coping with it that should be our focus'.[2] Small states or small powers are a special category since their specific position in relation to the big power may make them behave in a special way. As the American scholar Robert L. Rothstein writes, 'The problem of comprehending the behavior of small powers involves more than noting its weaknesses. It also involves understanding that the inferior power status of Small Powers, which they tend to imagine as a permanent feature of their existence, may have created consistent patterns of behavior as a response to that situation'.[3]

Most scholars come to the conclusion that there are basically two approaches available for a weak state choosing to compensate for its weakness—'policies to remove or isolate itself from power conflicts, or policies in which it chooses to draw on the strength of others to insure its own security'.[4] In other words, the available alternatives are neutrality/non-alignment or alliance/alignment. Much research has been done on neutrality as an option for small states, on the examples of the small European neutral countries. Non-alignment in the form of the Non-Aligned Movement, created in 1955, was a major option for Third World countries at the height of the cold war. Still, alliance/alignment is a far more common alternative. It consists of two very different options—*bandwagoning* and *balancing*. These concepts rest on distinct assumptions about how states will select their alliance partner—*with* or *against* the principal external threat. Stephen M. Walt defines them as follows: balancing is 'when states join alliances to protect themselves from states or coalitions whose superior resources could pose a threat'; while bandwagoning refers to alignment with the threatening or stronger state.[5]

Walt writes that 'The belief that states form alliances in order to prevent stronger powers from dominating them lies at the heart of traditional balance of power theory'.[6] A large power may be a threat to a small power in the sense that it constitutes a threat to its territorial integrity, or by preventing the small power from adopting an independent policy. At the same time this same power may provide guarantees against other kinds of external threat to the security of the small power. A balancing policy, according to Walt, can be 'part of a wider political strategy designed to avert the development of potentially dangerous configurations of power'.[7] It can also be part of an effort 'to curb a potential hegemon before it becomes too strong'.[8]

Most scholars agree that bandwagoning is more common among small powers than among large powers. The logic of bandwagoning is a form of appeasement, and for a small state in the neighbourhood of a powerful state which clearly demonstrates its power it is highly probable that it will try to appease the large one.[9] Roy Allison writes,

> ... the preoccupation of local governments with regime security has also been an important factor encouraging Central Asian states to bandwagon with Russia. This concern has been sufficiently strong for them to be prepared to delegate some of their decision-making prerogatives to accommodate Russian preponderance. Russia has been willing to make military and financial contributions to the domestic political survival of rulers and ruling coalitions, irrespective of their political complexion or of normative concerns. Indeed, one can argue that 'those governmental patterns of association that have made a positive contribution to the domestic survival of post-Soviet governments have been more likely to endure'.[10]

Tajikistan is a small power in relation to Russia. Russia has dominated its territory since the 1870s but incorporated it only in the 1920s. Russia also continued to dominate after Tajikistan became an independent state in 1991. Tajikistan is also a small power in relation to Uzbekistan, to which it was subordinated during the period 1924–29, as the Tajik Autonomous Soviet Republic under the Soviet Socialist Republic of Uzbekistan (see chapter 2).

Russia constitutes no physical threat to Tajikistan. Instead Russia has acted a guarantor of Tajikistan's security against external threats.

Nevertheless, as the old hegemon which had been used to dominating and manipulating, Russia continued to set the parameters of Tajik foreign policy also after the latter became independent. To understand Tajikistan's policy towards Russia these different aspects have to be taken into consideration.

Instead the physical threats to Tajikistan have come from its neighbours—first and foremost Afghanistan but also Uzbekistan. From the early 1990s Afghanistan was the more serious threat as a failed state; turmoil, radical Islamism, weapons, drugs, and rebel fighters spread out from Afghan territory. By military intervention and/or support to Tajik rebel commanders, Uzbekistan also constituted a direct threat to Tajikistan's national security. A strong power with a large population and Central Asia's largest army, Uzbekistan continued to take unilateral measures against Tajikistan in order to ensure its own national security, thereby meddling in Tajik affairs, using Tajikistan's energy dependence for political pressure, closing the Uzbek–Tajik border, and restricting Tajikistan's contacts with the outside world. With the overthrow of the Taliban regime in 2001, the threat to Tajikistan from Afghanistan was reduced, at least temporarily, but the Uzbek authorities' fear and concern about Uzbekistan's domestic security continued unabated.

This study includes an analysis of Tajikistan's policy towards these two neighbouring states, and how Tajikistan's relations with the big powers can constitute a guarantee against threats and challenges from the neighbours.

Can small states have any advantages when dealing with large powers? Many scholars have pointed to how often a 'strong' state experiences problems in achieving its objectives when it attempts to influence the behaviour of 'weak' states. This indicates that small states may have levers of their own. How, asks K. J. Holsti, 'have "small" states gained trading privileges and all sorts of diplomatic concessions from those nations with great economic wealth and military power?'.[11] This raises the question what assets a small power like Tajikistan may have to help it improve its own standing in international politics and in relation to the big powers engaged in Central Asia. What possible assets does the Tajik government have to hand, and how have they been used in the post-September 2001 world?

## Foreign Policy Change

In the Western academic literature, policy change has been roughly defined as major changes, which alter a country's policy fundamentally, and minor, natural adjustments to changing conditions, which governments always make. Charles Hermann identifies four different levels or degrees of change. The most drastic involves a change of the international orientation of a state, that is, a redirection of the actor's entire orientation to world affairs which requires a basic shift in the actor's role and activities. A less drastic level is change to the way in which major problems and goals are defined, which means that the original problems or goals that policy addressed may be replaced or simply abandoned. A lower level of change again is programme change, that is, change of methods and means (instruments of statecraft) while the purposes remain the same; and, finally, the lowest level consists of adjustment, changes or refinements while actual policy remains unchanged.[12] This study of Tajik policy looks for change at the three first mentioned levels according to Hermann's categories.[13]

Tajik foreign policy will be analysed from two aspects. First, Tajikistan's policy towards the large powers that are engaging in the region, and towards the two most relevant neighbouring states, will be examined in order to trace possible shifts with regard to bandwagoning and balancing Russia. Second, we will discuss possible shifts in foreign policy orientation based on identification with states and values.

It is an interesting question in what direction Tajikistan may orient itself in the long term. The answer can only be found by looking beyond the present constellations of the region, to history and the country's cultural affinities. After the break-up of the Soviet Union, the questions where the Central Asian countries would look for foreign partners, with whom they would identify and what kind of political model they would follow became topics of concern. Searching for guiding lights for their policy, the Central Asians looked to Muslim countries, and first of all to Turkey and Iran. They hoped that close cooperation with Muslim countries would help them overcome their own economic crisis. Turkey and Iran provided different political models—respectively, a secular state in a Muslim society and a theocracy. It soon became obvious, however, that 'in interstate relations ideologies were of minor importance compared to a sober pragmatic approach to the economic and political advantages of cooperation', as Russian scholar Aleksei Malashenko writes.[14] Does this hold true in a long-term as well as a short-term perspective?

In discussing Tajikistan's possible foreign policy reorientation in the future as related to shifts in the identification and values of the country, five orientations will be identified: (a) a pan-Islamic identity; (b) a secular European/Western identity; (c) a secular European/Russian identity; (d) a culturally–linguistically-based Iranian identity; and (e) a local Central Asian identity.

## The Determinants of Foreign Policy

In order to understand what factors may play a major role for change to Tajikistan's policy in the future, we will try to identify the major factors behind its change of policy during the first four years after 2001.

In line with several other studies which try to explain foreign policy, this study identifies external and internal factors, and adds historical–cultural factors. The external factors create the setting and conditions for foreign policy, but the actual choice of policy will be determined by internal factors. Among the domestic factors most often mentioned as determining foreign policy are internal threats, economic conditions and political factionalism.[15] External and internal factors are thus interwoven. 'The degree and the precise mode of an adaptation to outside pressures depend on the domestic and social structure of the respective country. External factors rarely influence the political priorities of a state directly without being modified by the internal structures and coalition-building.'[16] To these two sets, we add historical–cultural factors, focusing on the role of historical memory for forming a national identity and providing the framework within which Tajikistan's role and place in the world will be perceived. The historical–cultural factors are crucial for understanding the long-term changes of orientation and identification as Tajikistan shapes its future.

The analysis will be based on three possible explanations of why a government changes its foreign policy. They will be called the *regional system* approach, the *domestic consolidation* approach, and the *societal* approach. While the first focuses on the international system in the region, and the constraints it represents and the opportunities it offers to the Tajik state, the second gives attention to efforts by the government to consolidate the state and secure its own hold on power, and the third looks at the dynamics from within society, which may press the government to shift its foreign policy in one direction or another. These perspectives are not necessarily mutually exclusive; rather they complement each other. How they may complement each other is discussed in the final chapter.

### *The Regional System Approach*

This approach relates to the international environment of Tajikistan and the impact of the big powers engaging in the region and the neighbouring states most relevant to Tajikistan's national security. Changes at the regional level create both constraints and challenges for a government. Foreign policy change is the result of a government trying to make the best of a situation by adapting to new external circumstances or more actively promoting the interests of its country.

The regional system perspective focuses on the dynamics following from the big power impact on interstate relations, as well as the dynamics emanating from the domestic development of the neighbouring states. What trends and events does the foreign engagement set in motion relevant for Tajikistan?

The regional system as defined in this study consists of Tajikistan, Uzbekistan and Afghanistan, and can be considered a sub-complex of a larger Central Asian regional security complex. A security complex has been defined as a group of states whose primary security concerns 'link together sufficiently closely that their national securities cannot realistically be considered apart from another'.[17] The external powers that are engaging in the region (Russia, the USA, China, Iran, India and Pakistan, as well as European states) have to be analysed in this regional context.

The foreign engagement may contribute to strengthen the capability of individual states and governments in the region, thereby changing the power balance between them. It may influence patterns of friendship and hostility among the states. The impact of the external engagement may also set in motion domestic dynamics which become serious challenges to the governments. The very presence of Russia and the USA in Central Asia may strengthen or provoke and distance groups within Central Asian states. The interplay between the external engagement and local dynamics may work in both conflictual and cooperative directions.[18] While cooperative dynamics dampen conflicts and encourage peaceful relations between states and within states, conflictual dynamics aggravate conflicts and tensions between states and within states.

External powers engaging in a region often fall in line with already existing regional lines of division, but they may also shape new lines of alignment, thereby altering the old system.[19] By influencing the conditions of the region, the big powers affect the policy choices and policy making of these states and thus set off a further chain of events in the region.

The dynamics of the relations between external powers may also spill over into the region. This means that a changing power balance or increased tension between them may be transferred into the region and influence the regional and domestic dynamics.

The basic assumption of the regional system perspective is that changes in the international environment influence the foreign policy making of the individual state. Changes in the region thus provide opportunities and challenges, and thereby set the options for national foreign policy making. The logic of this approach indicates that a higher degree of tension in the region (between the big powers or the regional states), as well as a larger asymmetry in the power relations between them, will increase the probability that the foreign policy of the small state will be cautious and constrained. If relations between the big powers become more tense, a state which has hitherto pursued a bandwagoning policy can be expected to continue such a policy. Increased tension in relation to a neighbouring state may also force a government to seek support from a big power. If there is less tension in the system, this will create better conditions for the small state to pursue a foreign policy of its own choice. If the big power balance starts to shift to the disadvantage of the former hegemon, a small power may initiate a balancing policy.

### The Domestic Consolidation Approach

This perspective analyses foreign policy as following from a regime's efforts to strengthen its hold on power. Stephen G. Walker writes that 'in order to pursue or maintain domestic policy goals, a state may also act to establish, maintain or disrupt a shared set of expectations or the allocations of values among other states'.[20] Valerie M. Hudson, Susan M. Sims and John C. Thomas follow this up, developing the idea that foreign policy is often linked to the regime's attempts to maintain or regain control over the domestic political exchange process:

> [I]mportant foreign policy decisions are often linked to the regime's attempts to maintain or regain control over the domestic political exchange process. While this is not to say that a domestic political struggle is always the direct catalyst for such decisions, it may figure prominently in the regime's choice of foreign policy initiatives. As we may view governmental policy as the selective use of available strategies by the regime, how and why certain strategies or tactics are selected (i.e. how and why certain policy moves are chosen) will be intimately tied to the threat posed to the regime's pursuit of its agenda of needs, which necessitates control over the exchange process.[21]

The policy makers define the national interests and interpret them in terms of the interests of the regime. They may formulate foreign policy largely autonomously in relation to society in the sense that they try to reduce the other interests' possibilities to influence the choice of foreign policy. The insecurity of the ruling regime is fed by competing clan rivalry—as in the case of Tajikistan—as well as the potential threat of popular protests from some sections of society. The regime does its best to handle these challenges.

The logic of the domestic consolidation approach is that a regime will pursue the policy it initiated as long as it considers this policy to be in its own interests and is able to pursue it. Thus, if the government has taken on a balancing foreign policy, it will continue this policy as long as the policy is not threatened. While 'weak' states, as here defined, are states which are weak in relation to society and policy makers are therefore unable to exploit the full scope of their margin of manoeuvre in the international environment. In contrast, 'strong' states are relatively independent of societal demands and pressures. It is easier for them to extract resources from society in order to pursue foreign policy goals.[22] As Peter Katzenstein and Stephen Krasner argue, a state's 'strength' or 'weakness', as defined in relation to society, are central to explaining foreign policy.

## The Societal Approach

This perspective assumes that societal groups have an impact on foreign policy making either directly, as the impact of lobby groups, or indirectly, through the threat these groups may constitute to the survival or consolidation of the regime. David Skidmore and Valerie M. Hudson write that 'a societal approach assumes that many foreign policy choices, like those concerning domestic policy, evoke societal division and political mobilization. This occurs either because the material interests of various groups are affected differently—producing both winners and losers—or because foreign policy choices provoke ideological conflict over values and purposes'.[23] Thus, they conclude, foreign policy choices are judged first and foremost according to their effect on central decision maker's political standing at home.

Although most presidents try to postpone the transfer of power to a next generation of leaders by strengthening their own hold of power and silencing their opponents, problems in society demand more or less immediate solution. Tajikistan, like other Central Asian states, may face a choice between reforming and the regime being overthrown when discontented groups of people are set in motion. The new threats of radical Islamism and extremism are parts of a complex of problems following from eruptions of popular discontent, and normal political channels do not exist.

Although Tajikistan may seem not very receptive to public opinion, we will look at the impact of three possible directions of domestic protest—*secular-political, religious-political,* and *ethnic-national.* We will also discuss the spontaneous, non-articulated outburst of popular discontent. The basic assumption is that the dynamics within society may make the government change its foreign policy either to suppress the opposition or in order to listen to it.[24]

The analysis also gives an indication of value orientation and attitude change among broader groups of the population, with possible consequences not only for the development of domestic protest but also for the orientation of national identity and thereby also for the choice of foreign policy in the long term perspective.

The drug trade across Tajikistan from Afghanistan is a crucial factor determining the stage of the domestic scene in Tajikistan by providing a substantial source of revenues and influence. The drug trade feeds an overall corruption in society, and is often also a major factor behind twists and turns in political life. It adds to tension and rivalry between groups, which compete for power and wealth.[25] The impact of the narcotics trade on Tajik society is, however, not the focus of this study. Nevertheless, the following analysis of the Tajik political scene reflects the shadow cast on society from the ongoing drug trade.

## Possible Implications of Foreign Policy Change

What are the possible implications of Tajik foreign policy change? This question will be discussed from different angles.

First, what are the implications for Tajikistan's international standing and for its domestic scene? Foreign policy change may set various trends and dynamics in motion, eventually threatening the survival of the regime. The spread of transnational values of human and democratic rights may encourage the regime to reform, or produce a popular revolution. The regime may be strengthened by the international attention and economic support, or it may collapse due to discontent as it cannot live up to popular demands and international standards.

Second, what are the possible implications if the determinants of foreign policy take a drastically different course compared with the recent years? If the external factors shift—if Russia returns, the USA withdraws, Afghanistan falls back into civil war, or Uzbekistan descends into domestic chaos—how would such developments influence Tajik foreign policy? What impact would the uncertainties illustrated have on the domestic scene and thus on Tajik foreign policy?

Third, what may be the implications for the regional system of a change in Tajik foreign policy? Does the policy of a small state make a difference? If Tajikistan develops towards a stable democracy and sustainable economic development, this could have strong positive effects on Afghanistan and Uzbekistan. Both states have a difficult and thorny path to reform ahead. A stable Tajikistan that is able to pursue a balancing policy and to derive the benefits of international help and support from several big powers will be in a better position to contribute to stable development of the region as a whole. Moreover, if Tajikistan can balance Russia's position, this may have an impact on the power balance and the lines of friendship and suspicion between the states in the region, and support confidence and reduce conflict behaviour. In the worst of cases, Tajikistan may be too small an actor, and thus be left to the outcome of the intrigues of the big powers.

## The Structure of this Book

The first part of the book gives the background, introducing the history of the Tajik people over the centuries, which is now coming to the forefront as part of the nation and state formation that is going on (chapter 2), and the history of the first ten years of independence (chapter 3). Part II analyses Tajikistan's foreign policy since 2001, and consists of chapters on policy towards the big powers (chapter 4) and towards neighbouring states, Afghanistan and Uzbekistan (chapter 5). Part III (chapters 6 and 7) analyses the determinants of Tajik foreign policy. Part IV (chapter 8) draws the conclusions on trends and discusses the implications of Tajikistan's foreign policy change as well as prospects for the future.

## Sources

The sources for this study consist of research publications by Western, Russian and Central Asian scholars; Tajik, Russian and Western newspaper and news agency material; and interviews in Tajikistan. The chapters on contemporary events are based on the regular 'hoovering' of news material—first of all the Tajik news agencies Asia Plus and Avesta, and Tajik papers in Russian such as *Biznes i politika*; Central Asian and Russian web sites such as Fergana.ru; Russian newspapers, among them *Nezavisimaya gazeta*; and Western services such as the BBC Monitoring Service, *Jamestown Monitor*, and Radio Free Europe/Radio Liberty. The author was fortunate to have been able to visit Tajikistan four times since 1997 and to have had the opportunity to interview politicians, scholars and journalists during those visits. In most cases the choice has been made not to publish their names.

# 2

# BACK TO THE FUTURE?

Can history tell us about the future foreign-policy orientation of a state? 'History is no guide to the future, but its map ... still provides the best single guide we have available by which to discern possible future events', Graham E. Fuller writes.[1] History is a formative experience for any nation, but it also provides a rich material to make alternative choices for a state leadership in an ongoing nation- and state-building process—what the state is to identify with, and which lessons are to be drawn from history. For a young state this choice is crucial, especially if, like Tajikistan, it shares a common history with neighbouring nations of belonging to the same but shifting empires over the centuries. This chapter gives an overview of the richness of the past from which the Tajiks choose to trace their history and the alternative identities which are buried in their history.

The future can never be a return to the past, but the past may offer guidelines for future policy. Thus, formulating the framework for the national consciousness is crucial. In the first volume of the series entitled *The Tajiks in the Mirror of History*, written by a collective of scholars but published under the name of Tajik President Emomali Rakhmonov, we read:

> We live in a time when many nations and nationalities are challenged to make a choice and to decide that their fate may be. At this moment in time the Tajik nation, which so recently obtained its political independence, is faced with the necessity to analyse its recent and distant past, and to learn the lessons taught by history for the establishment of its new role and position in the international community.[2]

He strengthens his argument by quoting the Tajik scholar Yurii Yakubshokh who put it more directly: 'after the rebirth of independence, the history of the nation has to be revised and rewritten in conformity with the spirit of national consciousness'.[3] Several studies on the history of the Tajiks have followed in the footsteps of B. Gafurov, who was the first scholar to publish a history of the Tajik nation, in 1964–65.[4]

In the centre of Dushanbe stands the statue of Ismoil Somoni, the founder of the Samanid Empire of the 9th and 10th centuries AD. One theory is that his family was from Balkh in present-day Afghanistan, and he is buried in Bukhara in a tomb which is an outstanding piece of architecture. For more than 100 years the Samanids ruled most of Central Asia and parts of present-day Afghanistan, Iran, Pakistan and India. The Samanid Empire is regarded as the first Tajik state, but official Tajik historiography goes further back to trace a Tajik statehood. 'Long before the Samanid epoch, the Tajiks had already established a number of states.' 'We regard ancient Bactria and Sogdiana, the Graeco-Bactrian state, the Kushan and Ashkonid dynasties and the Khuttal kingdom as the chain of events which forged the history of the Tajik nation', write the authors of *The Tajiks in the Mirror of History*.[5] There is a problem here, however, since large parts of Central Asia share the same history. The Tajiks have a common history with the Uzbeks, first of all, and now both nations lay claim to what to a great extent is the same cultural heritage. As Edward Allworth writes, there is a search for 'retrospective proof' of nationality in a given territory.[6]

The Tajiks—the only national group of Iranian descendants in an otherwise Turkic-speaking environment in Central Asia—started after independence to spell out the specifics of this national identity, mainly defined in ethno-linguistic terms. To find the specifics of the nation, Tajik official historiography looked for the golden past when Iranian tribes still dominated Central Asia, going back to the second and first millennia BC. The search for a cultural self-identity took an ethno-national turn.[7]

The geographical area between the rivers Amudarya and Syrdarya was once at the very crossroads of traffic between East and West, and between civilizations and religions. Empires replaced one another and the rulers came from different geographical directions. Cultural, linguistic and ethnic elements of different people blended. Nevertheless, the cultural influences on this area are like layers which are unveiled as excavations proceed. Although some of these empires did their best to eradicate the culture and religion of the previous empire, new cultural syntheses appeared over time. The question is to what extent cultural affinities emanating from this shared history with states in the near or more distant neighbourhood determine identity and foreign policy orientation.

History provides several options in this regard. Here we will identify the following analytical alternative for Tajikistan's self-identification in international politics: (a) the pan-Islamic; (b) the Persian, or Iranian; (c) the local Central Asian; (d) the European/Western, following from the

Macedonian–Greek heritage; and finally (e) the European/Russian. All are embedded in the history of the Tajik nation.

Tajikistan is part of the geographical–historical area which the Greeks (using Latin) called Transoxania and the Arabs called Mawarannahr, 'the other side of the river'. Two rivers defined this area. The Amudarya is the river referred to here: it is called the Oxus in Latin (Jahun in Arabic, while Vakhshu or Wakshu is the old East Iranian or Aryan name). The other river delimiting the region is the Syrdarya (Jaxartes in Latin, and Sayhun in Arabic) to the north.

Like most rivers, the Amudarya did not divide people but connected them. It attracted people and stimulated exchange between them. For centuries the settlements on both sides of the Amudarya belonged to one and the same state entity, although these entities replaced each other over time. The famous Russian scholar Vasilii Barthold writes that there are 'provinces to the south of the Amu-Darya with which some portions of Transoxania were at times more closely connected than with Samarkand and Bukhara'.[8]

Iranian tribes populated Transoxania, and when the Arabs arrived in the early 8th century they regarded the Syrdarya as a border to the land of the Turkic nomads. They therefore named the territory to the north of the river Turkistan, since they called all non-Iranians to be Turks. There was no natural barrier against the inroads of the nomads from the north, and Transoxania was therefore subject to influxes of nomads from time to time.

Present-day Tajikistan is located north of the River Pyandzh, which is the main tributary of the Amudarya. The river is modern Tajikistan's southern border, which it shares with Afghanistan (it becomes the Amudarya at the confluence with the Vakhsh), and continues into Uzbekistan.[9] Through Tajikistan's northern city of Khujand runs the Syrdarya. It rises in Tianshan in eastern Kyrgyzstan as the Naryn River, and enters the Fergana Valley close to the town of Andijan, where the Karadarya runs into it and it becomes the Syrdarya. From Tajikistan it continues into Uzbekistan to end up in the Aral Sea as the Amudarya.[10]

Mawarannahr was surrounded also by high mountains, but, like the rivers, the mountains were no hindrance to trade and traffic in ancient times. Through the passes went traders, ambassadors, invaders and ordinary people. Svat Soucek explains:

> The Pamir ranges fan out through Tajikistan and Sinkiang into Afghanistan, Pakistan, Tibet, and India under such names as Kunlun, Karakoram, Hindukush, and Himalayas. Incredible though it may sound, this convergence of giant mountain chains was the crossroads, in antiquity and the Middle Ages, of the celebrated Silk Road—caravan tracks that linked Inner Asia and China with India, the Middle East, and the

Mediterranean world. Man found ways to penetrate them through passes some of which lie higher than peaks considered lofty elsewhere (for example ... Akbaital in Tajikistan 4,655 meters) ...[11]

The Tajikistan of today is the mountainous south-eastern part of what once was Transoxania.[12]

### Ancient Bactria and Sogdiana, and the Persian Conquest

The official Tajik historiography of today turns to ancient Bactria and Sogdiana, which in the 6th and 7th centuries BC constituted state entities, although no written records exist from that time. When they became part of the Persian Achaemenid Empire in the mid-6th century BC, this territory already had an ages-old history of its own. Roughly speaking, the territory of ancient Bactria corresponds to what is today northern Afghanistan, southern Tajikistan, and south-eastern Uzbekistan and Turkmenistan.[13] Uzbekistan and Tajikistan share the history of Sogdiana. This situation, of a shared heritage, clearly supports the contention of the authors of *The Tajiks in the Mirror of History* that 'neither history in general nor a history of culture can be studied within the limits of the territories of the contemporary states'.[14] Nevertheless, this is exactly what takes place today. Writing the national history today in Tajikistan and Uzbekistan is most often an exclusionary activity: its purpose is to separate the specifics of the writer's own nation from those of other nations.

Bactria connected people on both sides of the Amudarya. The territory of Bactria was defined in the north and the south by two mountain ranges, the Hissar range and the Hindu Kush. Without clear delimitation to the east and west, in the east it included Badakhshan and in the west it reached to the western part of the Surkhandarya Basin.[15] The central lands of Bactria were Balkh, Khutalon and Kabodiyon.[16] Balkh was a province to the south of the Amudarya, Khutalon was located to the north between the Pyandzh and the Vakhsh (present-day Kulyab), and Kabodiyon was located between the rivers Kafarnihan and Vakhsh. The vast expanses of the valleys of the Amudarya, Vakhsh and Pyandzh rivers provided a favourable environment for the rapid development of agriculture, as well as of towns and settlements. The results of excavations have shown that thousands of well-organized towns and large settlements of ancient Bactria existed on the lands stretching from Kabodiyon and Termez to Balkh and Herat, Merv and Nisa. In the region of the confluence of the Vakhsh and Pyandzh rivers, dozens of towns existed, such as Beshkent (Vashkand), Shahri Tus, Ayvach and many others. The banks of the Vakhsh were watered by a sophisticated irrigation system, traces of which have been discovered in the Beshkent Valley.[17]

Ancient Sogdiana was situated north of Bactria along the Zerafshan River and in adjacent regions, and, like Bactria, was populated by Iranians at the time of the Arab conquest.[18] In inverted commas, the term 'Bactria' was used to refer to both Bactria and Sogdiana.[19] The historical corridor between Bactria and Sogdiana was the 'Iron Gate', a defile about half-way between Balkh and Samarkand that breaks the low mountain range extending from the Hissar range southwards towards the Amudarya.[20]

The Tajiks adduce the Avesta, the famous Zoroastrian holy text from the 12–10th centuries BC, to trace their history back to the Iranian (Aryan) tribes living along the Amudarya in the 2nd and 1st millennia BC. The Avesta is the earliest written text of the Indo-Europeans and is based on the oral cultural heritage of Aryan tribes. It is the basic Zoroastrian text and is assumed to have been compiled by Zarathustra. Different nations lay claim to it, but Tajik historians identify the territory referred to in it as Bactria, Sogdiana and Khorezm. According to official Tajik historiography, 'Nowadays it is a well established fact that the Avesta was a product of the minds and spirituality of the Tajik people. A large body of commentaries on the Avesta mentions such cities and states as Bactria, Khorezm, Kabul, Sogdiana, Merv and Parakana (Fergana), ... The homeland of Zarathustra was Sogdiana and Bactria.'[21]

Early temples for fire worship have been found in Balkh and Bactria, and excavations in present-day Tajikistan and Uzbekistan show remnants of Zoroastrian fire temples. In a settlement in the vicinity of Darband, a town in the present-day Surkhandarya region in Uzbekistan, close to the Tajik border, there is a temple dating back to the Bronze Age. It is built in accordance with Zoroastrian traditions and dated to 1,600–1,500 BC on the basis of typical Bactrian building traditions.[22] As Barthold points out, the ancient Aryan name of the Amudarya—Vakhshu or Wakshu—is preserved in the name of the river Vakhsh (Surhab) in Tajikistan.[23] Archaeological finds in the lower reaches of the Kafarnihan in the Shartuz district and from the Vakhsh Valley close to present-day Kurgan-Tyube have yielded interesting information about the culture and life of northern Bactria of the time.[24] Penjikent in western Tajikistan demonstrates the location of an important city of Sogdiana at the time. Archaeological surveys have uncovered evidence for the early development of irrigation, commerce and fortifications.

The written history of the area dates from the conquest of Bactria and Sogdiana in the mid-6th century BC by the Achaemenid (Persian) king, Cyrus the Great. At its greatest extent, the Achaemenid Empire, which lasted for 200 years, ruled a territory extending from the Indus River in the east to Libya and Thrace in the west, and from Egypt in the south to the Caucasus and the Syrdarya in the north. It exerted a form of centralized control over the caravan and sea routes and was at the time the uncontested world leader in trade and a centre of culture and civilization. Bactria and Sogdiana occupied a prominent place in the system of trade as the cultural and commercial crossroads on the way to Babylon. Bactria, writes Frank Holt, was 'perhaps the key satrapy (government) on the eastern front'. It always played a role in struggles for power in the Achaemenid Empire. The region thus played a notable place in the political history of the Persian Empire, and was generally placed under the control of close relatives of the reigning king.[25]

Bactria was rebellious and not easily subsumed into the Persian Empire, but even so the Persians were able to integrate the area fully into the cultural and economic life of the huge empire.[26] The satraps (provincial governors), the leaders of the military and administrative districts, and many other top administrative appointees were usually Persian.

### Alexander, the Graeco-Bactrian State, and the Fall of Bactria-Sogdiana

Alexander, king of the Graeco-Macedonian empire, went to war against the Achaemenid Empire, defeated King Darius, and brought an end to Achaemenid rule at the battle of Gaugamela in 331 BC. He entered Bactria in 329 BC as ruler of Persia under the name of 'king of Asia'.

Alexander further developed Bactria as a central meeting-place of routes connecting China, India and the Western world. India could be reached either by a northern circuit through Bactria or by a longer southern route. The former took the traveller through Bactria and over the Hindu Kush through either the Bamiyan or the Panjshir Valley, which converge from opposite directions upon Alexandria-sub-Caucaso (near present-day Begram).[27] The latter took the traveller through Alexandria-Arachosia (near present-day Kandahar) to India. Alexander's reign did not stop with Bactria. In Sogdiana outside present-day Khujand in northern Tajikistan Alexander founded his new city, Alexandria-Eschate ('Alexandria the Furthermost') in 328 BC. The city was built as his outpost against the nomads in the north.

Alexander built new cities but most often he developed already existing ones. He developed Bactra (near present-day Balkh).[28] He also developed existing cities of Sogdiana, such as Maracanda (Samarkand) and Nautaca (located somewhere near present-day Shahr-i-Sabz, or possibly deeper into present-day Tajikistan).[29]

Alexander entered Central Asia claiming to be a legitimate successor of Darius and thus the last Achaemenid king. At first he met no local resistance in Bactria, and he easily defeated Bessus, Darius' satrap whom Alexander accused of murdering Darius after the latter had been defeated.[30] Alexander acted within the long tradition of Persian rule in the area, embraced the protocol of the Persian court, and incorporated Persian nobility into the royal retinue.[31] However, by the time he reached the Syrdarya and started building Alexandria-Eschate, he met fierce resistance from the local population. His direct interference in local affairs raised resistance, and his disruption of regional socio-economic patterns made the presence of his army unacceptable.[32] As Holt writes, Alexander's announced intention with Alexandria-Eschate—to keep the nomads out of his empire by means of a military colony—'ran counter to local, long-established conventions of close interaction between the diverse peoples on both banks of the Jaxartes'.[33] By building a military frontier against the nomads, Alexander thus provoked what he intended to avoid—a hostile alliance of Sogdians and the nomads. Alexander was forced to fight the longest and perhaps most costly campaign of his whole career.[34]

While the Persian kings had tried to control the cities through local princes, and had them exercise general authority over surrounding villages, Alexander destroyed the cities that resisted him, resettled the inhabitants in his own new city, and killed the local princes, whom he held responsible for the revolt.[35] The Sogdians fought under the leadership of Spitamen, a local noble, with support from the nomadic tribes. According to historians, the scale and savagery of the warfare all over Sogdiana were unequalled anywhere else in Alexander's empire.

As a result of the local resistance, Alexander changed his policy towards the local aristocracy. Instead of punishing them, he restored them to their ancestral positions, and fell back on his previous policy along Persian lines.[36] He had defeated Spitamen, and managed to calm the situation enough to be able to leave for India. The situation in Bactria-Sogdiana remained far from settled, however. By the time Alexander died in India, Bactria-Sogdiana was in full-blown revolt.[37]

After the death of Alexander in 323 BC a power struggle followed between his military commanders, who divided the empire between themselves. Central Asia came under Seleucus, who in 312 BC confirmed his position as satrap in Babylon. After 293 BC he started to 're-conquer' and 're-colonize' Sogdiana, but then encountered similar problems to those Alexander had met. He assumed the royal title in 304 BC, and marched towards India.

Seleucus became the ruler of an enormous empire stretching from the Aegean Sea to Afghanistan and coterminous with the Achaemenid Empire minus Thrace and Egypt.[38] Greek-Macedonian colonists settled in Bactria, and it remained an extremely important region of the empire, not only as a frontier area but also as a producer of grain, as it was covered by fields and pastures, was well watered by extensive irrigation works, and had a nexus of trade routes linking India and China to the west by the road from Bactria to Seleuceia in Babylon.[39]

After a series of raids by nomads in the north-west deep into the Seleucid territory of Margiana and Ariana, Seleucus handed over Bactria to his son, Antiochus.[40] Under Antiochus Bactria-Sogdiana became more autonomous, and, during the civil war for power within the Seleucid Empire, Theodotus (Diodotus), the satrap of Bactria, revolted.[41] Around 250 BC, Seleucid ties with Bactria and Sogdiana were cut off.

Instead a powerful Graeco-Bactrian kingdom now appeared, centred around Bactria, including Sogdiana to the north, Margiana to the north-west, and Ariana to the west. Whether Fergana was included in Greek Bactria is not clear, although much evidence points in that direction.[42] 'Over the next 130 years, this kingdom would not only thrive and prosper, but it would gradually expand beyond its original boundaries, to incorporate most of what is now Afghanistan, north-west Pakistan, and beyond.'[43] This period demonstrates a wide cultural exchange, including cultural–religious exchange, between Bactria and both India and the Hellenistic world. A characteristic feature of the Sogdian civilization was the vast number of religious beliefs, among them Zoroastrism, Buddhism and Manichaeanism,[44] although Zoroastrianism retained its dominant position when Buddhism spread in Central Asia.[45] Ai Khanoum, a Hellenistic city on the Amudarya, situated just inside what is now Afghanistan, unearthed in the 1970s, provides a 'clear picture of Greek and Oriental features side by side'.[46] Excavations have revealed cities of the Bactria period located outside present-day Kabodion and south of Kolkhozabad in what is now Tajikistan.[47]

The cultural patterns of the region came to be deeply influenced by the new Greek colonists. As the American scholar H. Sidky concludes, 'Alexander's invasion of Central Asia radically transformed the socio-political and economic picture of the region. No other Asian territory conquered by Alexander experienced the degree of socio-political, economic, demographic, and cultural transformations as did Bactria and Sogdiana'.[48] Alexander the Great played a crucial role for Central Asia in introducing Western culture and contributing to a cultural synthesis, which continued in Bactria up to the arrival of the Arabs.

However, the excessive territorial expansion and costly wars drained the resources of the Greek Bactrians and left them vulnerable to their enemies to the north and west.[49] The Graeco-Bactrian administration was dissolving into a number of autonomous cities and towns. At this point a new factor appeared on the Central Asian scene. The clashes along the boundaries of Central Asia and China had set in motion a complex movement of peoples, and these nomadic tribesmen 'took Bactria away from the Greeks'.[50]

Bactria and Sogdiana were conquered by nomads from the north-east, whose forces continued southwards and in AD 50 had created the Kushan Empire. They extended their rule to India by taking Punjab, Kashmir, Sind and Uttar Pradesh. The Kushan Empire (from the 1st to the early 4th centuries AD) came to include not only northern India but also almost all of present-day Afghanistan, large parts of Central Asia and East Turkistan.[51] Over Sogdiana, the empire maintained only a form of suzerainty.[52] It has not been possible to identify who the Kushans were except that they came from somewhere near Mongolia and were most probably tribes of Iranian descent. The most famous of the Kushan kings was Kanishka, who converted to Buddhism.[53]

Under Kushan rule Buddhism further spread to Central Asia through Afghanistan. One of the most important cities of the Kushan Empire was Termez, where large Buddhist monasteries have been excavated. Several cities in the neighbourhood were also important; many were located in what is today Tajikistan and Uzbekistan. Among them are Shahrinau, Kai-Kubad-shakh (not far from Kabodiyon) and Yavan in present-day Tajikistan, and Khalchayan in present-day Uzbekistan (close to Denau in what is now the Surkhandarya region).[54] The huge Sleeping Buddha in Nirvana, now exposed at the Museum of Ancient History in Dushanbe, was found at the Ajina-Teppa Buddhist temple in the Vakhsh Valley not far from present-day Kurgan-Tyube. This beautiful Buddha, the largest clay Buddha statue outside India, is from the 5th or 6th century AD. The temple was destroyed and the statue damaged during the Arab conquest. The remnants of hundreds of Buddhist temples and monasteries have been found in Tajikistan and Afghanistan.[55]

In the Kushan Empire, three important civilizations—the Chinese, Iranian and Indian—met. Sogdiana developed into a great commercial centre for Chinese trade with the West. Extensive finds of Roman coins and products bear witness to the economic exchange that took place between East and West along the Silk Road.

As Kushan rule was undermined, Central Asia underwent periods of turbulence. Local rulers extended their territories, and conquest enabled them to build up new large empires. Turkic-speaking nomadic tribes, which from time to time had entered the agricultural lands of ancient Sogdiana and Bactria, now started to expand their rule into Transoxania thereby contributing to the political turmoil which preceded the Arab conquest.

## The Arab Conquest

During the 630s and 640s AD the Arabs conquered Iran, and more than 400 years of rule of the Persian Sasanid Empire was brought to an end in

651. The Arabs expanded northwards; but to cross the Amudarya and conquer the territory on 'the other side of the river' (Mawarannahr as the Arabs called it) turned out to be a much more complicated operation. Svat Soucek writes in his study of Central Asian history that 'Compared with the conquest of the Sasanian empire of Persia ... that of Transoxania proved to be a laborious and protracted affair. The Arabs needed here almost a full century to bring the province beyond the river firmly into the Islamic fold'.[56] Barthold writes that 'The slowness of the conquest is explained partly by the fact that the Arabs themselves were satisfied at first with military booty and tribute, and had no intention of making a permanent conquest of the country, and partly by the struggle with natural obstacles'.[57]

By the time the Arabs conquered Transoxania the region had disintegrated into a mosaic of small fiefdoms formed into larger conglomerates or loose principalities—Tukharistan (as the Arabs named Bactria), Sogdiana, Ustrushan (located north of Zerafshan, and including modern Tashkent), and Fergana (the valley enclosed by the Tianshan and Pamir mountains on the north, east and south).[58] Tukharistan was under the suzerainty of the Persian Sasanid Empire, while Sogdiana and the other fiefdoms had been under the suzerainty of the Turkic khaganate (the Kök Turks), who came from the north-east, since the early 500s.[59] Tukharistan at the time consisted of present-day southern Tajikistan, the Surkhandarya region of Uzbekistan, and Balkh and northern part of Afghanistan.[60] Between the principalities there were competition and rivalry.

To the north-west of Transoxania lay Khwarazm, although geographically its north-eastern part belonged to Transoxania. South of Transoxania lay Khurasan, a province of the Sasanid Empire. Khurasan included the south-western part of Iran's present-day province of the same name, as well as parts of central Turkmenistan, north-western Afghanistan, and the cities of Nisa, Merv, Nishapur and Herat.[61]

In 651 the Arabs took Merv in Khurasan and made it a base for their attacks and offensives across the river, which they initiated in the 670s. In 673 the Arabs conquered Ramitan and the outskirts of Bukhara. After a first Arab offensive against Bukhara, the Bukharan empress paid tribute to prevent an Arab attack, and during the years that followed Bukhara paid tribute to the Arabs to avoid their attacks. Yet, in spite of repeated Arab offensives across the river, which in the 680s took them as far as modern Khujand, they were not able to establish their rule and had to return to their footholds in Merv.[62] Under Caliph Abd al-Malik ibn Marvane (685–705) a new determination to conquer Mawarannahr resulted in 706 in a series of offensives by the appointed Arab governor-general of Khurasan, Qutayba ibn Muslim. In 704 Termez was finally brought under Arab control, which made operations easier. Termez (close to the present-day Uzbek–Tajik–Afghan border) was situated at the crossing point where the Surkhandarya flows into the Amudarya. It was a historic passage between Bactria and Sogdia and a crossing point for caravan routes.

In 706 Qutayba turned against Bukhara. It was conquered in 709, as was the principality of Chaganian along the Surkhandarya River and the western part of the Hissar Valley (around Denau). In 712 Samarkand fell. Between the years 705 and 715 Qutayba lay the foundations of an Islamic Transoxania and Khwarazm through a series of campaigns. The Arabs were able step by step to extend their control over Transoxania since the principalities in Transoxania did not present a united front. Instead, the Arabs skilfully used the rivalry between the fiefdoms, as well as within them.[63] In order to stop the Arabs, in 712–13 the principalities of Sogd, Chach and Fergana entered a coalition with the Turk Khaganate.

In 715 the Arab offensive was stopped by a new turn of events. An Umayyad caliph, Sulaiman, came to power in Damascus, and Qutayba could not count on his support. Amid deep discontent among his troops, Qutayba was murdered in Fergana and the Arab troops returned to Khurasan.

A new stage in the Arab conquest began in the late 730s, when Nasr ibn Sayyar became governor general in Khurasan (738–48). He managed to appease the local princes and the population of Mawarannahr, and was able to retake control of Sogdiana.[64] Nasr turned to a policy of cooperation with the subject peoples and developed the agriculture of Mawarannahr,[65] but fell from power as a result of the general discontent in the caliphate against the rule of the Umayyads and the struggle for power by the Abbasids (the Alis) towards the mid-8th century. This was reflected also in Khurasan and Mawarannahr, when the Abbasids sent Abu Muslim to stir revolt in Khurasan in 747.[66] In 750 the Umayyad dynasty fell. Although Mawarannahr had also been against the Umayyads, the people did not want the Abbasids to take over, and rose in revolt. As a result of the internal troubles in the caliphate, Khurasan's hold on Mawarannahr weakened; and at this moment the Chinese went on the offensive. They had expanded their territory after the fall of the western Turkish empire, and no new powerful nomad state had arisen in the steppes of Turkistan to prevent them.[67] In a final battle in 751 near Talas, not far from what is now the city of Jambul, the Arabs defeated the Chinese army, and the Chinese never returned to Mawarannahr.

During the 150 years of Arab rule in Central Asia war and revolts were legion. The Arabs destroyed most of the pre-Islamic culture. Their clergy burned pre-Islamic literature and destroyed objects of culture and religion (sculptures and paintings) from previous periods. Pre-Islamic religious halls were destroyed and rebuilt as mosques. Contemporary official Tajik historiography tells us that 'The most disastrous setback of all [invasions] was caused by the Arab conquest'.[68] On the other hand the Soviet Tajik scholar Gafurov argues that on the whole Arab rule and the introduction of Islam contributed to the socio-economic and cultural development of Mawarannahr. The area, and especially the Zerafshan Valley, became one of the major granaries of Mawarannahr and Khurasan. Mawarannahr was included in the trade and economic exchange of the Arab state and with countries to the east. The Arabs acted to improve conditions for trade and during their rule *rabats* were built along the caravan roads where merchants could stay to rest and eat.[69] Cultural life expanded. The Arab language and alphabet were introduced in administration, religion and science and known among the elite, although not among the population at large. Many Arab words entered the local languages. The work of poets, writers and scholars in Mawarannahr spread across the Arab world.[70]

The caliph maintained his formal position as ruler over Central Asia after the Arab troops had left. Local Persian leaders gradually took back previous positions as they were appointed his ruling local representatives. According to Barthold,

> The complete subjugation of the country to Muslim rule, and the establishment of entire immunity from danger both internal and external, was attained only when, instead of constantly changing governors at the head of the province, hereditary rulers were appointed from among the native aristocrats, well acquainted with local conditions and enjoying the confidence of the population. It follows as a matter of course that these governors acted more in their own interests than in those of the Caliphs, and that their dependence on the latter rapidly became purely nominal.[71]

The further penetration of Islam deeper into Central Asia, however, was taken over by the Persians, while Central Asia remained part of the wider cultural, scientific and religious community of the Islamic Middle East, Asia and North Africa.

## The Samanids

The Samanid Empire, from the mid-9th century to the end of the 10th century (879–999), is considered the golden age of Iranian culture in Central Asia and present-day Tajik official historiography identifies it as the first period of Tajik statehood. '[I]t was only during the reign of the Samanids that the whole country became a unified national state and remained united during the whole century',[72] according to the authors of *The Tajiks in the Mirror of History*, although it can be questioned whether at the time a Tajik state or a nation existed at all.

The caliph in Baghdad, Mamun, appointed four brothers of a local Persian family (descendants from the village of Saman in Balkh province) as local rulers of Mawarannahr, subordinated to the governor of Khurasan. The family had converted to Islam, and the brothers helped to end a revolt against the Arabs in 819–20. The caliph therefore made them rulers of Samarkand, Fergana, Shash and Ustrushan, and Herat. After a violent power struggle within the family, Ismoil Somoni took over and created a united Samanid Empire, of which the core area included Transoxania and Khurasan.[73] It was the Samanids who carried out the final subjugation of Mawarannahr to Muslim rule.[74]

During the 120 years of the Samanid Empire, the Samanids never ceased to acknowledge the caliph as their 'suzerain' and regularly sent tributes to Baghdad.[75] Nevertheless, they acted independently of the caliph. Barthold writes that 'If in the eyes of the Bagdad Government the Samanids were only amirs (governors) "clients of the Commander of the Faithful", or even only "amils" (tax collectors), within their own territories they were undoubtedly independent rulers'.[76]

The Samanid rule in Transoxania and Khurasan played a catalytic role in creating a new Iranian identity which was Islamic at the same time. A new Persian language, Dari, came into being and replaced the kindred Sogdian and Khwarazmian idioms as the language of statecraft (alongside Arabic) and literature.[77] Among its writers were the poets Abu Abdallah Jafar Rudaki and Abulkasim Firdawsi, writing in Dari.[78] Simultaneously, Arabic continued as the language of religion and the exact sciences, and the works of Central Asian scientists, philosophers and theologians spread all over the Islamic world. Among them were the mathematician and astronomer al-Kharezmi, al-Marvazi from Merv, al-Fergani, Abdulmahmud Khujandi, Abu Ali Ibn Sina, and Abu Raihan al-Biruni.

The Samanid Empire fell into turmoil and confusion towards the end of the 10th century, and thereby became an easy prey to conquerors, the Turks, approaching the empire from the north.[79]

## The Turks, Genghis Khan, and the Timurids

An army of Turkic tribes brought an end to Samanid rule. In the 9th century and the first half of the 10th century the Samanids dispatched armies to the steppe to subdue the invading Turkic Qara-Khanids. Turkic tribes had previously entered Transoxania, but there was no extensive immigration into the area, and those who moved there soon became assimilated in the predominantly Iranian population. The exception had been the steppe empire of the Kök Turks, which from the mid-6th to mid-8th centuries claimed suzerainty over the petty rulers of

Central Asia.[80] When the Samanid Empire was brought to an end by the invading Qara-Khanids, this, writes Barthold 'for ever put an end to the dominion of the native Aryan [i.e. Iranian] element'.[81] The origin of the different population groups in the area at the time (whether Iranian or Turkic) is, however, still disputed.[82]

In contrast to the Turkic tribes that had entered Transoxania previously, who were nomads and whose lifestyle and psychological orientation remained those of the steppes of Inner Asia, the Qara-Khanids were Muslims and declared themselves 'clients of the commander of the faithful'. On their minted coins they had a picture of Caliph Qadir.[83]

The arrival of the Turks set in motion a demographic and ethno-linguistic shift in the region. The Iranian culture and language continued to play a dominant role in Central Asia,[84] but a Turkicizing wave had started. In contrast to the previous Persian rulers in Transoxania, the Qara-Khanids practised the Turkic kind of tribal family or clan rule rather than rule under a single monarch.[85]

The Qara-Khanids were overrun when in 1220 Genghis Khan conquered Transoxania coming from the steppes of Mongolia into which Turkic nomads had moved. He had in 1206 become ruler of a coalition of Mongol and Turkic clans and tribes.[86] When he died in 1227 his son Chaghatay was assigned Central Asia. The final phase of Mongol expansion occurred during the third generation of the Genghisids. Mongol rule was a period of destruction in Central Asia. About a century after the Mongol invasion some Chaghatayid khans began to convert to Islam. They lived in Transoxania among a population which had maintained its Islamic creed. Soucek writes that 'Islam played a fundamental role in the resilience of native identity, and renaissance during these years of Mongol rule, and an especially seminal part was assumed by its Sufi dimension'.[87]

In 1370 Timur, a Muslim Turk, seized power in Transoxania, ending Chaghatayid rule in the area. The borders of the Timurid state of 1405 stretched from the Black Sea coast almost as far west as the Mediterranean, across the Caspian Sea and the Aral Sea, down into India, and into the Persian Gulf and the Arabian Sea. The Timurid period is characterized by 'the co-existence of two strains of high culture, the established Persian one and the new Turkic one'.[88] As Soucek puts it, there was also a 'remarkable symbiosis of Perso-Islamic administrative and cultural traditions with the customs and methods of the still largely tribal and Turco-Mongols came to full fruition'.[89] Ulugh Beg, the grandson of Timur, developed Transoxania into a cultural centre and Samarkand into its very heart.[90] He encouraged the Persian cultural heritage, and sponsored a critical edition of Firdawsi's great epic poem *Shahname*, including a biography of the poet. During the Timurid reign both the Persian and the Turki languages were used, and gradually Turki (a branch of the Turkic family of languages) took its place as a language of literature besides Persian. Yet the Persian language and culture continued to dominate.[91]

In 1500 the Timurid dynasty was brought to an end by an Uzbek khan, the founder of the Shaybanid dynasty (1500–99) and a descent of Genghis Khan. The greater part of Central Asia now passed to the control of the nomadic Uzbeks from the Kipchak steppe. They were Sunni Muslims and 'had been sufficiently exposed to Arab-Persian Islamic culture to ensure a fundamental continuity', writes Soucek.[92] Tukharistan (former Bactria) became Shaybanid territory and Balkh in northern Afghanistan became the Shaybanids' capital. Balkh played a central role for communications and commercial links between Central Asia and India under Timurid rule.

The Shaybanids represented a period of economic and cultural development, but during the 16th century a fundamental transformation started which gradually led Central Asia into decline. The Europeans opened up a sea route which bypassed the land route across Transoxania and Sinkiang (Xinjiang). The decline that followed for Central Asia was gradual but definitive. Another important factor at the time was, as Soucek puts it, the 'confrontational stalemate' between Shia Iran and Sunni Central Asia, which was to last for 300 years up to the conquest by Russia in the late 19th century. This antagonism isolated Central Asia from Turkey and the Near East. Iran, hostile and powerful, 'to a considerable degree blocked direct communications of merchants, pilgrims and scholars between the eastern and western part of the Muslim world'.[93]

## The Emirate and the Russian Conquest

In the 17th and 18th centuries local khanates emerged—the Bukhara Emirate, the Khiva Khanate and the Kokand Khanate. Most of the territory of modern Tajikistan is located in the territory of Bukhara, and a smaller part in what was Kokand. The Bukhara Emirate was the largest and was ruled by the Manghit dynasty from 1785. It was the first dynasty since the Timurids not to use a Genghisid genealogy to legitimize its rule. The title of the ruler changed from khan to emir. ('Emir' is the same word as 'amir', 'commander of the believers', which was the Arab title of the caliph.) This was an Islamic way to legitimize the dynasty rather than a Turco-Mongol tribal way. The Manghits, the scholar Svat Soucek writes, reduced the power of Uzbek tribal chieftains (who had become more independent), relied on a small, partly non-Uzbek standing army and on a Persian-speaking bureaucratic class often recruited from the emir's Iranian slaves, and sponsored the religious class in order to consolidate Manghit authority.[94]

During the second half of the 19th century Russia expanded into Central Asia, and the despotic and conservative nature of the Bukhara Emirate made it incapable of grasping the dramatic changes as this expansion proceeded. In 1864 Russian troops conquered Tashkent, which became the administrative centre of Russian rule on conquered territory in Central Asia. The Russian government regarded Tashkent under Russian control as a buffer against surprise attacks from the Bukhara Emirate and the Khiva Khanate, as well as a convenient base for further action in Central Asia. Russia played on the contradictions and clashes between and within the khanates, waiting for the weakest party to turn to itself for support.[95] In 1866 Russian troops invaded the Bukhara Emirate and conquered Irdzhar on the road to Samarkand and Khujand further to the east. Russia saw Russian domination of Bukhara as a necessity: there was no middle way, one of the officers of the General Staff asserted in a memorandum of July 1866. It was necessary 'either to take possession of the Central Asiatic khanates, or else to put the khans in such a position that they would not dare to take a step without the agreement of Russia'.[96]

In the 1860s and 1870s the emir of Bukhara and the khan of Khiva were forced to sign treaties with the Russian tsar that made them Russian protectorates de facto, although they remained independent entities de jure. The external pressure by Russia on the emirate and khanate exacerbated their internal contradictions. In Bukhara the Islamic clergy demanded that the emir stood up against the Russians and declared a 'holy war' against the Russian troops. Other groups within the emirate wanted to regularize the situation with the Russians as soon as possible. In September 1867 the emir refused to sign a Russian proposal for a bilateral treaty. When in April 1868 Bukharan troops went on the offensive against the small principalities in the Zerafshan Valley, they weakened their own defence of the city of Samarkand by diverting their troops. Following a plan of action to take Samarkand, the new Russian governor-general and military commander of the newly organized Turkestan government, General K. P. Kaufman, crossed the river and occupied Samarkand.[97] The Bukharan troops capitulated in May 1868.

Russia demanded that the emir of Bukhara recognize its territorial conquests; cede Khujand, Ura-Tyube and Jizzak; open up the emirate to privileges for Russian merchants on an equal footing with native merchants, and guarantee their security; and pay a huge sum of money as military reparations. As a guarantee that the money would be paid, Russia continued its occupation of Samarkand and Kattakurgan. As the emir could not pay the amount specified, these areas were handed over to Russia.[98] Formally, Russia's treaty of 1868 with the Bukhara Emirate was a trade agreement. As Hélène Carrère d'Encausse writes, it gave Russia 'everything that for almost three centuries Russia's envoys had been unable to obtain'.[99] The agreement did not touch upon the issue of Bukhara's formal status as an independent state entity.[100] It did not give Russia the right to intervene in the domestic affairs of the emirate and, since the emirate bordered on the British zone of influence, the Russian government avoided to take further measures, which could have complicated relations with Britain at the time. In 1873 a second treaty was signed between Russia and Bukhara, which confirmed the status of the emirate as a Russian protectorate de facto. The Russian government did not intervene directly in the domestic affairs of the emirate, although there were repeated tensions between Bukhara and Russian-ruled Tashkent. The emir flirted with the anti-Russian rulers of Afghanistan, Khiva and Turkey; the slave trade continued in Bukhara; and Russian merchants had difficulty expanding their businesses in the emirate.

Developments in the Khiva Khanate were similar. After a treaty with Russia in 1873 Khiva became de facto a Russian protectorate. In 1876 the khanate was dissolved and its territory incorporated into the Russian Empire after Russian troops had intervened in response to internal instability in the khanate.

Russia allowed the emir of Bukhara to conquer the small principalities to the east. The independent principalities of Shahrisabz and Kitab were incorporated into the emirate, as were Karategin and Darvaz.[101] Russia was happy to see the emir strengthen his position, hoping this would reduce the risk of domestic turmoil in the khanate.[102] Russia also gave Bukhara Chorjui, which it had conquered from Khiva. Moreover, Russian troops helped the emir to crush a revolt led by the feudal lords of Hissar and Shahrisabz, who wanted to free themselves from the emir's rule.[103]

In the 1880s and 1890s Russia strengthened its control further. In 1884 the emirate was included within Russia's customs frontier by an agreement, and Russian troops took control of Bukhara's borders with Afghanistan, which were now to be guarded by Russian troops and customs officials.[104] The Russian customs frontier was established along the Amudarya in 1885.[105] In early 1895 Britain and Russia signed an agreement in London defining 'the Spheres of Influence of the two countries in the Region of the Pamirs'. According to the agreement Roshan, Shugnan and northern Vakhan, to the east of the Afghan–Bukharan border, were to be transferred to the Bukhara Emirate, while southern Darvaz, on the left bank of the River Pyandzh, was to be transferred to Afghanistan. Russia gained direct control of the eastern Pamir, and Russian garrisons were established in 1897–98 at Khorog in Shugnan and at two locations in Vakhan.[106] The agreement of 1895 was further strengthened by the 1907 Anglo-Russian Convention which created a strip of territory between the Pamir and Kashmir (the Wakhan Corridor) and attached it to Afghanistan.[107]

The emirate continued its isolated life. Strong resistance of the emir and the clergy to the modern world kept Bukhara in its old-fashioned, feudal condition. The Muslim clergy played a considerable political role over the years both in putting pressure on the emir to take a firmer stand in relation to the Russians and in resisting the advances of the modern world. The building of the Central Asian railway in 1886–88 did bring some change in this respect.[108] It brought both goods and ideas to the emirate, and stimuli from the outside world. These ideas, however, had difficulty penetrating the mountainous eastern part of the Bukhara Emirate.

In 1918 the British occupied Ashgabat and the Bukharan emir Alimkhan tried to strengthen his position by negotiating with the British and with the emir of Afghanistan. The final breakdown of the emirate did not come until after the Bolshevik revolution of 1917 in Russia proper. In October 1920 the emirate was replaced by the People's Soviet Republic of Bukhara, established with the help of Russian troops intervening in the domestic turmoil of the emirate.[109]

A reformist cultural revival in opposition to the emir had developed in the late 19th century. Akhmad Donish (1826–97), a Bukharan scholar and civil servant, was very influential in introducing the idea of need for modernization and reform in Central Asia. Donish realized the need for profound social and economic transformation in society and issued a number of reformist treatises, which the emir of Bukhara rejected.[110] The Jadidi reform movement gained strength at the beginning of the 20th century, and played an important role in bringing down the emir in 1920. The movement raised the demand for a political reform of the emirate but was also part of a trend of growing pan-Turkic nationalism among the Turkic-speaking peoples of Russia. Its founder was a Tatar, Ismail Beg Gaspirali, who advocated the unity of the Turkic peoples around a common literary language, a common culture and a common political organization. The Jadidis visualized the 'nation' of Turkic peoples not along ethnic lines but along religious and geographical lines as the 'Muslims of Turkistan', thereby including both Turkic and Iranian elements. Nevertheless, the Jadidis contributed to the strong trend of pan-Turkism in Central Asia at the time.

As Alexandre Bennigsen writes, the Jadidis developed 'from progressive Jadid democracy, to national socialism, national communism, and finally to nationalism'.[111] Thus, as a first step the radical Jadidis broke away and became Young Bukharans. They sought allies against the emir, collaborated at first with the Bolsheviks, joined the Tashkent Soviet of People's Commissars, formed the major section of the Turkestan Central Executive Committee, and played a role in the formation in 1918 of the Autonomous Turkestan Republic (ATR) from the former Russian Turkestan governor-generalship. In 1921 some former Jadidis broke away and joined the Basmachis fighting Soviet power. Further contributing to the chaotic situation was the renegade Turkish general Enver Pasha, who had arrived in Turkistan in 1921 from Turkey after he promised the Bolsheviks that he could put down the Basmachi revolt. Instead he joined the revolt and took over the leadership.[112]

In 1924 the People's Soviet Republic of Bukhara was incorporated into the Soviet Union, the ATR was dissolved, and Central Asia was delimited into territories defined on a national basis. By then the pan-Turkic school of thought was dominant—also attracting Tajik intellectuals, with consequences for the delimitation of Tajik territory under the Soviet Union. From 1924 to 1929 Tajikistan was an autonomous Soviet socialist republic (ASSR) under the Soviet Republic of Uzbekistan. It did not become a Soviet socialist republic on a par with Uzbekistan until 1929, when the Tajikistan Soviet Socialist Republic (SSR) was created. The discussions during these years, when the Uzbek language and the Turkic cultural heritage were emphasized, and the Tajik language and the Persian heritage were disregarded, left a dissonance between the republics when they became independent states in 1991. We will return to this in chapter 5.

It was Soviet rule, however, that gave the Tajiks statehood and own geographical and political territory, and reinstated the Tajik language. Under Soviet power a modernization process was initiated. The wider context of the Soviet Union helped Tajikistan to develop as a nation, although within the strict framework of the Soviet ideology. Moscow provided long-term economic investment and the Tajik SSR developed economically. In the 1970s and early 1980s Moscow made major investments in power stations for hydro-energy in order to exploit the riches of the republic, its water. These construction works started but had not been completed by the time the Soviet Union broke up. To Tajikistan the break-up of the Soviet Union was a heavy economic blow. To Gorno-Badakhshan, which lived on subsidies from Moscow thanks to its strategic importance, the end of the USSR was a disaster.

During the Soviet ideological offensive, which was launched against Muslim leaders and infrastructure, the traditional Muslim religious establishment in Central Asia was destroyed.[113] The Soviet Union reoriented Tajikistan away from contacts with southern Muslim countries towards Russia in the north. The Soviet leadership made it its objective to cut Central Asia off from the Muslim world and from the neighbours to the south—Afghanistan and Iran.[114]

As soon as the Soviet Union fell apart, the statue of Lenin in the central square in Dushanbe was replaced by a monument to Abulkasim

Firdawsi, the 10th-century poet and author of the national epos *Shahname*. The search for a national identity formulated through a return to the past had started.[115] A religious revival was on its way by the time the Soviet Union broke up, and an Islamic political movement had formed in opposition to the Communist regime. These trends were to give the direction of the development that was to follow.

## Conclusions

There is in the Tajikistan of today an ongoing process of national self-identification through the creation of a national past of the Tajiks. As in other Central Asian states, a search for 'retrospective proof' of a nationality on a given territory is going on. The history of Transoxania is one of invasions and empires replacing each other, but also of strong local resistance to the invaders. The official history, as formulated in *The Tajiks in the Mirror of History*, presents a history of invaders who time after time destroyed the Tajik nation, which 'like a mythical Phoenix will always rise from ashes, return to life and move forward towards the future decided by fate'.[116] The highest military award of today's Tajikistan, the Order of Bravery, is named after the Sogdian rebel leader Spitamen, who fought the invasion of Alexander the Great. Thus, history gives nourishment to a struggle for national identity.

Most of the invasions left an imprint and over time enriched the cultural heritage. The religions, ideologies, cultures and other influences that were brought by the invaders were taken over by the locals and assimilated into a common cultural heritage of the region. To a cultural heritage of East Iranian descent, Alexander the Great contributed the Greek–Macedonian culture, the Arabs brought Islam, the Uzbek khans added Turkic elements, and Tsarist and Soviet Russia brought European ideas and modernization. In this way the cultural heritage of the Tajik nation was complemented by different components, thereby creating room for different possible identities and foreign policy orientations of the state.

There are two aspects of the process of national identity-building and foreign policy orientation that are of special interest.

First, as pointed out in this chapter, the reading of history may either emphasize the common heritage of the Iranian and Turkic cultures and peoples or emphasize the specifics of each people as the state tries to trace the national–ethnic roots of the nation. This is something of direct concern to Tajikistan and Uzbekistan. Their history and culture are closely interwoven, yet official Tajik historiography perceives the nation to have been threatened through history almost to extinction. According to this view, two factors have been decisive: (a) that a Turcophone population came to dominate Transoxania as a result of invasions and movements of people over the centuries; and (b) that the national–administrative delimitation of Soviet Central Asia in the 1920s denied Tajikistan territories that were regarded as historic Tajik land. Tracing the national–cultural heritage of one state is a highly complicated matter. In Tsarist Russia and in the Soviet Union national groups were classified first and foremost with the help of ethno-linguistic criteria. Ethnic groups merged and the Turkic culture blended with the Iranian cultural heritage. While the Persian language remained the language of state administration and literature during the periods of Arab rule, as well as under the Timurids and the Uzbek khans, it later had to coexist with the Turkic languages. Literature later flourished in both the Iranian and the Turkic languages. These circumstances contribute to complicate the issue of what the specific national–cultural heritage of Tajikistan and Uzbekistan is. We will return to this in chapter 5 on Tajik policy towards Uzbekistan.

Second, the reading of history in this chapter shows possible options for foreign policy orientations that are available to independent Tajikistan. The options are embedded in the history of the territory. At the beginning of this chapter five possible analytical options for Tajikistan's foreign policy orientation were introduced: (a) the pan-Islamic; (b) the Persian; (c) the local, Central Asian (mostly with a pan-Turkic bent); (d) the European/Western; and (e) the European/Russian. We will save the final discussion of these options and where Tajikistan is heading to the concluding chapter. Suffice it here briefly to point out the characteristics of the different options.

The pan-Islamic option is based on the identity of Islam as a common religion and Arabic as the language of religion. This option had strong support in the late 19th and the early 20th centuries. The Bukhara Emirate was inclined towards a pan-Islamism that included Afghanistan; the reform-minded Jadidis, on the other hand, looked for a pan-Islamic movement that was oriented towards Turkey. Pan-Islamism is contrary to the nationalism that dominates the Tajik discourse after the 1920s, which is a kind of particularism in the sense that the interests of the individual nation state are in focus. The contemporary official Tajik discourse points to Islam as a common basis for the nation but emphasizes that no single political–social model follows from the Islamic faith; instead, it is said, the Islamic world is 'a conglomerate of different peoples and cultures'.[117]

The Persian option is based on the cultural affinity between the speakers of the Farsi language, which means Tajikistan, Afghanistan, Iran, and the north-western part of former India, nowadays Pakistan and India. This Persian identity blends with the Islamic component since the Samanid Empire continued the mission of the Arabs to spread Islam in

Central Asia. Yet the fact that the Persians have also been the conquerors makes this option difficult to reconcile with present-day nation-building in Tajikistan. Moreover, in spite of the cultural affinity with Iran, the fact that the Shia maintained power in Iran while Central Asia stayed Sunni also resulted in a distance between the two peoples. Nonetheless, the national Tajik heritage has to be defined from the general Iranian heritage since the Tajikistan of today seeks its roots in the distant past of the East Iranian tribes, the Aryans.

The local Central Asian option is based on the common experience of Transoxania/Mawarannahr—of the peoples of Iranian and Turkic descent which share a cultural heritage for almost 2,000 years. This common history is shared not only by Tajikistan and Uzbekistan but also to a substantial degree by other Central Asian countries. In the Tajik official discourse, emphasis on the closeness of Tajikistan and Uzbekistan is often perceived as being equivalent to Turkic dominance, and thus to the detriment of the Tajiks (see chapter 5 for a more detailed discussion of this).

A European/Russian option exists in the form of Russia's cultural influence, and above all Russia as symbolizing the modernization and industrialization efforts of the Soviet Union. Although it continues to regard Russia as a desirable partner, the Tajik national elite is trying to define the Tajik national interest as being separate from Russia's in order to shape a new national future for Tajikistan.

The European/Western option can be traced to the cultural heritage of the Macedonian Greeks. Although this may seem to be going too far back in time, the democratic values which the present Tajik regime defines as Western and European. As the authors of *The Tajiks in the Mirror of History* write,

> At the beginning of the twentieth century, Rudyard Kipling … expressed his deep regret at the fact that the civilisations of the East and West were divided by an insurmountable barrier. Fortunately enough, towards the end of the twentieth century this barrier has now become obsolete, and cultural and friendly exchanges between the countries have become a reality. Nowadays, Tajikistan is a full member of many influential international organizations, including the UN, the [Organization for Security and Co-operation in Europe] OSCE, the Economic and Social Commission for Asia and the Pacific, … . [118]

Thus, history provides layers of cultural and religious identification, and thereby alternative options for the future foreign policy orientation of Tajikistan. To which of them will Tajikistan turn?

In the short-term perspective, pragmatic evaluations often determine in what direction the leadership of a state will look. It will orient itself towards the foreign power that in the short run brings the best opportunities for national security, economic development and a thriving culture. The long-term endeavours of the state, on the other hand, will most probably be anchored in the way history is read. To the discussion of this question—in what direction Tajikistan is orienting itself—we will return in the concluding chapter.

# 3

# THE FIRST TEN YEARS OF INDEPENDENCE

Soviet power gave Tajikistan a state identity, although with the framework of the USSR, and brought schools, factories and new alphabets (first Latin in the 1920s and then Cyrillic in the 1930s). Tajikistan was well integrated into the Soviet system and, although its development was not entirely free of problems, Tajikistan still benefited from it. Gorno-Badakhshan has already been mentioned as an example of a region that lived on subsidies from the central government in Moscow. The break-up of the Soviet Union meant an end to this, and was thus a heavy economic blow. Adding to the picture at the time was the fierce political struggle that ended in civil war between 1992 and 1997. The first ten years of independence can therefore best be characterized, in the words of American scholar Rafis Abazov, as 'ten lost years'. By the time the citizens of Tajikistan commemorated their first ten years in September 2001, this took place 'in such misery and terror as no other state on former Soviet territory', he says.[1]

## The Disaster of the Civil War

Tajikistan, like the Baltic states, became the scene of lively debate political debate early on during the years of Gorbachev's perestroika. In July 1989 the Tajik language was given the status of state language by law after large demonstrations had taken place in the capital, Dushanbe, at the beginning of the year. In September the same year the Rastokhez (Renaissance) opposition movement was set up, and during the following year, 1990, the major opposition political parties—the Islamic Revival Party (IRP), and the Democratic Party (DP)—were established. Demonstrations against the communist regime started in January 1990 and became frequent. The failed August 1991 coup attempt against President Mikhail Gorbachev triggered a wave of opposition activities as the Tajik communists supported the coup plotters. The opposition held a ten-day meeting demanding a ban on the Communist Party and tore down the statue of Lenin on Shakhidon Square in Dushanbe, outside the building of the Supreme Soviet. The communist leader was forced to resign.

The first Tajik presidential elections ever took place in November 1991. As much as 31 per cent of the vote went to the opposition candidate, film producer Davlat Khudonazarov, whose family came from Gorno-Badakhshan in eastern Tajikistan. The former communist leader and representative of the Leninabad region, Rakhmon Nabiev, won. Nabiev formed his government in the Soviet tradition with people mainly from the north of Tajikistan (the Leninabad region). The opposition, which accused the regime of falsifying the vote, refused to recognize the outcome. The political atmosphere was wound-up and tense.

During spring 1992 political tensions resulted in demonstrations that went on for weeks. A physical front line was established between two camps in Dushanbe, with the opposition on Shakhidon Square and those loyal to the regime on Ozodi Square, both along the former Lenin Avenue (later to be renamed Rudaki Avenue). The opposition sent a resolution to President Nabiev demanding that parliament be dissolved, work on a new constitution be speeded up, and persecution of the opposition parties be ended.[2] The political situation had become sharply polarized. To calm the situation, in May 1992 Nabiev agreed to create a coalition government with one-third of its members from the opposition—descendants of families from the east and south of the country. This provoked a strong reaction, especially from the Leninabad region, which did not recognize the new government. The country erupted in armed violence. In September 1992 Nabiev was forced to resign, and the civil war was in full swing. The major force fighting the Democratic and Islamic opposition was the so-called People's Front.

It was against this background of chaos that a special session of the parliament was held in Khujand in November 1992. Different pro-nomenklatura groups of the People's Front joined forces and had a relatively unknown former kolkhoz chairman from Kulyab, Emomali Rakhmonov, elected acting head of state.[3] At about the same time their troops launched an offensive against Dushanbe and a brutal campaign of 'ethnic' cleansing of Pamiris and Karateginis.[4] Those who had helped to install Rakhmonov had considered him a temporary figure who could be their instrument, but once in power Rakhmonov consolidated his position. In spring 1993 different factions of the opposition joined forces and created the United Tajik Opposition (UTO). The civil war continued until 1997. It claimed between 40,000 and 80,000 lives and forced 800,000 people to seek refuge abroad, mostly in Afghanistan but also in Iran and Russia.

Why did Tajikistan erupt in civil war? There are at least three important factors that shaped the political scene and made the political struggle much fiercer in Tajikistan than in any other former Soviet republic at the time. First, there were the regional divisions and tensions in Tajikistan that became a basis for political factions and movements; second, there was the turbulence around neighbouring Afghanistan, which provided inspiration and later weapons and a safe haven for the opposition fighters; and, third, there was the factor of radical Islam, which for at least a part of the opposition was an additional motivation.[5]

Soviet policy had sharpened regional contradictions and thereby paved the way for the civil war. Regional division has always characterized Tajikistan. The topography of the country, with high mountains dividing people in the valleys, contributed to strong local identification, expressed in distinct regional dresses and customs, local languages, and the pronunciation of the Tajik language. These local identities were classified as Leninabadis from the north (nowadays the Sogd region); the Pamiris from Gorno-Badakhshan in the east; the Garmis from the Garm and Karategin valleys to the north-east of Dushanbe; the Kulyabis to the south-east of Dushanbe; the Hissaris from the Hissar district to the west of Dushanbe; and finally those from Kurgan-Tyube to the south-west of the capital.[6] Huge programmes of forced labour resettlements drawn up by the Soviet government from the early 1920s up to the 1960s contributed to create tension between regional groups. Thousands of households from the Garm region and from relatively densely populated districts in the Fergana Valley were resettled in the south of Tajikistan, in Kulyab and Kurgan-Tyube, especially the Vakhsh Valley. They were sent there to cultivate cotton for the Soviet Union in the newly irrigated lands. These new 'settlers of cotton and irrigation migrants'[7] did not meld easily into the society around them but settled in isolated enclaves. People already living in the Vakhsh Valley considered that the newcomers were given preferential treatment and superior agricultural land. Mistrust between the groups built up. It strengthened against the background of the general economic decline of post-Soviet Union, a demographic boom, high rural unemployment, and an evolving vacuum of central government power in the later years of the Soviet Union.[8]

During the last years of Soviet rule the people from Karategin increased their economic strength in the republic by trading their local agricultural products all over Soviet territory. The people from Pamir had gained greater weight in the state structures as the Gorno-Badakhshan Autonomous Region became strategically more important to Moscow and was therefore heavily subsidized. At the same time neither Karategin nor Badakhshan had any political influence in Dushanbe, since in Soviet times people from the industrialized and more developed Leninabad region always dominated the government. When the political opposition took form, people from Garm and Karategin, as well as Badakhshan, became the backbone of the opposition. The core of the government side under Rakhmonov during the civil war was the pro-nomenklatura People's Front with supporters in the south of the country, especially in Kulyab, but also in the Turzunzade and Hissar districts in the west. The Leninabadis supported the People's Front but without participating in the fighting. The epicentre of violence during the civil war was Dushanbe and the Kurgan-Tyube region. The fiercest clashes during the civil war took place in the south of Tajikistan, where the Kulyabis mobilized the Popular Front against the Garmis living in the area. The majority of people killed during the civil war were ethnic Tajiks of Garmi and Pamiri origin.

The outcome of the civil war was a victory for the Kulyabis. By 1999 the Leninabadis, who had dominated Tajik political life throughout the Soviet period, found themselves replaced in the top positions by Kulyabis from Rakhmonov's home region.

There was an Afghan factor in the Tajik civil war from the very beginning. The Soviet occupation of Afghanistan between 1979 and 1989 reopened Tajikistan to influences from Afghanistan. Since the late 1960s the Soviet Union had used the Muslim population and the government-controlled Muslim establishment to penetrate the Arab/Islamic world. In the 1970s the Soviet authorities organized conferences on Islamic themes and sent delegates to such conferences in other Muslim countries. The outcome had both benefits and drawbacks, as the American scholar Shireen Hunter writes: 'Contacts with the Muslim world awakened Soviet Muslims to their secondary position. It also facilitated the penetration of new ideas, including politicised Islam, into the USSR's Muslim regions, a process that later proved disruptive'.[9] In this context the encounter of Soviet Central Asians and Afghan Muslims took place in Soviet-occupied Afghanistan. What in Afghanistan had started as a reaction to the modernizing efforts of the Afghan regime in the 1970s had developed into a jihad against the Soviet occupation of Afghanistan. This development in Afghanistan went parallel with an Islamic revival in Central Asia.

By the time the pro-communist regime of Afghan President Mohammad Najibullah fell in 1992, three years after the Soviet occupation of Afghanistan had ended, and the Islamic Republic of Afghanistan was established, the political situation in Dushanbe had become very tense. During demonstrations by the Islamist flank of the opposition, when thousands of people gathered in central Dushanbe on Shakhidon Square, they shouted slogans such as 'Down with the USA', 'Down with Russia', but also 'We have an army of 27,000 Mujaheddin' and 'In Afghanistan our brothers have taken power'.[10] During the Tajik civil war thousands of Tajiks, among them many members of the Tajik opposition, fled to Afghanistan and stayed as refugees during the years that followed.

The Islamic revival that was already emerging in the 1970s intensified during the years of perestroika, and the process accelerated during the break-up of the Soviet Union as the societies in Central Asia searched for their heritage, identity, norms and values.[11] The IRP, at the time it was created in 1990, was the outcome of the Islamic awakening among Soviet Muslims that had taken off in the late 1970s. In this process a 'politicization of Islam' took place as Islam was used for political purposes by the opposition, as well as later by the regimes, to legitimize claims and demands. The derogatory term used for the opposition fighters during the years of civil war was *vovchiki*, which was the derogatory term used for the Wahhabites and referred first of all to the Islamist flank of the opposition.[12]

Religion was not the major factor; the regional factor was the most important. Nevertheless, as it was perceived at the time, radical Islam was a crucial factor, and many feared the outcome of this radicalism.

Russia's role during the Tajik civil war can be described as initially passive from the side of the government, while the local Russian military engaged in the conflict against the opposition. When civil strife turned into civil war in May 1992, the Russian 201st Motorized Rifle Division (MRD), deployed in Tajikistan since Soviet times, was ordered to remain neutral. Informally, however, it started to transfer weapons to the Popular Front. According to most commentators, Rakhmonov might never have come to power without the help of the Russians. Once in power, Rakhmonov received Moscow's official recognition and blessing, and the Russian military presence increased. Russia's prime concern was to support a regime that would bring stability and guarantee a continued role and influence for Russia in Tajikistan irrespective of the fact that the democratic opposition in Russia had previously supported the Tajik democrats. Now there was no room for any Russian consideration as to what would advance democracy. After opposition fighters killed 25 Russian border troops in July 1993 during an attack at the Tajik–Afghan border, Russia assumed primary responsibility for Tajikistan's security and increased its military presence. In September 1993 Russian troops took on the role of 'peacekeepers' in line with a decision by the member states of the Commonwealth of Independent States (CIS). In April 1994 Russia as a 'third party mediator' succeeded in getting the warring parties to the negotiating table. Under the pretence of being neutral, Russia continued to back the Rakhmonov regime and his efforts to defeat the opposition.[13]

In 1994 Rakhmonov hastily arranged a referendum on amendments to the constitution and presidential and parliamentary elections in order to legitimize his government. Both the United Nations and the

Organization for Security and Co-operation in Europe (OSCE) criticized the presidential election of 1994 and the 1995 parliamentary elections: the opposition parties had been banned in 1993 and were not allowed to participate. Nevertheless, after the elections the Rakhmonov regime began to act with confidence as if it were a legitimate elected government, and it repeatedly referred to the 'existing constitutional framework'. By referring to the new constitution, both Rakhmonov and Moscow turned down all the UTO's proposals at the negotiating table for a political compromise as unconstitutional. Thus, Moscow's official support for Rakhmonov continued as previously.

The situation in Tajikistan reached stalemate in autumn 1995; the inter-Tajik negotiations under the aegis of the UN made no progress, and on the ground the opposition began to advance militarily in the interior of Tajikistan, in Tavildara and Garm. Moscow was seriously concerned at this, especially since the Taliban had swept to victory in Afghanistan after their first appearance in 1994. By the time Yevgenii Primakov became Russian foreign minister in January 1996, a change in the Russian approach had started. Primakov, a former head of the Foreign Intelligence Service (Sluzhba Vneshnei Razvedki, SVR) and an orientalist by academic training, fully understood the threat of the Taliban on the offensive in Afghanistan and the possible disastrous implications for neighbouring Tajikistan in the midst of a civil war. He saw stabilization and an end to conflicts as his first priority. During 1996 Moscow together with Iran began seriously to seek a political compromise that would end the civil war in Tajikistan. On 23 December 1996 an agreement was signed between President Rakhmonov and the UTO leader, Said Abdullo Nuri, on the creation of a Commission of National Reconciliation (CNR). The protocol of the agreement prescribed a referendum on a new constitution, a new electoral law, reform of the executive powers to include representatives of the opposition at all levels, and suggestions for the date of new elections to take place under UN and OSCE monitoring.

## Light at the End of the Tunnel

The General Peace Agreement was signed in June 1997. Not only did Russia and Iran play an important role in the peace negotiations; so did the international community, represented by the United Nations, which moderated the peace negotiations from their start in April 1994.[14] In 1992 the UN Security Council had authorized the UN to find a negotiated settlement to the conflict.

The peace agreement thus prescribed the creation of the CNR to oversee its implementation and to design a set of reforms to the government structure. It was to be composed of equal numbers of government and UTO representatives and chaired by the UTO leader, Said Abdullo Nuri, while his deputy would be Abdulmajid Dostiev from the government side. The CNR was to work out guidelines for constitutional reform and the forthcoming presidential and parliamentary elections, in which opposition parties were to participate. As Rahmatullo Zoirov and Scott Newton later wrote, the CNR had the chance to prepare far-reaching constitutional reform, yet the outcome of its work was structurally biased in favour of the existing system.[15]

The peace agreement dealt with the issue of how to agree on an end to the war, but did not specify what was implied by 'national reconciliation' or what political forces would be included. As Arne Seifert has pointed out, while the UN and the OSCE understood 'national reconciliation' as meaning the inclusion in the peace settlement process of the widest possible circle of political forces, in the event the mechanisms of conflict resolution concentrated only on the warring sides, the government side and the UTO.[16] The result was that no other political forces in the country were represented. As a result the Leninabad region was never part of the power-sharing agreement as it had not participated in combat. When Abdumalik Abdullodjanov from the Leninabad region made an effort to articulate the interests of the region and create a 'Third Force', it never became part of the power-sharing arrangement.[17] His efforts to put forward regional interests were crushed.[18] There were also other kinds of minor contradiction that were never dealt with, for example, between the Islamist part of the UTO, many of whom lived outside Tajikistan during the civil war, and those of the Democratic flank who remained inside the country.[19] The two parties to the conflict, however, had limited popular support since neither the government nor the opposition had a majority behind them.

The CNR set up four subcommissions—on refugee-related, military, political and legal issues. The most rapid progress was made on the Protocol on Refugee Issues, and UN bodies played an important role in its implementation. The Protocol on Military Issues aimed to integrate the many armed forces into a unified military and to promote decommissioning and demobilization. It centred on integrating the UTO fighters into a national army, and crucial to this was the work on a law on a general amnesty to release opposition members from prison and grant amnesty to more than 5,000 UTO fighters.[20] By March 2000 the process of military integration of the former fighters was completed.

The Political Protocol was more difficult to implement, since it was based on power-sharing between the two former opposite sides of the civil war. According to the agreement, 30 per cent of the government posts at all administrative levels were to be distributed to the UTO. The appointment of two members of the UTO's Islamist flank was delayed.

These were the UTO's first deputy chairman, Hodji Akhbar Turajonzoda, who was to become first deputy prime minister, and the UTO commander-in-chief, Mirzo Ziyo, who was to head the Ministry of Emergency Situations. The UTO feared that Rakhmonov would try to avoid implementing all parts of the peace agreement. This was right in the sense that at the regional or district levels the 30 per cent quota was never fully implemented.[21] Only at the ministerial level was the UTO given representation up to the level stipulated.

Work on the Protocol on Legal Issues consisted first of all of drafting constitutional amendments and new legislation. Step by step the process continued in spite of many difficulties. On 30 June 1999 the Tajik parliament adopted the amendments to the constitution (prepared by the CNR), and a referendum in September confirmed the revisions. The main changes included the creation of an upper house of parliament representing the regions, an extension of the president's term of office to seven years (with a limit of one term), and allowing political parties based on religion. The 1993 ban on the opposition parties was lifted in August 1999.

In November 1999 the presidential elections took place. The UTO could not agree on a joint candidate; instead there were three candidates—Davlat Usmonov of the IRP, Saiffidin Turayev of the Party of Justice, and Sulton Kuvvatov of the DP. The registration of an IRP candidate resulted in a split within the party when Turajonzoda came out in support of Rakhmonov. Rakhmonov was elected president with large majority, and in the parliamentary elections in February and March 2000 his party won most seats. The opposition charged that the presidential as well as the parliamentary elections had been rigged. In the parliamentary elections the IRP received less than 8 per cent of the vote on the party list part of the voting, and was represented by two delegates in parliament. This was a great disappointment to the party members, many of whom considered that the IRP leadership had given in to the Rakhmonov regime too easily. The DP did not pass the 5 per cent threshold of the party list part of the vote to parliament and did not receive representation.

The transition period prescribed in the General Peace Agreement thus came to an end in spring 2000, when constitutional reforms had been carried out and presidential and parliamentary elections had taken place. Rakhmonov could now feel much safer. Yet the political situation remained fragile, and armed warlords who did not recognize either the peace agreement or the authority of the government continued to challenge the government. This created 'pockets' of warlord territory over which the government had no control. This was true especially of the inner parts of Tajikistan to the east of Dushanbe, where commanders of the opposition had control. However, there were rebel commanders on the government side as well. Among them was Makhmud Khudoberdiev, an ethnic Uzbek and a former head of the Presidential Guard, who led a series of mutinies against Rakhmonov beginning in 1996, until he was driven out of Tajikistan into Uzbekistan in 1997. In November 1998 he returned for the last time, leading some 1,000 armed supporters into the Leninabad region, and was stopped only by the joint efforts of government and UTO forces. Khudoberdiev was accused of receiving Uzbek support and being the instrument of Uzbek interests.

Tajik society was still generally unstable as late as 8 September 2001, when the minister of culture, press and information was assassinated on the doorstep of his home. This was the last in a chain of political murders and kidnappings that had dominated life in Tajikistan for many years. In the same month, the government successfully completed its campaign against the warlord Rakhmon Sanginov and his band of supporters, initiated in early summer 2001.

By autumn 2001 the situation in the country remained fragile although it was slowly stabilizing after the 1997 peace agreement. The situation during the year and a half after the parliamentary elections of spring 2000 was characterized by two features: (a) the power-sharing arrangement of the General Peace Agreement was violated, as power was concentrated in the hands of the president and he tried to marginalize the opposition; and (b) the regional imbalance that was the result of Rakhmonov's takeover of power was confirmed.

The economic situation remained catastrophic, although by 2001 it had started to recover somewhat compared with the late 1990s. A basic reform strategy had been drawn up in 1992 but the government could only start the process seriously after the civil war had ended. Statistics reflect the situation: by 1992 the economy was just 60 per cent of its size in 1988. Between 1992 and 1996 the economy shrank by a further 50 per cent, and the total volume of industrial production contracted by nearly 70 per cent between 1990 and 1997. In August 1998 Tajikistan received its first World Bank credits. The late 1990s were characterized by moderate growth as traditional industries, such as the aluminium sector, increased production.[22] But all this was far from enough.

## Foreign Policy: Bandwagoning with Russia

Tajikistan's foreign policy focused on surviving as a state by securing international assistance for (a) national security and (b) economic development. During the years of civil war and turmoil Tajikistan had been too weak to have any active foreign policy of its own. The Rakhmonov regime was dependent on Russia. Tajikistan was embedded in bilateral and multilateral cooperation with Russia and the CIS after the CIS was created in late 1991, and in the Collective Security Treaty (CST) after 1992. Because of its domestic situation it was a mainly passive member of these organizations, and only in 1998 did it join the CIS Customs Union of Russia, Belarus, Armenia, Kazakhstan and Kyrgyzstan, and in March the same year the Central Asian regional organization (the Central Asian Economic Union, CAEU, which later became the Central Asian Cooperation Organization, CACO).

Thus, the ending of the civil war provided the basic conditions for a more active foreign policy. During 1999 Dushanbe became a venue for international summit meetings for the first time since the break-up of the Soviet Union, as the Central Asian regional organization and the Shanghai Five (later renamed Shanghai Cooperation Organization) met there. 1999 was also the year when Tajikistan signed a Joint Declaration of Friendship and Cooperation with China regulating their common border.

The end of the 1990s was also the time when the regional situation seriously deteriorated, first of all in Afghanistan but also in Uzbekistan. As the security situation in Afghanistan deteriorated after the Taliban took power in 1996, Tajikistan took on a high profile in the Russian-led CST military and security cooperation. From 1998 it became the major transit country for Russian material support for the anti-Taliban Northern Alliance under Ahmad Shah Massoud. After Uzbekistan left the CST in April 1999, Tajikistan became a major ally of Russia on the southern flank of the CIS. When most Central Asian governments started to waver in relation to the Taliban regime, as they wished to normalize relations, the Tajik government continued to regard the situation in Afghanistan as a major threat to its national security. The tensions in the security situation in the region increased following the bombings in central Tashkent in February 1999, reflecting the complex domestic situation in Uzbekistan. The incursions into southern Kyrgyzstan by Uzbek militant Islamists of the Islamic Movement of Uzbekistan (IMU) in August 1999 increased the pressure on Tajikistan from the side of Uzbekistan.

The regional security situation, Tajikistan's own domestic fragility, and the large Russian military presence in Tajikistan contributed to the strong Russian orientation of Tajik foreign policy. Although Tajikistan was willing in principle to develop relations with different states, as other Central Asian governments did, its vulnerability made it dependent on Russia. Russia was a guarantor of both Tajikistan's national security and the survival of its regime. Cooperation with Russia and integration with states in the CIS, and first of all Central Asian states, were priorities for its foreign policy. The Tajik scholar Z. A. Dadabaeva reflected the hopes of the time that such an orientation would bring Tajikistan economic benefits. She referred in 2000 to the concept of 'Eurasianism', and to Russian thinkers of this school, to explain Tajikistan's identification and orientation, although she also noted Tajikistan's efforts to reach out to the world market and to individual countries, among them European countries and the USA.[23] The idea of Tajikistan creating its own room for manoeuvre in foreign policy by extending its international contacts had already existed during the civil war. By 1997 Iran was regarded as an important foreign partner, although it was in no way comparable to Russia. Circumstances, however, did not yet allow an independent Tajik foreign policy.

The Russian military presence in Tajikistan was far larger than the presence in any other CIS country. The 201st MRD in Tajikistan, which in September 1993 had been formally labelled 'CIS peacekeeping troops' after a decision of the CIS, consisted of about 8,500 men at its most but was reduced to approximately 6,500 men after the General Peace Agreement. The division was formally subordinated to the Russian Volga–Ural Military District and consisted of Russian contract personnel. As Russia's most important forward post to the south, its troops were deployed not far from the border with Afghanistan as a back-up to the Russian border troops (a second echelon) along the Tajik–Afghan border in the towns of Dushanbe, Kurgan-Tyube and Kulyab.[24] Since the peacekeeping mandate given to the 201st MRD by the CIS was to come to an end in summer 2000, Tajikistan and Russia signed an agreement in April 1999 on a Russian military base to secure the Russian military presence in Tajikistan in the future. The devil was in the detail, however, and the negotiations on the conditions for such a base continued for the following five years.

The Russian border troops remained in Tajikistan according to a bilateral agreement of May 1993. Article 29 of this agreement envisaged the possibility of a handover of responsibility for the border to a national Tajik border service at the end of a ten-year period. The Russian border troops, which numbered about 16,000 men in 1997, were reduced to about 11,500 in 1997. They were mostly Tajik citizens, but of the officers as many as 93 per cent were Russian.[25] Either side could opt out of the 1993 agreement on border protection with six months' advance notice, but if they failed to do this the agreement was automatically extended for a new five-year period. In other Central Asian countries national border services had taken over responsibility for the protection of their borders by early 1999. In February 1997 a Tajik State Border Protection Committee was set up but its troops were few in number, and badly trained and equipped.

In spite of this substantial Russian military presence there was a degree of Western engagement in Tajikistan before 2001. This relates in particular to the work being done by the UN and OSCE missions in the country. Western assistance implied humanitarian aid and assistance. In April 1999 President Rakhmonov visited the USA where he met with First Deputy Secretary of State Strobe Talbott, the deputy secretary of state for South Asia, and the head of the US Anti-Drug Agency. Otherwise his visit was dominated by the humanitarian situation in Tajikistan and the assistance the country could receive from international organizations. Rakhmonov met representatives of economic and financial organizations such as the International Monetary Fund (IMF) and the World Bank, but also the US Agency for Trade and Development, the Eurasia Foundation, the US Department of Agriculture, and US business circles. This assistance was followed up in May when the USA assigned 800,000 dollars (USD) to support the peace process in Tajikistan.[26] The visit had a low political profile but was nevertheless highly important for Tajikistan for receiving international credits and economic assistance. It was in stark contrast to the high profile of Rakhmonov's first official visit two and a half year later.[27]

Thus, Tajikistan was outside the security cooperation that the USA was encouraging between the Central Asian states and the North Atlantic Treaty Organization (NATO) countries under NATO's Partnership for Peace (PFP) programme. Tajikistan did not join the PFP when other Central Asian states did so in 1994. It did not contribute to the PFP-supported Central Asian peacekeeping battalion set up by the other member states of the Central Asian Union (CAU), and did not participate in the PFP-sponsored exercises of the Central Asian Battalion (Centrasbat) from 1997. Western governments and international organizations kept a low profile in Tajikistan both because of the Russian dominance in the country and because of the lack of security for international representatives and staff members.

Although a US embassy was set up soon after then US Secretary of State James Baker visited Dushanbe in spring 1992, for long periods there was no US ambassador. The USA did not pay much attention to Tajikistan. US policy in Central Asia reflected an interest in the region that was anchored in the geo-strategic location of the region in relation to Russia and in an interest in the energy resources of the region. The US administration demonstrated an ambition to help strengthen the independence of these states against Russia and a policy of democratic reform, human rights and economic liberalism.[28] Tajikistan, however, was not one of the Central Asian countries with large oil and gas resources.

Thus, although President Rakhmonov and the Tajik parliament officially stated a desire to develop cooperation with any state independent of ideology, political system and religion, Tajikistan's exchange with the outside world remained limited.[29]

## Conclusions

Tajikistan was a case of a civil war being successfully ended through negotiation and political compromise. It also was a case of a state plunged into deep poverty.

Against this background it is not surprising that during its first ten years of independence Tajikistan was bandwagoning with Russia in its foreign policy, and continued to do so after other Central Asian states had started a balancing policy in relation to Russia by extending their contacts with foreign governments. Although there was an interest in creating room for an independent Tajik foreign policy (as reflected in discussions with official Tajik representatives in the late 1990s), Tajikistan's foreign policy was an answer to its difficult internal and external security situation—a fragile regime in an external environment of turmoil and political radicalism on the rise in neighbouring countries. From 1998 Tajikistan tried to carve out a niche for itself as an active promoter of security cooperation within the Russian-led CST. The Tajik leadership tried to establish a foreign policy role which would make the country more valuable to Russia and thereby hopefully also allow it to become a beneficiary of Russian economic assistance.

The vulnerability of Tajikistan followed from the difficult security situation both in the country and in the region. It also followed from the disastrous economic situation as a result of the break-up of the Soviet Union and then five years of civil war. To reduce its vulnerability and get the wheels of the economy started, substantial international assistance and investments were needed. So far, however, international interest seemed low, and the prospects for any large-scale international economic assistance seemed bleak. This was the situation as the terrorist attacks on the Twin Towers of the World Trade Center in New York and the Pentagon in Washington, DC took place on the morning of 11 September 2001.

# PART II

# TAJIKISTAN'S FOREIGN POLICY SINCE 2001

# 4

# BIG-POWER ENGAGEMENT AND
# TAJIK POLICY

## Introduction

The 11 September 2001 terrorist attacks on the United States changed
the international context for Tajikistan drastically. From having had only
few contacts with Western countries, a few Western and Asian embassies
and two or three foreign journalists, Dushanbe was suddenly bustling
with foreigners. Although most of the journalists soon left, the
international attention to Tajikistan remained, and so did the interest of
the big powers. Tajikistan welcomed this foreign engagement.

This chapter deals with the way in which the pattern of big-power
engagement shifted in Tajikistan and in the sub-region, including
Afghanistan and Uzbekistan, and how Tajikistan responded to the
foreign interest, trying to reduce its vulnerability and perform the major
tasks of the state in the security and economic spheres. How did
Tajikistan's relations with foreign the powers that engaged in the
country—first and foremost Russia and the USA, but also European and
Asian powers—change? Where did Tajikistan turn for assistance and
guarantees with regard to its national security and economic
development? The chapter thus deals with Tajikistan's policy and
relations with Russia and the USA, first of all, but also China, Iran,
Pakistan and India, and European states, in the security and economic
spheres after September 2001.

In relation to Tajikistan's relationship to Russia, the trends in Tajik
foreign policy will be defined in terms of *bandwagoning* with Russia or
*balancing* Russia.

Weakened by the five-year-long civil war, the Tajik leadership's
capacity to influence its international environment during the 1990s was
minimal. Tajikistan could at best react to events. Its vulnerability in
security terms can be compared to that of states of the Third World that
are described as 'small or undeveloped nations, often susceptible to
intimidation or manipulation by external powers'.[1] Nevertheless, at a

certain moment history may give a country a chance to break away from the previous patterns of regional power configurations and enter into cooperation with new partners. The period after 11 September 2001 provided such a 'window of opportunity' for Tajikistan.

Substantial changes took place in Central Asia after September 2001, especially with regard to the increased US engagement in the region as a whole, and above all in what is here called the sub-system of Afghanistan, Uzbekistan and Tajikistan. These years saw a new 'axis' arise of the USA in cooperation with all these three states, while Russia was left with Tajikistan as an ally. Russia did not manage to attract Uzbekistan back to the 1992 Collective Security Treaty (CST), which Uzbekistan had left in 1999, and in Afghanistan Russia continued to lose political influence as the old guard of ethnic-Tajik Afghans of the Northern Alliance was squeezed out of central positions in the government of President Hamid Karzai from 2002. Thus the general trend of decline in Russia's influence in Central Asia since the late 1990s accelerated after 2001.

The trend of reduced Russian influence was also visible in Tajikistan. However, in October 2004, Russia and Tajikistan signed a series of agreements which secured a strong Russian presence not only in the military sphere but also in the economic sphere. They concerned huge Russian economic investments in the Tajik hydro-energy and aluminium sectors during the next five to seven years. What impact would this increased Russian presence have on Tajik foreign policy making? Was this a sign that Russia was again rising as a power in Central Asia, or had the foreign engagement in the region already contributed to a fundamental change in the geopolitical situation, which Russia would not be able to dominate again? Uncertainties surrounded these question as Russia's political influence in Central Asia seemed to increase after President Askar Akaev was forced from power in Kyrgyzstan in March 2005, riots followed in Andijan, Uzbekistan, two months later, and in June 2005 Uzbek President Islam Karimov told the US military to leave Uzbekistan within 18 months.

The analysis of the policy changes of the post-2001 period will be divided into three brief periods defined by changes in the Russian factor in Tajikistan: first, immediately after September 2001, here called 'the turn of events in 2001'; second, the years 2002 up to the summer of 2004, here called the 'backdrop of Russia' (although Russian policy towards Central Asia and Tajikistan was activated at the time); and, third, the period after summer 2004, called 'a Russian return?', with the question mark indicating the uncertainty of the outcome of Russia's new foreign policy.

## The Turn of Events in 2001

More or less immediately after the terror attacks in September 2001 the Tajik government understood that the new situation was opening up favourable prospects for Tajikistan.[2] Although cautious not to provoke a Russian reaction, it expressed its interest in participating in the US-led anti-terrorist coalition and opening up its territory for the US military. On 16 September the Uzbek foreign minister had declared that Uzbekistan was open to 'any form of antiterrorist cooperation with the United States', including the possible use of Uzbek territory for strikes on terrorist camps in Afghanistan.[3] The Tajik foreign minister was more cautious but clearly indicated interest in cooperation with the USA. Since he was not sure what line Moscow would take, he stated that consultations with Russia would take place first.[4] In late September the Tajik government announced to the US administration its willingness to open up its territory, if needed, for overflights, landing and basing, offered all available sites, and left it to the USA to state its preferences.[5]

The Tajik reaction reflected the regime's clear interest in using the opportunities of the post-11 September situation to increase cooperation with the USA. This positive reaction was made possible since Russian President Vladimir Putin had expressed his understanding and support for US President George W. Bush and the USA's right to respond to the new threat. Putin used the post-11 September situation to make a breakthrough in Russia's relations with the USA, but he had to find a formula for building a consensus in Russian government structures, where opinions were divided on how to respond.[6] On 14 September the *New York Times* alleged that there had been negotiations between US and Russian officials over the use by US forces of Russian military facilities in Tajikistan and of a former Soviet airfield in northern Afghanistan for attacks on Taliban troops in Afghanistan. Russian Defence Minister Sergei Ivanov and Chief of the General Staff Anatolii Kvashnin denied that any such discussions had taken place.[7] As reported on 18 September, Ivanov excluded the possibility of US forces being allowed to use Central Asian territory and stated that 'Central Asia is within the zone of competence of the [Commonwealth of Independent States] CIS Collective Security Treaty. I see no reasons whatsoever, even hypothetical, for any suppositions about NATO operations being conducted from the territories of Central Asian countries which are members of the CIS'.[8] Nevertheless, in a speech on 24 September Putin announced that Russia and its Central Asian allies would allow the US military to use Central Asian airfields during operations in Afghanistan. He spelled out, however, that only foreign humanitarian, rescue and intelligence operations would be allowed to take off from these countries. His statement was a compromise which took into account both the Central Asian states' strong interest in cooperating with the USA and the resistance from the Russian military.

The Tajik government, which had a clear interest in cooperating with the USA, made public its offer to the US government on 8 October, one day after the US bombings of Afghanistan were initiated and three days after President Rakhmonov had had a telephone conversation with Putin. In mid-October, Foreign Minister Talbak Nazarov followed up on this, stating that Tajikistan 'does not rule out the stationing of US forces in the country'.[9] Visits by top-level US military followed to hammer out the details of the US presence, for example, the commander of the US operation in Afghanistan, General Tommy Franks of the US Central Command (CENTCOM), met Rakhmonov in Dushanbe on 31 October to discuss the situation in Afghanistan.[10] On 3 November, during a visit to Dushanbe by US Secretary of Defense Donald Rumsfeld, Rakhmonov publicly gave his consent to the use of three military airfields in Tajikistan by the USA and its allies.[11] Rakhmonov agreed to regular exchanges of information on anti-terrorist operations and to the establishment of permanent military-to-military contacts between the USA and Tajikistan. Rumsfeld confirmed that Tajikistan would provide assistance with regard to 'overflights, intelligence gathering and various types of military-to-military cooperation'.[12] Tajik officials underlined, however, that this did not mean that Tajikistan would allow any US military operations to take off from Tajikistan.[13]

The Tajik government was willing to host a US military base. A US assessment team soon found that, of the three airfields under discussion (Dushanbe, Kulyab and Kurgan-Tyube), only Dushanbe could be used, and only for refuelling cargo planes, but not for heavy aircraft.[14] Western troops began arriving in December. Among the first were French marines, arriving on 6 December en route to Afghanistan. The US military followed. The Western military presence in Tajikistan was small (there were 150 US troops at the most during spring 2002; in September 2002 this number was down to 50; and there were 500 French troops at the most, and 150 half a year later) but the Western presence changed the strategic situation and initiated a new era of international cooperation.[15]

In interviews in December 2001 Rakhmonov predicted that the stationing of Western air power in Tajikistan would continue long after the end of active US military operations in Afghanistan, and stated that it would take several years to achieve the pacification and stabilization of Afghanistan.[16] The new Tajik–US security cooperation was unique. Although the US military had participated in exercises of the Central Asian peacekeeping battalion (Centrasbat) of Kazakhstan, Kyrgyzstan and Uzbekistan in cooperation with the North Atlantic Treaty Organization (NATO) Partnership for Peace (PFP) programme since

1997, US military had never previously been located on Central Asian territory. (Tajikistan had never been involved, since it was not a member of the PFP.)

This was an 'extraordinary geopolitical situation' with both Russian and Western military on Tajik territory, writes an analyst of the Tajik Foreign Ministry.[17]

The new international situation and Tajikistan's participation in the US-led anti-terror coalition initiated a chain of events. In January 2002 the USA lifted its ban on the export of weapons to Tajikistan. In February Tajikistan formally joined the PFP programme—as the last of the states of Central Asia to do so—and this provided further impetus to cooperation with the USA and the other countries. Membership of the PFP included Tajikistan undertaking to work together with the PFP in civil emergency planning, scientific affairs, environmental programmes and military reform.[18] In August 2002 an agreement was signed giving immunity to the US military contingent in Tajikistan in relation to the International Criminal Court. In November 2002 President Rakhmonov participated for the first time in a NATO summit meeting. In his speech he stressed that participation in the PFP programme was considered one of the most important parts of Tajik foreign policy. In early December 2002, Rakhmonov went on his first official visit to the USA and together with President Bush expressed a will for 'long-term strategic partnership' and future cooperation against the threats to security from international terrorism, the spread of weapons of mass destruction, and the drugs trade.[19] Bush praised Rakhmonov for his stand in the international fight against terrorism. Rakhmonov for his part stressed that he was in favour of maintaining the anti-terrorism coalition with regard to Afghanistan, and that Tajikistan was ready to be a reliable and stable long-term partner of the USA and to develop cooperation in all directions.[20]

This drastic improvement in relations between Tajikistan and the USA reflected Tajikistan's unique chance to implement a policy of reaching out to the world and to start pursuing a kind of multi-vector policy, which it had previously been unable to pursue. In his speech at the end of December 2002, President Rakhmonov for the first time used the concept the *open door policy* to characterize Tajik foreign policy.[21] He thereby formulated a policy which had been in the making for some time but could only take off after September 2001.[22] An open door policy reflected a pragmatic policy of cooperation with all states that were willing to cooperate with Tajikistan, above all economically. The Tajik government saw Western interest as an opportunity to strengthen the regime, improve the security situation, and secure assistance and investment for the economic development of the country. Two months later, in February 2003, Rakhmonov for the first time used the term 'national interests' of Tajikistan.[23] Slowly the concepts and strategies of an independent policy were taking form.

Thus the Tajik government took the opportunity to develop its external relations. Although it remained embedded in security cooperation with Russia, the developments after September 2001 set Tajikistan off on a new trajectory. The US military presence was not large, but it was a dynamic factor that strengthened Tajikistan's aspiration to take responsibility for its own foreign policy—and for the protection of its border with Afghanistan.

## 2002–mid 2004: The Backdrop of Russian Influence

Russia, which had seen its position and influence reduced during the 1990s and at first seemed to stand by passively as the US administration engaged in Central Asia after September 2001, tried to take up the challenge. There was a strong media reaction in Russia to what was considered a Russian retreat from Central Asia. The Russian government tried to respond to this, and Russian Central Asia policy became more active from the autumn of 2002.[24]

During 2002–2003 there was uncertainty about what the USA's intentions in the region and in Tajikistan were. The huge task of pacifying Afghanistan after the fall of the Taliban regime in November 2001, the growing US concern about what was assumed to be Saddam Hussein's access to weapons of mass destruction in Iraq, and the US–British military invasion of Iraq that followed in March 2003 seemed logically to divert US interest from Central Asia towards what in US political parlance became the 'Greater Middle East'. Yet, contrary to what many commentators believed at the time, the US engagement in Afghanistan, Uzbekistan and Tajikistan developed further during the following years. The small US presence brought a new element into Tajik political life and debate. The new international attention brought hopes and expectations of future Western assistance, but also an awareness on the part of the Tajik government that there were other options besides close alliance with Russia. From this time the beginnings of a more critical stance towards Russia became more pronounced.

This more critical stance was reflected in particular in the strong Tajik reaction to statements in the Russian Duma, which in early 2002 discussed how to regulate the presence of foreign migrant labour in Russia. In the debate there were emotional outbursts against Tajiks in Russia from top-level Russian officials, arguing in favour of strict regulation of migration. President Putin's representative in the Duma, Aleksandr Kotenkov, created a scandal when he claimed that 'Moscow is full of Tajik beggars'.[25] The mayor of Moscow, Yurii Luzhkov, followed suit, accusing Tajiks in Moscow of crime and theft. After a strong reaction from the Tajik government, Kotenkov was obliged to apologize, and sent a letter to President Rakhmonov. The exchange of statements that followed was a sign of a new climate in Tajik–Russian bilateral relations. The conflict deepened when the Russian authorities began to deport Tajiks who did not have the correct documentation allowing them to stay and work in Russia. What further complicated the issue, as the Tajik media pointed out, was that Russia and Tajikistan already had agreements on the free movement of labour. In November 2002 Rakhmonov stated that Russia's deportation of Tajiks was 'a major violation of their rights, including their financial rights'.[26] Although Russian politicians watched their language after this, the issue of migrant workers was a hot one on the Russian domestic scene, and the Tajiks became targets of populist and xenophobic Russian politicians.[27]

Voices critical of Russian policy were heard both in the Tajik media debate and in official statements. President Rakhmonov repeatedly expressed disappointment at the level of economic exchange with Russia, which he considered far too low. Disappointment with Russia in this regard was reflected in an article by Rakhmonov's adviser Sukhrob Sharipov just before President Putin visited Dushanbe in April 2003. Sharipov pointed to a 'quite contradictory development in the relations between Tajikistan and Russia'. Hundreds of documents had been signed without being implemented. His explanation was that Russia's interest in Tajikistan was geopolitical, while Tajikistan was interested above all in Russian participation in the economic reconstruction and development of Tajikistan and the launching of joint investment projects.[28] Russian policy in Tajikistan was struggling with an asymmetry of a large military presence but an almost negligible economic presence. Although Russia's Central Asia policy was activated during 2002, this pattern seemed difficult to change.[29] Russia's lack of interest in investing in Tajikistan caused major frustration in Dushanbe. From now on rumours started to surface that the Tajik authorities had claimed compensation for the presence of Russian troops, although this was officially denied.

Tajikistan gradually learnt how to bargain in relation to Russia, and demonstrated this knowledge during negotiations with Russia. While Tajikistan before 2001 had been too dependent on Russia to make its voice heard when making requests, the post-2001 situation put it in a stronger position as new patterns of foreign engagement emerged.

## The Security Sphere

As early as the autumn of 1999, Russia under Vladimir Putin had initiated a policy of strengthening the Collective Security Treaty as part of a general anti-terrorist struggle in Central Asia.[30] Although this organization was sidestepped in the immediate aftermath of 11 September, it continued to build up its institutions and structures, with a Rapid Reaction Force, an anti-terror centre, and a Russian military base at Kant in Kyrgyzstan. Tajikistan continued to keep a high profile in the CST, supported the development of the treaty into an international regional organization (the Collective Security Treaty Organization, CSTO), and frequently hosted summits and meetings.

For Tajikistan, however, bilateral security agreements with Russia were more important than CST agreements. As mentioned in chapter 3, the Russian military presence in Tajikistan included the largest contingents of Russian military and border troops anywhere on former Soviet territory. As these agreements were to be renegotiated, the Tajik government now used the post-September momentum to put forward Tajikistan's interests during the negotiations to an extent that had not been seen previously. A minuet of negotiations began which included several twists and turns.

By the time the 1993 Tajik–Russian agreement on the protection of the Tajik–Afghan border was close to renewal, the Tajiks understood that there might be Western assistance to be had if only Tajikistan were to take on responsibility for the border itself. This started a period of intense negotiations with Russia—a move the Russian government had not expected. Parallel to the complicated negotiations on the Russian border troops, negotiations also continued on the setting up of a Russian military base.

Already in April 1999 Tajikistan and Russia had agreed on the Russian base (rather a reorganization of the Russian 201st Motor Rifle Division, MRD), and the documents were ratified in due course by both parliaments, but the specific details were to be hammered out in separate agreements, and the parties could not agree on the conditions. The question was not whether there would be a base or not, since both sides had already agreed on that. Rather it concerned costs and benefits. There were repeated announcements that these agreements were soon to be finalized, but it became obvious that there was serious disagreement. Before President Putin went to Tajikistan in April 2003 it was announced that discussions were well on the way to completion and that the final signing of the agreement was to take place the following month.[31] No signing took place, however, and the media reported that Tajikistan had increased its demands in exchange for allowing Russia to have the base.[32] Tajikistan was demonstrating a new willingness to assert its national interests.[33]

In July 2003 Tajik Defence Minister Sherali Khairullaev admitted publicly that there were several questions to be sorted out in the bilateral talks before the four framework agreements could be signed. As one point of disagreement related to the military base, he mentioned the location of its headquarters.[34] The 201st MRD had been located in the very centre of Dushanbe and the Tajik government wanted them out from there in order to build a huge Palace of the Nation on the land. Russia rejected the Tajik government's offer of a 15-hectare piece of land.

In early August 2003 the Russian side declared that Tajikistan's requests in the negotiations on the base were completely unacceptable.[35] As was reported later, the Tajik demands included Russia writing off Tajik debt worth 300 million US dollars (USD) in return for permission for Russia to have a military base in Tajikistan; President Rakhmonov would get 'the right to assume command of Russia's 201st MRD and use it for the protection of national interests'; the Tajik side would get the right to dispose of the movable property of the 201st MRD in the event of the Tajik leadership deciding that the division would withdraw from Tajikistan; and Tajikistan would receive Russian weapons, military hardware and infrastructure located on Tajik territory that were formerly the property of the Soviet Union. The Tajik government also requested compensation for Russia's use of the Okno space surveillance station at Nurek.[36] The Russian deputy defence minister and commander-in-chief of the Russian ground forces, General Nikolai Kormiltsev, stated that these demands were completely unacceptable.[37]

Meanwhile the negotiations on the future of the Russian border guards seemed no closer to agreement. In accordance with the 1993 bilateral treaty on border cooperation, a process of handing over responsibility for stretches of the border to Tajikistan was initiated in spring 2002. An agreement was signed to the effect that the section of the border with China was to be transferred to Tajik hands before the end of the year. However, disagreement soon appeared on the issues of the timetable for the handover of the rest of the Tajik border and of future border cooperation with Russia. During his visit to Tajikistan in April 2003 President Putin had declared that Russia was to maintain its military presence in the country as well as its presence on the border.[38] 'Russian–Tajik border interaction is an irreplaceable element in the joint struggle against international terrorism and international drug trafficking', he said, stressing that the Afghan conflict was far from settled and that the Taliban movement and the al-Qaeda network had intensified their activities in Afghanistan.[39]

On 18 September 2003 disagreement between Tajikistan and Russia over the future of the Russian border troops in Tajikistan was made public when the first deputy chairman of the Tajik State Border Protection Committee, Major General Nuralisho Nazarov, revealed that his committee had already submitted to Russia a proposal for a gradual transfer of the whole border to Tajik troops. In an interview with Iran's

Radio Mashhad he stated that Tajik border troops were ready to assume responsibility, and that it was time to end the dual authority on the country's southern border. 'I am 100 per cent sure that [Tajik soldiers] are ready to guard the front line of this border [without the Russians].'[40] Nazarov used the term 'front line' since Tajiks already made up a second echelon. He stated that the Tajik authorities had submitted a proposal for manning the border, that a joint commission of the two countries had been set up to discuss the issue, and that the issue of responsibility for the border would be resolved during the coming year.[41]

Nazarov's statement was repudiated a week later by the deputy prime minister responsible for the law enforcement agencies, Saidamir Zukhurov. Zukhurov said that Nazarov had been expressing his personal opinion and not the official position of the Tajik government. The Russian border guards were there to stay, he said.[42] The war of words escalated when on the following day the chairman of the Russian Duma's Defence Committee, General Andrei Nikolaev, threatened that Tajikistan would have to bear the full costs if the Russian border troops were forced to withdraw.[43] Although the Duma committee has no direct decision-making power on issues of foreign policy, his statement was important since Nikolaev was a former director of the Russian Federal Border Guard Service. Official Russia announced its counter-move a few days later.

The Russian government, represented by the Russian ambassador to Tajikistan, Maksim Peshkov, acted as if Nazarov's statement had been his personal views.[44] The Russian authorities declared that they counted on an extended Russian presence on the border. On 10 November 2003 the new commander of the Russian border troops in Tajikistan, Lieutenant General Aleksandr Markin, said that Russian border troops would have to remain in Tajikistan for at least 10–15 years to counter the threat of drug trafficking from an unstable Afghanistan.[45] This was followed up by a statement by the head of the Russian Federal Border Guard Service, Vladimir Pronichev, that 'Russian border guards have been present, are present, and will remain in Tajikistan. The question is on what conditions Russian–Tajik efforts to guard the Afghan border should be focused'.[46]

Although the Tajik government had been quick to declare that Nazarov's statement was his personal view and not the view of the government, the different Tajik statements did indicate that there was a shift on the way in the Tajik position. There was clearly a new readiness to put forward requests in negotiations with Russia when the Tajik government saw new possibilities for cooperation with NATO countries.

Many Tajiks feared that the national border troops would not be ready to take over the defence of the border with Afghanistan. In 2004 the Russian border troops in Tajikistan still consisted of about 11,500 men, while the Tajik State Border Protection Committee had only some 2,000 men, and the Tajik soldiers were neither properly trained nor adequately equipped. Their salaries were extremely low (15–20 USD a month), which made them easy targets for bribery and was considerably less than what the Russian troops paid their Tajik personnel (50 USD a month for an officer in the Russian troops).[47] Drug production in Afghanistan and its drug exports had increased dramatically after the fall of the Taliban regime in Afghanistan. While the hectarage used for opium poppy cultivation in Afghanistan had increased during the 1990s, and in 1998–2000 reached approximately 6,000 hectares, it dropped substantially in 2001—only to increase drastically in 2002 to almost 10,000 hectares. After 2002 drug production continued to increase and the Tajik border troops thus faced a tremendous task.

Still, Tajikistan seemed determined to raise its demands in the negotiations with Russia. It now had a chance to strengthen its position in relation to Russia and did not want to miss it. In December 2003 the official Tajik newspaper *Narodnaya gazeta* carried an article which argued strongly in favour of cooperation with Russia, but at the same time pleaded that Russia must give more attention to Tajik interests in the difficult bilateral negotiations. The author wrote that Russia needed Tajikistan no less than Tajikistan needed Russia and pointed to the value of Tajikistan for Russian interests in Afghanistan; Tajikistan's role as an important partner for Russia and a strong supporter of all Russia's integration-related initiatives; its value for Russia as the only Persian-speaking country in the otherwise Turkic-speaking community of Central Asia; and finally its geo-strategic location, which was crucial to Russian interests in Asia.[48]

In January 2004 an article published under a pseudonym in the independent Tajik paper *Asia Plus* sharply criticized the Russian position in the negotiations over the Russian military base, and demanded the full handover of the border to the Tajiks.[49] The article presented the arguments behind several of the Tajik claims. Although it was not official it seemed to have the blessing of the government and indicated the seriousness of Tajikistan's demands. The author argued that the country's debt to Russia was not a real debt but a result of Tajikistan being loyal and remaining in the rouble zone when Russia itself carried out its monetary reform in the early 1990s. When Russia made a loan of 9 million roubles available to Tajikistan, the author stated, it had imposed an interest rate of 7 per cent per year, while no other country at that time charged such a high rate of interest. Now, he continued, the interest payments on that loan had increased Tajikistan's total debt to Russia to about 300 million USD. Why, he asked, is not Russia remitting the Tajik debt, when it is generously remitting the multi-billion debts of other countries? He pointed out that Russia used all the infrastructure of Tajik facilities, which he estimated to be worth more than 2 million USD for the past 12 years, at no cost, and demanded that Russia pay rent to Tajikistan for the military base and for the use of the Okno space surveillance station at the rate of 250–300 million USD per year. He concluded that Tajikistan had to realize that to a small country economic issues must have first priority, and it must therefore make demands on the larger power for which strategic military–political aspects are more important. Tajikistan, said the author, faced a choice between staking its interests on the rich developed countries of the West, which were willing to make large investments in Central Asia, or on the 'traditional partner' with its mainly military and security interests. 'On the one side there are rich advanced countries in the West ready to commit large investments in Central Asia, while on the other side there is a "traditional partner" with tremendous ambitions and operating according to old principles. Suppose', said the author, that the traditional partner 'offers nothing'.

A Tajik–Russian working group was to meet in spring 2004 to sort out the issues surrounding the future of the Russian border troops, but before it did so Russia's pressure on Tajikistan seemed to intensify. Thus, the chairman of the Tajik State Border Protection Committee, Abdurrahmon Azimov, having stated publicly in February that it was time for the Tajik government to take responsibility for the whole of the border with Afghanistan, changed his mind two days later, declaring instead that Russian troops were not to be withdrawn.[50] By the time the Russian delegation came to Dushanbe in March 2004 for another round of negotiations on the Russian military and border troops presence, the disagreements were deep. The Russians returned without any progress in the talks having been made.

On 30 April 2004 Rakhmonov stated in his annual speech to parliament that withdrawal of the Russian border guards from Tajikistan was necessary.[51] He thanked the Russian troops for the job they had done, but said that the Tajiks were now taking over. So far, he said, the 500 kilometres (km) of the Tajik–Chinese border had been handed over, and a 70-km section of the Tajik–Afghan border was next. The rest of the border was to follow, he said.

Proof that there were internal disagreements on the Russian side on this issue came on 12 May when Russian First Deputy Minister of Foreign Affairs Vyacheslav Trubnikov confirmed that Russian border troops were to be withdrawn from the Tajik–Afghan border.[52] He did this by warning loudly that the situation at the border would deteriorate seriously and drug trafficking would increase, since Tajik troops were unable to protect the border, thereby creating a 'leaky border', and that the quantities of drugs entering Russia would increase. Russia would therefore have to create a security belt elsewhere in order to handle the drug threat from Afghanistan, he stated. His words had a certain resonance within Tajikistan, where many questioned the capacity of the Tajik border troops.[53] However, four days later the deputy chief of the Russian Federal Border Guard, Lieutenant General Aleksandr Manilov, declared that the Russian border guards were not leaving completely and repeated that only the format of cooperation was changing.[54]

The seriousness of the diplomatic tension was underlined when Tajik Foreign Minister Talbak Nazarov, in an interview for *Nezavisimaya gazeta*, tried to play down the disagreement with Russia, claiming that it was all part of a normal process of establishing the Tajik border troops and gradually placing the Tajik–Afghan border under Tajik jurisdiction. There was no need to make a fuss about this, he said, thereby indirectly confirming that there was disagreement over the conditions for the base. He took the opportunity to criticize the fact that former Soviet property had not been transferred to Tajikistan in spite of the 1999 agreement, which had prescribed this.[55] A few days later Konstantin Kosachev, the deputy chairman of the International Affairs Committee of the Russian Duma, complained that Tajikistan was putting heavy pressure on Russia to get the Russian border guards to leave the border within a year.[56]

Finally the summit meeting between presidents Putin and Rakhmonov at Sochi on 4 June 2004 ended months of haggling and produced a compromise. In Tajikistan, press comments were divided as to how far the outcome was a victory for Tajik diplomacy, or whether Russia had forced Rakhmonov's hand, using among other things the conditions on which Tajik migrant labour could travel to Russia to work as leverage. With about 600,000 Tajiks in Russia, and given the large amounts of money they regularly remitted to their families in Tajikistan, the issue of their right to go and work in Russia was important for Tajikistan. At first glance Russia seemed to have got the upper hand in the Sochi agreement, but the deal was in fact a compromise. Its long-term implications were not immediately clear. Russia turned down some Tajik proposals—for example, writing off the Tajik debt and giving the Tajik president the right to take command of the 201st MRD in 'emergency situations'. Putin's foreign policy adviser, Sergei Prikhodko, seemed satisfied with the package and confirmed that it was favourable to Russia.[57] The details of the agreements were not made public until they were signed four months later.

Parallel to this, Tajikistan intensified its cooperation with NATO countries, above all with regard to strengthening Tajikistan's capacity on 'soft security' issues—preventing the transit of drugs, weapons and rebel Islamists across the border from Afghanistan.

The deeper US strategic engagement in Afghanistan and Uzbekistan was accompanied by sizeable increases in US government assistance to Tajikistan and Uzbekistan. Total US assistance to Central Asia in US fiscal year (FY) 2002 (580 million USD) was twice what it had been in 2001, as was the US assistance to Tajikistan: it increased from 78.39 million USD in 2001 to 162.55 million USD in 2002 (see table 4.4).[58] Promises of international economic assistance to Tajikistan played a considerable role in Rakhmonov's interest in accepting a US military presence.

The USA never built a military base in Tajikistan, as it did in Uzbekistan and Kyrgyzstan. Instead it used the Dushanbe airport. The US administration initiated bilateral security coopera tion with Tajikistan while at the same time doing its best to tie Tajikistan to Western security arrangements. The assistance included the training and equipping of Tajik border troops and military but did not take the form of deliveries of military supplies. French troops remained and continued to use the Dushanbe and Kulyab airports for cargo transport to Tajikistan. French training of Tajik military and joint military exercises followed.[59]

The USA focused on border protection as the key issue in security cooperation. Already for FY 2000 the USA had initiated limited cooperation with Tajikistan under its Export Control and Border Security (EXBS) programme. This programme focused on enhancing Tajikistan's counter-proliferation capabilities in order to strengthen intra-governmental coordination on border security to prevent the transit of drugs and weapons of mass destruction, and the movement of international terrorists.[60] For FY 2001 the EXBS assistance amounted to 0.5 million USD, but it jumped to 7.5 million USD for FY 2002.[61] In early 2002 an agreement was signed on extended US assistance to Tajikistan's border security. Under a bilateral agreement signed on 5 February, the USA was to provide support to the Tajik Border Force with training and the purchase of technical and communications equipment. As part of Tajikistan's participation in the US-led anti-terrorist coalition, Tajikistan and the USA also developed cooperation in intelligence-gathering, especially with regard to movements and events on both sides of the Tajik–Afghan border.

The Iraq invasion in March 2003 did not reduce the US engagement either in Central Asia as a whole or in Tajikistan, as many observers had expected. The US administration worked to mobilize PFP and European Union (EU) support in building up Tajikistan's capacity for border protection. Tajikistan was greatly appreciative of these efforts. In late March 2003, at about the time of the US–British invasion of Iraq, when President Rakhmonov visited Brussels for talks with NATO Secretary General George Robertson, among others, he again expressed his hope that NATO would provide 'bilateral and multilateral assistance to Tajikistan' under the PFP.[62] This he repeated when Robertson visited Dushanbe in September 2003, mentioning in particular cooperation on combating drug trafficking and international terrorism, and he 'positively assessed' the programme to equip the armed forces and strengthen the border forces in Tajikistan under the PFP.[63] He also welcomed the idea of opening an Organization for Security and Co-operation in Europe (OSCE)–NATO training centre in Dushanbe in future, where personnel from the border services of Central Asian countries were to be trained.[64]

The EU General Affairs Council decided in December 2001 to strengthen the EU's bilateral relations with Central Asian countries, to double the budget for the TACIS programme (of technical support for countries of the former Soviet Union), and to resume TACIS assistance to Tajikistan. One important aspect of the TACIS programme was to build border control capacity and improve border management—first of all in Tajikistan and Kyrgyzstan—in order to come to grips with arms smuggling, the proliferation of weapons, and the trafficking in drugs. The TACIS programmes dealt with issues of border security capacities, surveillance and control. The EU Strategy Paper 2002–2006 and the Indicative Programme 2002–2004 for Central Asia described a strategy for the development and training of the border services, the construction of adequate border crossings and border management facilities, the provision of necessary infrastructure, modern border procedures, and last but not least modern radio and telecommunications equipment and data transmission networks.[65] In spring 2003 the TACIS programme allocated 12 million euros (EUR) to Tajikistan to enhance its security along the border (Border Management in Central Asia, BOMCA).[66]

The US administration was cautious not to provoke Russia when providing security assistance to Tajikistan. It therefore offered no military deliveries but support, training and equipment to the Tajik State Border Protection Committee, the Customs Directorate of the State Revenues and the Tax Collection Ministry. At the same time it let Tajikistan understand that the West had a clear interest in assisting it if it took over responsibility for the border from Russia. This US interest played a crucial role for the Tajik negotiations with Russia. Although individual Tajik officials and officers expressed their doubts that the Tajik border troops were ready for such responsibility, the Tajik government pressed for a takeover in the negotiations with Moscow.

Whether the Tajiks had overestimated the future contribution of the USA and the EU was as yet too early to say.

## The Economic Sphere

While Russia was a major partner in security and military affairs, its economic engagement in Tajikistan was small. As mentioned above, Rakhmonov brought up this issue repeatedly. Developments after

September 2001 opened new prospects for economic cooperation in other directions. Western countries had contributed humanitarian aid through international organizations during the 1990s, and this aid increased drastically after 2001 and was complemented by economic assistance of different kinds. Tajikistan had been the poorest republic in the Soviet Union and as a result of five years of civil war still ranked bottom among the former Soviet republics on all economic measures. After September 2001 international governmental and non-governmental organizations opened in Dushanbe.

Different indicators show the decline in Russia's economic presence in Tajikistan, above all the data on trade and investment. Although Tajikistan's overall external trade decreased in absolute figures as a result of the civil war, a reorientation of its trade started in the late 1990s, and the post-September development strengthened this pattern.

Thus, Tajikistan's trade turnover with the CIS countries as a whole shrank after 1991. By 2002 it accounted for only slightly over 50 per cent of its total trade. By then the EU countries as a group had become Tajikistan's largest partner outside the CIS area, even surpassing its trade with its largest individual CIS partners, Russia and Uzbekistan. The USA, meanwhile, was insignificant, according to the statistics, with less than 1 per cent of total trade turnover (see table 4.1).

**Table 4.1: Tajikistan's Trade Turnover, 1991–2004**
Figures are percentages of total trade.

|               | 1991 | 1997 | 1998 | 1999 | 2000 | 2001 | 2002 | 2003 | 2004 |
|---------------|------|------|------|------|------|------|------|------|------|
| CIS countries | 80.3 | 50.3 | 49.6 | 61.4 | 64.0 | 56.0 | 50.5 | 43.9 | 49.0** |
| of which:     |      |      |      |      |      |      |      |      |      |
| Russia        | 40.5 | 11.9 | 11.4 | 15.3 | 24.9 | 17.5 | 17.2 | 13.7 |      |
| Uzbekistan    | 8.0  | 29.0 | 26.9 | 32.9 | 19.4 | 17.7 | 14.1 | 11.9 |      |
| EU countries* | –    | 19.9 | 21.8 | 24.5 | 17.1 | 19.0 | 20.3 | 16.4 | 28** |
| USA           | –    | 0.5  | 0.2  | 0.2  | 0.1  | 0.3  | 0.5  | 0.4  |      |

* The Netherlands has been Tajikistan's largest EU trade partner due to its imports of Tajik aluminium.
** Avesta News Agency (Dushanbe), 6 February 2005.

Source: *Vneshneekonomicheskaya deyatelnost' Respubliki Tadzhikistan: Statisticheskii sbornik* (Dushanbe: Gosudarstvennyi komitet statistiki Respubliki Tadzhikistan (Goskomstat), 2004), pp. 23–26. Figures for 1991 are from *Ezhegodnik Respubliki Tadzhikistan 2003* (Dushanbe: Goskomstat, 2003), pp. 264–65.

A more complex pattern appears, however, if we look at the inter-annual changes that took place and the pattern of exports and imports. Thus, exports to Russia increased during 1999 and 2000 but fell back during 2001, and continued to fall during the following years. Russia's share of Tajikistan's imports is far larger than its share in Tajikistan's exports. There was a peak in imports from Russia in 2002 but they started to fall again the following year (see tables 4.2 and 4.3).

**Table 4.2: Tajikistan's Exports, by Destination, 1991–2004**
Figures are percentages of total exports.

| | 1991 | 1997 | 1998 | 1999 | 2000 | 2001 | 2002 | 2003 | 2004** |
|---|---|---|---|---|---|---|---|---|---|
| CIS countries of which: | 78.8 | 36.6 | 34.0 | 45.7 | 47.7 | 32.4 | 26.6 | 17.4 | |
| Russia | 46.4 | 8.5 | 8.0 | 16.7 | 32.9 | 16.0 | 11.8 | 6.5 | 6.6 |
| Uzbekistan | 6.1 | 23.1 | 21.0 | 26.2 | 12.5 | 13.3 | 9.9 | 8.4 | 7.2 |
| Rest of the world of which: | 21.2 | 63.4 | 66.0 | 54.3 | 52.3 | 67.6 | 74.4 | 82.6 | |
| EU countries*– | | 36.1 | 43.3 | 36.1 | 28.1 | 32.8 | 32.4 | 28.1 | |
| Turkey | – | 1.0 | 0.0 | 0.1 | 7.4 | 11.5 | 16.0 | 24.2 | 15.3 |
| USA | – | 0.6 | 0.3 | 0.1 | 0.1 | 0.2 | 0.1 | 0.1 | |
| China | – | 1.8 | 0.8 | 0.4 | 0.4 | 0.2 | 0.3 | 0.7 | |
| Iran | | | 2.3 | 2.0 | 1.6 | 4.6 | 3.8 | 6.4 | 3.2 |

* Of the EU countries, Tajikistan's largest trading partner is the Netherlands (aluminium).
** Avesta News Agency (Dushanbe), 6 February 2005.
Source: *Vneshneekonomicheskaya deyatelnost' Respubliki Tadzhikistan: Statisticheskii sbornik* (Dushanbe: Gosudarstvennyi komitet statistiki Respubliki Tadzhikistan (Goskomstat), 2004), pp. 23–26. Figures for 1991 are from *Ezhegodnik Respubliki Tadzhikistan 2003* (Dushanbe: Goskomstat, 2003), pp. 256 and 261.

Analysis of the figures for foreign direct investment (FDI) in Tajikistan also shows that the Russian presence was minimal. In 2002 total FDI amounted to only 36 million USD, of which Russia (the only CIS country to invest in Tajikistan that year) invested almost 8.5 million USD. This is modest compared with the major investments of the United Kingdom (UK), of 14.5 million USD in the same year.[67] The largest foreign investors in 2002 were the Nelson Gold Corporation (gold and silver), Gulf International Minerals (gold), and Crédit Suisse First Boston (cotton).[68] US companies invested less than 3 million USD. One year later, in 2003, total FDI was about 31.6 million USD, of which only one-third came from CIS countries, that is, from Russia. Half of the investment from outside the CIS area came from Cyprus, which probably means Russian or Russian–Tajik capital.[69] At the beginning of 2004 the Tajik Institute for Strategic Studies reported that the largest foreign companies with a presence in Tajikistan came from Canada, the USA, the UK, South Korea, Germany, Switzerland, Italy, Hungary and Russia. Nevertheless, in total foreign inward investment remained small.

### Table 4.3: Tajikistan's Imports, by Source, 1991–2004
Figures are percentages of total imports.

| | 1991 | 1997 | 1998 | 1999 | 2000 | 2001 | 2002 | 2003 | 2004** |
|---|---|---|---|---|---|---|---|---|---|
| CIS countries | 82.0 | 64.3 | 62.8 | 77.6 | 82.9 | 78.2 | 76.0 | 68.0 | |
| of which: | | | | | | | | | |
| Russia | 34.1 | 15.3 | 14.3 | 13.9 | 15.5 | 18.8 | 22.7 | 20.2 | 24.2 |
| Uzbekistan | 9.9 | 34.8 | 31.9 | 39.8 | 27.5 | 21.9 | 18.4 | 15.1 | 12.3 |
| Rest of the world | 18.0 | 35.7 | 37.2 | 22.4 | 17.1 | 21.8 | 24.0 | 32 | |
| of which: | | | | | | | | | |
| EU countries*– | | 3.8 | 3.7 | 12.5 | 4.3 | 6.0 | 7.9 | 5.9 | |
| Turkey | – | 0.6 | 0.5 | 0.2 | 0.6 | 1.3 | 1.4 | 3.3 | |
| USA | – | 0.3 | 0.2 | 0.2 | 0.1 | 0.1 | 0.8 | 0.6 | 5.8 |
| China | – | 0.2 | 0.1 | 0.3 | 1.7 | 0.8 | 1.0 | 3.0 | 4.1 |
| Iran | – | 1.6 | 1.5 | 1.5 | 1.1 | 1.4 | 2.1 | 2.7 | 1.9 |
| India | – | – | 0.1 | 0.2 | 0.0 | 5.0 | 4.4 | 0.4 | |

* In 2002, of the EU countries, Italy and Greece were the largest exporters to Tajikistan.
** Avesta News Agency (Dushanbe), 6 February 2005.
Source: *Vneshneekonomicheskaya deyatelnost' Respubliki Tadzhikistan: Statisticheskii sbornik* (Dushanbe: Gosudarstvennyi komitet statistiki Respubliki Tadzhikista (Goskomstat), 2004), pp. 27–30. Figures for 1991 are from *Ezhegodnik Respubliki Tadzhikistan 2003* (Dushanbe: Goskomstat, 2003), pp. 264–65.

From these statistics it is obvious that Russia's economic presence in Tajikistan was quite modest, which quite naturally was of concern to the Tajik government. To Tajikistan, attracting investment was a most important issue, and Russia was the most promising partner as the old ally and the leading member of the Eurasian Economic Community (EEC). Since Russia was not investing, the Tajik government hoped that its new open door policy would attract foreign investment.[70]

Tajikistan has potential with its rich natural resources, above all water, but also minerals of all kinds. Its water resources create the basis for a future hydro-energy sector that is capable not only of satisfying the country's own needs but also of exporting electricity to neighbouring countries. Water is Tajikistan's 'oil'. The Soviets had started the construction of large hydro-power stations in the 1970s but never finished them. International investors therefore had to be found in order to complete them. The country's aluminium factory was another unique resource, although bauxite had to be imported for its production. Intense and bloody fights for control of the aluminium plant at Turzunzade had taken place since the early 1990s, and the plant was in need of new investment. Aluminium and cotton remained Tajikistan's major exports. Cotton cultivation was state-controlled but the land was leased by individual peasants and was in need of foreign money and expertise in order to make production rational and more effective.

Tajikistan was in desperate need of assistance and investment in order to develop the economy. The extreme situation was clearly reflected in the fact that a share of its labour force as high as about 600,000 men were labour migrants in Russia. For a country with a total population of 6.5 million (in 2003) this is the starkest sign of high unemployment. Factories were standing idle and the countryside could not feed the rural population. Even if Russia's economic presence in Tajikistan was remarkably small, the fact that so many Tajiks went to Russia as migrant labour created a strong economic bond between the countries. They supported their families with the money they earned in Russia, and the money they remitted to Tajikistan was comparable to three or even four times the state budget.[71] This also constituted a substantial sum of money outside the Russian sphere of taxation.

With serious difficulties in the economy it was obvious that a foreign country that would help Tajikistan improve its economy would also play a major role in the orientation of Tajikistan in the future. An economic presence in the country was thus an issue that could determine the future strategic constellation of powers in Tajikistan.

In the spring of 2002 there were signs that Russia was to give more emphasis to developing its economic cooperation with Tajikistan. In March 2002 the Russian minister for emergency situations, Sergei Shoigu, just appointed new co-chairman of the Russian–Tajik Inter-Governmental Commission, went to Dushanbe as the head of a sizeable government delegation. As he is a close ally of Putin, it was expected that his appointment would mean a fresh injection of energy into bilateral relations. More than 30 agreements were signed at the meeting, yet no breakthrough was made. However, from this time Russia's policy towards Central Asia was activated, and it was now directed in particular towards the energy assets of Tajikistan, Kyrgyzstan and Uzbekistan, which had hitherto been in the shadow of the large oil and gas producers of Kazakhstan and Turkmenistan.

At its March 2002 meeting the Russian–Tajik Inter-Governmental Commission also discussed Russian investment in Tajikistan's hydro-energy sector. The Russian side declared an interest in building up Tajikistan's electricity capacity, which would allow the export of electricity to Afghanistan. This would mean completing the construction of the huge Tajik hydroelectric power stations that the Soviet Union had started.[72]

At the centre of the Russian interest was the Sangtuda hydroelectric power station, located 120 km south-east of Dushanbe on the Vakhsh River. Sergei Shoigu, however, declared that a third partner must be found to finance the project. He spoke of developing a model of international cooperation by which Tajikistan would offer the energy infrastructure, Russia the production and scientific–technical potential, and a third partner the financing. If the Sangtuda project worked, Shoigu said, the model could also be used to complete the construction of Rogun—the largest hydroelectric power station in Tajikistan, located like Sangtuda along the Vakhsh River—as well as other hydro-complexes if and when the international community engaged in the development of Afghanistan.[73]

In October 2002 Russia and Tajikistan struck a preliminary agreement on Rogun.[74] When completed, the plant will be the second-largest hydroelectric power station in the world and the electricity it produces will have a significant impact on the economy of the whole of Central Asia. Experts predicted that 1.3 billion USD would be needed to complete it.

In March 2003 the Russian electricity monopoly, Russian Joint Stock Company Unified Energy Systems (RAO UES), declared its interest in creating an electricity market and buying electricity generated by Tajik hydro-energy facilities.[75] One month later, in April, at the EEC summit meeting, a memorandum was signed on a joint project to complete the construction of Sangtuda as a first step, with Russia a major and Kazakhstan a minor investor.[76] Iran soon became involved as the third partner in an international consortium, together with Russia and Tajikistan, for financing the construction work. Russia and Iran were now partners, but competition developed between them over who was to take the lead.

In May 2003 a 25-year agreement was signed between the Russian gas state monopoly Gazprom and Tajikistan which gave Gazprom the right to explore and develop the gas fields of Sargazon (in Dangara district), Sari-Kamysh (in Shahrinau district) and Rengan (in Rudaki district). Tajikistan's gas reserves are small but they are of interest to Gazprom as part of the former Soviet gas system.[77] Gazprom also began to repair Tajikistan's damaged infrastructure, its gas and oil wells, and pipelines. Gazprom linked the agreement to its general upgrading of the Central

Asian pipeline systems connecting Central Asia with Russia.[78] However, when the talks on gas production cooperation were renewed in November 2004 no concrete steps had been taken in the meantime.[79]

As pointed out above, trade between the USA and Tajikistan remained at a low level. Although Tajikistan's imports from the USA increased after 2001, in 2004 trade turnover with the USA was still less than 1 per cent of Tajikistan's total trade turnover (see table 4.1). US investments in Tajikistan were insignificant.

The Tajik government had difficulty attracting US businesses to invest in Tajikistan. US businessmen were cautious, fearing the risks of investing in a country like Tajikistan which they believed to be still politically unstable and lacking in mechanisms for the proper protection of investments. When President Rakhmonov visited the USA in December 2002 he discussed the development of the Tajik hydro-energy sector as a major factor for reducing poverty in the country. He did not manage to interest the Americans in investing, but the Americans did encourage major international financial organizations to contribute to the economic development of Tajikistan. Among them were the World Bank and the International Monetary Fund (IMF). The Asian Development Bank and the European Bank for Reconstruction and Development (EBRD) followed suit. Rakhmonov's meeting with the World Bank during his 2002 trip to the USA resulted in an agreement that the bank was be the major organizer of the financing project for the construction of Rogun.[80]

Although small where trade and investment were concerned, the USA remained a major contributor of development aid to Tajikistan, which includes economic and technical assistance (through the US Agency for International Development, USAID) and humanitarian and military assistance programmes. This assistance peaked in 2002 (see table 4.4), the peak being explained by the large volumes of humanitarian aid delivered after the severe drought of 2001. Since then the share of development projects in total US assistance, and thus USAID's share of the total, has increased: USAID now accounts for the lion's share of the US assistance. Thus, while USAID's budget for aid to Tajikistan in 2001 was only 7 million USD, it increased to 40 million in 2002, and levelled out to 30 million in 2003.[81]

**Table 4.4: US Government Assistance to Tajikistan for Fiscal Years 2001–2004**
Figures are in million USD.

| 2001 | 2002 | 2003 | 2004* |
|------|------|------|-------|
| 72.09 | 162.55 | 96.28 | 50.7 |

Source: US Department of State, http://www.state.gov/documents.
* *Asia Plus*, February 2005

As the Tajik statistics show, the EU countries together, in contrast to the USA, had already developed into a major trading partner of Tajikistan in the 1990s. However, this was the result of Tajikistan's large aluminium exports to the Netherlands. An agreement on trade and cooperation had been signed by the EU and the USSR in 1989 and concerned Tajikistan as a former Soviet republic. Tajikistan endorsed the agreement in 1994.

Between 1991 and 2001 the European Commission allocated about 370 million EUR to Tajikistan to overcome humanitarian, economic and social problems.[82] Cooperation of other kinds was minimal, however. In December 2003 work on a Partnership and Cooperation Agreement between the EU and Tajikistan started, and in October 2004 it was signed. The agreement ensured cooperation on a broad range of issues 'from trade to security', including political dialogue on democracy, human rights and foreign policy issues.[83] The Tajik side suggested EU investment in mining and the mining industry, energy, agriculture, tourism and transport, according to the minister for the economy and trade.[84]

In 2001 Tajikistan had applied for membership of the World Trade Organization, and was coordinating these efforts with Russia and other partners of the Eurasian Economic Community.


## 2004–2005: A Russian 'Return'?

On 16 October 2004 a package of final agreements covering most aspects of Tajik–Russian bilateral relations was signed when President Putin visited Dushanbe. The Russian side seemed to have been in something of a hurry to get these agreements through. However, the possibility could not be excluded that Rakhmonov also had his own reasons for coming to a compromise with Putin. Were we seeing a Russian 'return' to Tajikistan, or was the engagement of other big states already changing the basic parameters of Tajikistan and its environment?

*The Russian Factor*

The October 2004 agreements consisted of 14 documents in all and included huge Russian investments in Tajikistan, of 2 billion USD in total, over the coming seven years; the establishment of the Russian military base and the withdrawal of Russian border troops; an agreement on the Okno space monitoring station at Nurek; the regulation of Tajikistan's debt to Russia; and finally an agreement on Tajik labour migrants to Russia.[85] With so many issues both sides were able to play different aspects off against each other but also had room to make compromises. Several Tajik commentators believed that Putin had put Rakhmonov under pressure by using the issue of Tajik labour migrants.

Although the two presidents had agreed on the substance of the agreements in June 2004 at their summit in Sochi, there were uncertainties right up to the last minute before the documents were signed in October. As Anatolii Chubais, the director of UES, later admitted, there had been a major confrontation (*stolknovenie*) between Russia and Iran which both wanted to invest in Sangtuda. He said that if Russia had been delayed by only three months Iran would have taken over Sangtuda-1.[86]

There was thus a competitive situation, which the Tajik government used to get things moving faster. When in summer 2004 Rakhmonov and Putin agreed to regulate the Tajik debt to Russia, RAO UES expected to get a controlling share of 51 per cent of Sangtuda, and Russian specialists estimated the value of that share at 100 million USD. Tajikistan, however, was not satisfied with the evaluation. What followed seemed to be the Tajik government playing Iran and Russia off against each other.[87] When then Iranian President Mohammad Khatami visited Dushanbe on 14 September, he suggested that Iran take the controlling 51 per cent of Sangtuda-1 for 250 million USD. Within Rakhmonov's administration it was admitted that Iran had proposed much more than expected.[88] During Khatami's visit a memorandum was signed on the creation of a project company for Sangtuda-1. Rakhmonov stated at the press conference on the same day that Iran had promised to invest 250 million USD in Sangtuda, while Russia was to invest 100 million USD and Kazakhstan 30 million USD.[89]

However, when Putin signed the documents in Dushanbe on 16 October, Russia was the only investor in Sangtuda-1 and was to invest as much as 250 million USD, of which 50 million were to be deducted from Tajikistan's debt (Kazakhstan was to make a small contribution). Iran was to be the investor in the smaller Sangtuda-2 instead. The construction work on Sangtuda-1 was to be completed by the end of December 2008, and Tajikistan would then pay off the remainder of its debt by giving Russia a share in the power plant.[90] The two stations would together have a capacity of 670 megawatt (MW) and allow Tajikistan to secure its own electricity production and export as much as 50 per cent of its production (25 per cent to CIS countries and 25 per cent to non-CIS countries, including Afghanistan, Pakistan and Iran).[91]

Thus, Russia had increased its stake in order, it seemed, to avoid playing second fiddle after Iran. The Sangtuda-1 station was three times larger than Sangtuda-2. Putin had decided to make a breakthrough in the economic presence of Russia in Tajikistan.

Remarkably, the October 2004 agreements also included investments in the completion of the Rogun hydroelectric power station over the following seven years. The Russian company RusAl and its director, the Russian aluminium oligarch Oleg Deripaska, were to modernize the huge Tajik aluminium factory at Turzunzade,[92] thereby increasing its capacity, and to build a second aluminium factory. In order to secure the electricity supply to the energy-intensive aluminium smelters, Deripaska was to invest in the Rogun power station.[93] While the aluminium factories were to be completed by 2008, Rogun would be operational at full capacity in 2010.[94] Deripaska took responsibility for the training of altogether 50,000 Tajik specialists. There had been rumours of Deripaska's interest in the aluminium sector in Tajikistan since spring 2004, when he accompanied Putin to Dushanbe.[95] He owns 75 per cent of RusAl, Russia's biggest aluminium company, while Roman Abramovich, the governor of Chukhotka, owns 25 per cent. RusAl is the world's largest producer of primary aluminium. Deripaska's willingness to take on such large investments in Tajikistan's aluminium sector can be explained by the enormous increase in world prices for aluminium, from 42 USD a tonne in 1993 to 1,300 USD at the end of 2001 and 1,850 USD in September 2004.[96] Deripaska announced that he was to invest altogether 1.5 billion USD in Tajikistan.[97] All in all, this meant Russian investments of 2 billion USD by Russian state structures and private companies.[98]

Both Russia and Tajikistan were satisfied with the planned Russian investments in the energy sector. RAO UES was interested in securing its control of the former Soviet electricity infrastructure and getting access to cheap electricity in anticipation of the time in the future when the oil reserves would shrink. Tajikistan was pleased that investments were finally to come to the crucial energy sector.

These large Russian investments in the energy sector of Tajikistan fell into the larger pattern of Russia taking control of the energy assets in countries on former Soviet territory. However, if its investments in Tajikistan's hydro-energy sector are to be successful and profitable in the future, several difficult issues have to be resolved. Among them is the transit of Tajik electricity destined for Russia across Uzbekistan in particular, but also across Kyrgyzstan and Kazakhstan. With altogether

2,000 km of power grid, Uzbekistan constituted a problem for Tajikistan's electricity exports.[99] Another issue was the distribution of water from the upstream countries (Tajikistan and Kyrgyzstan)—the producers of electricity—and the downstream countries (Uzbekistan and Kazakhstan) which needed a regulated supply of water for their agriculture and the cultivation of cotton. As Russia was to invest in Tajik hydro-energy, it would have to act as the broker and mediator in Central Asian regional affairs.

Russian private capital in general, however, was hesitant about investing in Tajikistan. By the beginning of 2005 there were 55 Tajik–Russian joint ventures in Tajikistan, most of them run by Tajiks with Russian citizenship.[100] Nevertheless, in November 2004 a bilateral business forum was organized, where Russian business people from more than 19 Russian regions participated. The Russian regions with the largest economic exchange with Tajikistan were Moscow and Sverdlovsk.

The October 2004 agreements also regulated the Russian military base on Tajik territory. The headquarters of the base was to move to the outskirts of Dushanbe, to Giprozem. The base was to consist of 5,000 men, which was fewer than the 201st MRD had included, and was to include a strong aircraft component.[101] The base, which was to be named the Fourth Russian military base (no longer the 201st MRD), would maintain its previous tasks. Although this was not decided at the time, it could thus be assumed that the base would be given a similar function to that of the 201st MRD to act as a second echelon to the Russian border troops on the Afghan border. Half a year later Russian Defence Minister Sergei Ivanov announced that Russia was to make major investments in the base during the coming two to three years.[102]

The October 2004 agreements made the facilities of the unique Okno space monitoring station up in the mountains at Nurek to the east of Dushanbe Russian property for 242 million USD, which were deducted from the Tajik debt to Russia of 300 million USD. Russia was allowed to lease the land at Nurek for 49 years, not free, but for a symbolic sum equivalent to 30 US cents a year. The remaining 50 million USD of the Tajik debt was to become part of the planned Russian investment of altogether 250 million USD in the Sangtuda hydro-power station.[103]

The agreement on border protection stated that the gradual handover of responsibility to the Tajik border troops was to be completed by 2006. The Pamir section, with the Iskashim, Khorog and Kalaikhum border posts, was to be transferred during 2004, the Moskovskii border post was to follow in 2005, the Pyandzh post before October 2005, and at the end of 2005 the garrison in Dushanbe. The Russian border troops were thus to be gone by 2006. The Russian Education Centre of border troops under the Russian Federal Security Service (Federal'naya Sluzhba Bezopasnosti, FSB) was handed over to the Tajiks in March 2005.[104] The

Russian presence at the border would continue in the form of a Russian operational group, which was to be set up in January 2006 and consist of about 200 Russian advisers to assist the Tajik border troops and be located along the border. On 4 January 2005 the first group of advisers from the Russian FSB Border Department arrived in Tajikistan, offering practical help on increasing the security of the border areas that were now under direct Tajik control.[105] A few Russian officers stayed on with Tajik units as advisers. A year later, on 1 January 2006, a Russian operational group was to start working in Tajikistan as a liaison and assistance mission.[106] Although a small group of Russian advisers was to remain, the more than 100-year-long history of a Russian military presence along the 1,344 km-long border with Afghanistan was now coming to an end.

With a very small Russian presence on the Tajik–Afghan border after 2006, Russia had to find new forms of cooperation to meet the threat from the drug trade, which was a major challenge to Russia as well. Russia declared that it was now to create so-called security belts closer to Russia. A turn towards a greater emphasis on fighting drug trafficking had already been noticed both in Russia's bilateral policy on Tajikistan and in its policy on the CSTO. Russia was intensifying its efforts to build up new structures for international cooperation on the drug trade and encouraged cooperation between the border services of the CIS countries, in particular the Central Asian states. In summer 2004 a first coordinated operation between the border troops of the CIS countries took place. Called Dostyk (Friendship), the operation dealt with the trafficking from Afghanistan across Central Asia to Russia of drugs, terrorists and illegal immigrants. All the ministries and agencies concerned from Russia, Kazakhstan, Kyrgyzstan, Uzbekistan and Tajikistan participated. In all 13,500 persons participated at all vital crossing points along the route from Afghanistan into Russia. Cooperation took place between the CSTO, the CIS Anti-terror Centre, and the Shanghai Cooperation Organization (SCO) Regional Anti-Terror Structures (RATS).[107]

The challenge for the Tajik border troops as they took over responsibility on the border was substantial. The Moskovskii section of the border in the Khatlon region was considered the most difficult. The Tajik authorities declared, however, that they expected no deterioration of the situation along the border as they took over responsibility.[108]

Although Russia maintains a substantial military presence, Tajikistan managed to get the Russian border troops withdrawn by pursuing tough negotiations. Independently of what Putin had said—that Russia was to increase its military presence in Tajikistan—actual developments went in a different direction.[109] A page had been turned in the history of Tajikistan. Although the Tajik leadership regarded security cooperation with Russia as a crucial factor for regional stability in the region in the future, it had clearly demonstrated its desire to cooperate with Western countries. Tajikistan was slowly learning the art of the policy of balancing.

## The Western Factor

Only a few days after presidents Putin and Rakhmonov, in Sochi in June 2004, agreed in general terms that the Russian border troops were to leave Tajikistan by 2006, an expert group from the USA and the EU arrived in Tajikistan to study the Tajik borders and the question how to provide assistance to Tajikistan's border protection.[110] The US Department of State representative stated that a joint US–EU–Russian–Tajik team was soon to be set up to work out plans for providing technical assistance. The group of experts stressed that they had no plans to meddle in the negotiations between Tajikistan and Russia, arguing that the negotiations were a bilateral issue for the two countries. Although the USA and the European states kept a low profile, it was obvious that they were determined to build up Tajikistan's border capacity. In late July the commander of CENTCOM, General John Abizaid, announced that the USA and the international community were to help Tajikistan protect its border with Afghanistan.[111] He mentioned that a treaty on military–technical assistance had been signed under which the Tajik army would be provided with communications equipment worth 1.7 million USD.[112] President Rakhmonov welcomed the US initiatives and declared that 'The development of all-round cooperation with the USA is among the priorities in our foreign policy strategy'.[113]

The plans for broader Western assistance to Tajikistan's borders were being worked out during the following months. At its summit in Istanbul in June 2004, NATO stressed Central Asia's importance to Euro-Atlantic security and decided to increase its presence in Central Asia. This included appointing a special representative on the region, and plans to send liaison officers to Central Asia and to open NATO training centres. The new NATO Secretary General, Jaap de Hoop Scheffer, was dispatched to the region in October to encourage an intensification of bilateral cooperation within the PFP framework and to obtain transit rights for NATO forces going to Afghanistan via Central Asian countries.[114]

Scheffer's tour of Central Asia in October 2004 initiated a review of the implementation of NATO's PFP Programme, the Planning and Review Process (PARP), and the Individual Partnership Action Plans programmes with Central Asian countries. These programmes were aimed at helping Central Asian militaries become increasingly interoperable with NATO forces, offering them the possibility of participating in NATO-led operations. They included joint exercises for peacekeeping troops, officer training, reform of military establishments, preparedness for natural disasters and emergencies, the conversion of military industry to civilian production, and the NATO-funded Virtual Silk Highway providing Internet connectivity for Central Asian countries.[115] During Scheffer's visit President Rakhmonov stated that Tajikistan was interested in cooperation with NATO of all kinds and that such cooperation was an important part of Tajikistan's foreign policy.[116] On 20 October 2004 Tajikistan—the first Central Asian country to do so—signed an agreement with NATO on support for NATO's International Security Assistance Force (ISAF) troops in Afghanistan and allowed the transit for NATO troops to Afghanistan.[117] By doing so it took an important step towards further security cooperation with the USA and NATO.

The US administration now acted more openly to promote military cooperation. In November 2004 the first bilateral Tajik–US consultations on defence issues took place when a senior Tajik delegation visited Washington to discuss military cooperation, defence, border security and military contacts. The delegation included the Tajik deputy defence minister and representatives of the Tajik National Guard, the National Border Committee, and the Ministry for Emergency Situations and Civic Defence.[118]

The visits of Steven Whitcombe and Lance Smith, commander and deputy commander of CENTCOM, in November and December only confirmed the new US determination to assist Tajikistan through military and security cooperation.[119] US soldiers already went regularly to Tajikistan to train the Tajiks in counter-terrorism, and the USA financed the construction of the first counter-terrorist training range in the country, at Fakhrabad.[120] Further bilateral security cooperation was discussed during Whitcombe's visit in April 2005. A new chapter in Tajik–Western security cooperation seemed to have opened.

Numerous initiatives now materialized. In January 2005 representatives from the security ministries and agencies of Tajikistan together with representatives from Afghanistan, Pakistan and the Central Asian countries met to discuss regional security, including border security.[121] The UN regional representative on narcotics and crime, James Callaghan, announced increased international support for capacity-building for the Tajik border troops in order to prepare for the departure of the Russian border troops. He mentioned in particular financial support from the EU and from other Western countries. In February 2005 a round table meeting took place under the aegis of the EU to discuss international cooperation to assist Tajikistan on the border with Afghanistan.[122] As announced at the meeting, the EU and the USA together were to provide 20 million USD over the following three years (2005–2008) to strengthen the border between Tajikistan and Afghanistan.[123] Moreover, the European Commission suggested the setting up of a Central Asian Border Service Academy in Dushanbe, within the TACIS programme, to train officers of the border troops of Central Asian countries.[124] The TACIS programmes for border management in Central Asia (BOMCA) and on the struggle against drugs in the region (CADAP) were the largest of the TACIS programmes in the region.

President Rakhmonov made the most of the need to build up Tajikistan's capacity to fight terrorism and the drug trade. After meeting Putin again in Sochi in April 2005 he proposed the setting up of an international anti-drug coalition to fight the international drug trade. 'International efforts are needed on this issue', he said.[125] At an EU conference in Dushanbe in February 2005 the chairman of the Tajik State Border Protection Committee declared the importance of assistance from donor countries and stated that it is 'necessary to activate the participation of donor countries in programmes and projects connected to the defence of borders, illegal migration, weapons contraband, and drug trade'.[126] It seemed that this kind of cooperation would pave the way for closer military cooperation in the future.

Although no major Western investments were announced during 2004–2005, Tajikistan's economic relations with Western countries developed. The signing in October 2004 of the Partnership and Cooperation Agreement between Tajikistan and the EU opened a new era in relations. Later the same month a joint committee meeting between Tajikistan and the EU took place in Dushanbe to discuss Tajikistan's economic performance, economic reforms, privatization and the general conditions for investments in the country.

By 2004 US businessmen's interest in Tajikistan had awakened, and in February 2004 the US Trade Department started activity in Tajikistan through the Service for Business Information on the New Independent States (BISNIS).[127] In October 2004 a US delegation arrived in Dushanbe from the US Agency on Trade and Investment to discuss US investment. As the US ambassador to Tajikistan, Richard Hoagland, said, the situation in the country had stabilized, economic growth was high and the investment climate was attractive.[128] In February 2005 a high-profile US business conference took place in Dushanbe to discuss the establishment of trade and investment relations between the USA and Tajikistan, and contacts between companies. The conference was organized by the US embassy in Tajikistan, together with different US departments and agencies, and the Tajik government.[129] In 2005 the first signs of a US interest in the Tajik hydro-energy sector appeared. The USA financed feasibility studies of the sector and discussed participation in smaller hydro-energy projects and a large project, to include both Tajikistan and Afghanistan, on the Pyandzh River.[130]

To sum up, the increased US engagement in Tajikistan was a dynamic factor in Tajikistan. The very fact that the United States was deeply engaged in pacifying and rebuilding Afghanistan and was the 'strategic partner' of Uzbekistan in the international fight against terrorism created a completely new environment for Tajikistan. It made the US factor in Tajikistan central, as Afghanistan and Uzbekistan were both key countries for the future of Tajikistan. The US engagement in Tajikistan was not as large as its engagement in the other two countries, but all in all this was a completely new strategic situation.

Disappointment with Russia's lack of initiatives to engage economically in Tajikistan had led to Tajikistan announcing its open door policy in December 2002 in order to attract investment from other countries. The Tajik government willingly developed security cooperation with the USA and other NATO countries. Although the developments in Tajikistan of 2002–2004 can be seen against the backdrop of Russia's presence and influence in the country, Russia's policy became more active in order to maintain a presence in Tajikistan in future. What is important, however, is that Russia tried to come up with economic tools to support its presence in Tajikistan, to complement its military presence. This was a shift in Russian policy which the Tajik leadership, naturally, welcomed but, as long as the investments had not materialized, no one could be sure about Russia's actual presence in the future or about its intentions.

The US security engagement never took such a form as to indicate that it might replace Tajikistan's military–security cooperation with Russia. This was carefully avoided. Moreover, the Russian military presence remained substantial in Tajikistan even after the Russian border troops left. If Russia were to stage a return in the economic sphere, this could shift the newly evolving Tajik policy of balancing Russia back to bandwagoning with Russia again. Uzbekistan's sudden decision in summer 2005 to have US military leave the Khanabad base within 18 months raised the question whether this would mean an opportunity for Russia to step in.

To discuss these questions we have to look first into the engagement of the regional powers in Tajikistan and Afghanistan. In order to understand the changing geopolitical pattern in the region, the emerging engagement of the regional powers has to be taken into account.

## Tajik Policy and the Engagement of Regional Powers

Although regional powers such as Iran, China, Pakistan and India have a security interest in Central Asia and in maintaining stability in the region, they have engaged mainly in the economic sphere. This does not exclude the signing of bilateral memoranda and agreements, dealing in particular with promoting technical, logistical and educational cooperation. China was an exception, however. As a member of the Shanghai Cooperation Organization, which included China, Russia, Kazakhstan, Kyrgyzstan, Tajikistan and, since 2000, Uzbekistan, China had a legitimate framework for developing bilateral security cooperation with Tajikistan.

The 'Shanghai Five' group goes back to the agreements on troop reductions and confidence-building measures in 1996–97 between Russia, China, and China's Central Asian neighbours. (It became the SCO in 2001.) In 1999, when Uzbek Islamist fighters from the Islamic Movement of Uzbekistan (IMU) made incursions into Kyrgyzstan and Uzbekistan from Afghanistan over Tajik territory, this gave the organization new impetus, and the Bishkek Declaration of August 1999 placed the fight against religious extremism, separatism, terrorism and the international flow of drugs at the heart of the Shanghai Five's cooperation.[131] By September 2001 this cooperation was still not fully developed, and the SCO, like the CST countries, stood on the sidelines as the USA engaged in Central Asia. Since then, both the SCO and Tajik–Chinese bilateral security cooperation have developed. In general, however, Tajikistan's neighbour Kyrgyzstan was more interesting as a partner for Chinese bilateral security cooperation.

Tajikistan and China share a common border on the high plateau of the Pamir but their respective territories near the border are thinly populated. A border dispute between them in the Pamir was mainly resolved by an agreement in 1999, and the remaining disagreements were overcome in 2002.[132] These agreements normalized relations between the two countries, and in 1999 construction work started on a road between Khulma in eastern Gorno-Badakshan and Karsu in the Chinese Xinjiang region. Since Soviet times Tajikistan had had no direct exit to China, and the new road would open new prospects for bilateral relations. It was completed by 31 August 2001, although its opening was postponed for two and a half years without reasons being stated. In the spring of 2001 a Tajik–Chinese joint economic and trade commission had its first meeting. China gave economic assistance to Tajikistan in 2001, but economic cooperation developed only slowly and trade remained on a fairly low level. Tajikistan's imports from China were above all light industrial goods (food, clothes and shoes) and telecommunications equipment, while its exports to China consisted of metal, cotton fibres and aluminium.[133]

China has a direct interest in developing cooperation with Tajikistan, as it has with Kyrgyzstan and Kazakhstan, which border the Chinese province of Xinjiang. For years the economically underdeveloped Xinjiang had been a major problem for the Chinese leadership. China feared separatism, extremism and terrorism from the Uighurs, a Turkic-speaking Muslim population group in the region. In 1999 China had started to emphasize the development of trade with Central Asian countries as part of a development programme for Xinjiang. Developing Xinjiang and interesting the Central Asian neighbours in good-neighbourly relations with China became major priorities of China's Central Asia policy.

The year 2004 was a breakthrough for Tajik–Chinese relations in several regards. In late May 2004 the stretch of highway from Murgab to Khulma finally opened, thereby connecting Khorog and Kashgar, and a direct flight started between Dushanbe and Urumchi.[134] Whereas Tajik 'shuttle' traders had previously travelled through Bishkek and Kazakhstan to Xinjiang (most often by air from Bishkek and Almaty to Urumchi), they now got direct access. In June the first passenger bus arrived in Khorog in Gorno-Badakhshan from Kashgar in Chinese Xinjiang, after a 700-km journey through mountainous terrain in about 24 hours. The opening of the border between the countries was initially limited to five days every ten-day period from May to October; it was expected to stay open more in the future.[135] Stretches of the road from Khorog to Kulyab inside Tajikistan needed repairs, which would not be completed until around 2006.[136] Still, the road opened up important new prospects for Tajikistan to reach out to the world: it connects to the Karakorum Highway, running through China to India, and thus also opens up the prospect of linking Tajikistan to Pakistan and of access to the sea.

Trade between Tajikistan and China was expected to increase drastically as a result of the opening of the road. Cheap Chinese goods already represented a substantial share of the goods in the bazaars in Tajikistan, and many Tajiks feared that they would flood the market and prevent the domestic light industry producing consumer goods from developing. The volume of goods exported from China to Tajikistan greatly exceeded Tajikistan's exports to China. As the Chinese leadership in summer 2004 announced a programme for extending contacts with Central Asia, several analysts feared that China would promote trade aggressively as a way to extend its geopolitical influence in Central Asia. In June 2004 the Chinese president spoke about the need to boost China's ties with Central Asia, stepping up economic and technological cooperation.[137] A month later Tajikistan was promised 6 million USD in Chinese aid with no strings attached. In early 2005 China announced that it was to invest 900 million USD in Central Asia during the coming years, including more than 11 million USD in construction work in Gorno-Badakhshan.[138] By early 2005 there were 15 joint Tajik–Chinese ventures in Tajikistan. Unofficial estimates, however, gave a total number of Chinese businessmen as high as almost 1,000.[139] The Chinese were arriving on a broad front—but as traders.

China also had a clear interest in in Tajikistan's energy sector. When President Rakhmonov met Chinese Prime Minister Wen Jibao in China in November 2003 they discussed China's possible participation in the construction of the Rogun hydroelectric power plant.[140] In August 2004 China again expressed interest both in the hydro-energy sector and in the exploitation of Tajikistan's oil and gas resources.[141]

After 2001 the SCO broadened its field for regional cooperation to include issues of transport infrastructure, investment, water and energy. Anti-terrorism remained a priority issue. In October 2003 an anti-terrorist centre, the Executive Committee for Regional Anti-Terror Structures opened in Tashkent, Uzbekistan. In June 2004 the SCO members agreed on joint measures in fighting drug trafficking which gave greater emphasis to it.[142] Several observers saw China as the driving force pushing for an expansion of the SCO's capabilities and range of activities, since the organization legitimizes a larger Chinese role in the security and economic fields of Central Asia.[143] At the SCO summit meeting in June 2004 the Chinese president declared that China was ready to promote ties with Central Asia 'to a new high'.[144]

During 2004 bilateral security cooperation between Tajikistan and China developed. This can be explained by the opening of the Murgab–Khulma stretch of highway, which had direct security implications for both countries. Direct access to each other's territories and the free movement of people across the border increased the risks of cross-border crime and smuggling. A bilateral agreement signed in 2004 provided for joint investigations and exchanges of information between their security agencies in fighting cross-border crime and smuggling, and also permitted the Chinese agencies to pursue suspected terrorists on Tajik territory, to be present during trials in Tajikistan, and to ask questions of defendants.[145] China had already signed similar agreements with Kazakhstan, Uzbekistan and Kyrgyzstan for the purpose of fighting Uighur separatists, the major national security concern of the Chinese central authorities.

Tajikistan's problems with protecting its border with Afghanistan after the Russian handover were an issue of direct concern to China. In 2004 Tajikistan therefore opened a dialogue with China aimed at bringing Chinese expertise to bear on its border protection problems. A senior delegation from the Chinese army visited Tajikistan in late December 2004, meeting Tajikistan's defence minister, Sherali Khairullaev, as well as people from the Tajik National Guard and the

Tajik Border Service, to discuss how to deepen the bilateral military cooperation and cooperation within the SCO.[146] China thus seemed to be taking its first steps towards a more active and direct engagement in the security of Tajikistan.

Tajikistan developed security cooperation with other regional powers, above all on the 'soft security' issues of terrorism, separatism, religious extremism and crime. Iran, Pakistan and India have no direct borders with Tajikistan (although India did before the end of the 19th century, when a small strip of land, the Wakhan Gorge, was given to Afghanistan, hereafter to separate India from what later became independent Tajikistan; and when Pakistan was created as a sovereign state in 1949 the territory to the south of the Wakhan Gorge became Pakistani). Even so, they all share a common history, as parts of them once belonged to one and the same empire. To Pakistan, stability in Tajikistan and along its borders is relevant both with regard to Pakistan's interests in Afghanistan and also, of course, for the possible implications for the conflict in Kashmir. In the mountain regions of western Pakistan, Waziristan, followers of al-Qaeda and the IMU found refuge for years after the fall of the Taliban. Moreover, as a result of their rivalry, both India and Pakistan were eager to develop relations with Central Asian countries. After September 2001 India agreed to assist in restoring the military airport at Aini outside Dushanbe.[147] In 2003 a contingent of Indian paratroopers participated in a joint exercise held in Kurgan-Tyube in Tajikistan as part of a military training programme. The same year the Indian government gave no-strings-attached aid to the Tajik Defence Ministry in the form of equipment to a value of 700,000 USD,[148] although this engagement was only on the margins of defence cooperation.

Tajikistan's trade with India and Pakistan remained more or less insignificant. Moreover, in 2003 the volume of trade between Tajikistan and India fell by nearly 90 per cent compared to the 2002 level. There was, however, a clear interest on the part of both in developing their relations, and in November 2003 a friendship and cooperation agreement was signed. The same year a direct air flight from Delhi to Dushanbe started.[149] Rakhmonov called for Indian participation in the construction of Tajik hydro-energy facilities, although without success.[150] India was more interested in the prospects for energy transit across Afghanistan.

Official Tajik statements reflected a desire to develop cooperation with both India and Pakistan. The prospects for improved relations with Pakistan increased after 11 September 2001 when President General Pervez Musharraf, under US pressure, stopped supporting the Taliban. Tajikistan, for which the threat from the Taliban regime was the most important issue, had quite naturally viewed Pakistan with suspicion.

During 2004 specific aspects of cooperation in the fight against terrorism and the drug trade were worked out between Tajikistan, India and Pakistan. In early 2005 an agreement was signed between Tajikistan and Pakistan which included in particular joint investigation, warning, and the exchange of information between the security agencies of the two countries.[151] The opening of the Tajik–Chinese highway and the prospects for Tajikistan connecting with the Karakorum Highway, and thereby also with Pakistan, contributed to move security cooperation between Tajikistan and Pakistan up on the agenda.

When bilateral relations between Tajikistan and Pakistan improved after 2001, Pakistan cautiously expressed interest in Tajikistan's hydro-energy sector and in importing electricity from Tajikistan. When President Rakhmonov visited Pakistan in May 2004 he urged it to take part in the international consortium for the construction of the Rogun hydro-power station.[152] President Musharraf stressed the sphere of power engineering as a key area for cooperation. According to the Tajik presidential spokesman, Pakistan showed interest in initiating an international consortium for completing the construction of Rogun, and in importing cheap electricity from Tajikistan. In spite of the Russian investment, an additional 1.2 million USD were requested but Pakistan was not ready to make any commitments.[153]

Plans for cooperation developed, however. In March 2005 a memorandum of intent was signed between the two countries to construct a power transmission line from Rogun to Peshawar through the Wakhan Gorge.[154] Pakistan was also interested in expanding the transport infrastructure of Tajikistan, and in May 2004 plans were discussed for the construction of the approximately 1,200 km-long road linking Pakistan and Tajikistan through the Wakhan Gorge, in other words, parallel to the future possible electricity grid.[155]

The largest economic actor in Tajikistan among the regional powers was Iran. It had played a most constructive role during the intra-Tajik peace negotiations, and was an important economic partner of Tajikistan. Like the other regional powers, Iran avoided military–security cooperation with Tajikistan. Instead cultural and economic exchange developed. Although its share of Tajikistan's trade turnover was larger than that of other regional powers, it was only around 3 per cent in 2001–2002.[156]

Iran, like Pakistan, had a clear interest in developing the hydro-energy sector of Tajikistan and in the prospects for importing Tajik electricity. Both Iran and Pakistan were members of the Organization for Economic Cooperation (ECO) of several Muslim countries, created in 1977 (Tajikistan joined it in 1992).[157] The ECO and the Islamic Bank discussed the financing of projects in the hydro-energy sector, and in June 2004 the Islamic Bank decided to give Tajikistan credits worth 9.2

million USD for a 25-year term for the construction of five small
hydroelectric stations to solve the problem of interruptions to the power
supply to rural areas.[158] Iran became a large investor in the hydro-energy
sector of Tajikistan. In December 2003 a memorandum of understanding was signed between Iran and Tajikistan for completing the
construction of the Sangtuda hydroelectric power station.[159] According
to the memorandum, Iran was to be the guarantor of the international
financing consortium for completing the construction work.[160] (As
mentioned above, in September 2004 President Khatami announced his
interest in a 51 per cent share in Sangtuda-1. After Russia in early
autumn 2004 made it clear that it was taking over full responsibility for
completing the construction work at Sangtuda-1, and signed the
agreement with Tajikistan on 16 October, Iran was left with investing in
the smaller Sangtuda-2.[161])

Iran saw the prospects of importing electricity from Tajikistan across
Uzbek and Turkmen territory, and in September 2004 announced plans
for laying a high-voltage electric power grid from the Turkmen city of
Mary to Mashhad in Iran. It also was very interested in the prospects of
tripartite cooperation on hydro-energy transit across Afghanistan. In
September 2004, during a visit by Khatami to Dushanbe, a
memorandum was signed whereby Iran also undertook to participate in
the construction of 15 small power plants in Tajikistan and cooperate in
the training of Tajik energy personnel.

Iran also engaged in developing Tajikistan's transport infrastructure.
In September 2003 it won a tender to complete work on the Anzob
tunnel connecting Dushanbe with the northern city of Khujand, thus
making it possible to keep the road open the whole year round.[162] (The
north of Tajikistan becomes isolated from the south as soon as the
mountain passes fill with snow, and are not reconnected until late spring
when the snow melts.) The construction of the Anzob tunnel was to be
completed in 2006, although endless interruptions to the electricity
supply threatened to delay the work. The 5 km-long tunnel was in line
with the Iranian plan to construct a road connecting Tajikistan with Iran
and the Persian Gulf through Afghanistan (via Herat, Mazar-e-Sharif and
Sherkhan Bandar) and also linking up with the road to China across
Tajikistan.[163] During President Khatami's visit to Dushanbe in March
2004 a project was discussed for connecting Tajikistan to such a road.[164]
In early 2005 Iran announced a guarantee fund of 50 million USD for
Iranian investments in Tajikistan.[165]

All these plans and projects that developed after 2001 for economic
cooperation between Tajikistan and the regional powers were only in
their very beginning, or still under preparation in late 2005. Still, they
indicated a new trend in regional development. There was a clear interest

on the part of the regional powers in engaging in Tajikistan economically.

## Conclusions

Developments after 2001 provided new opportunities for the Tajik government to develop relations with foreign countries and get international assistance for its national security and economic development. The US military presence in Afghanistan, Uzbekistan and Tajikistan (as well as Kyrgyzstan) created a completely new strategic context for Tajik policy. The US engagement in Tajikistan attracted the interest of other Western countries as well as international organizations. The new strategic situation in Western and Central Asia after the fall of the Taliban also stimulated the interest of regional powers to engage economically in Tajikistan. Thus, Tajikistan, which had previously been more or less isolated and reliant on Russia, was now more or less at the centre of international attention.

We divided the few years after 11 September 2001 into three periods and named them in relation to the Russian factor in Tajikistan: 'the turn of 2001'; '2002–mid-2004: a backdrop of Russian influence'; and '2004–2005: a Russian return?'. The concept of an open door policy coined by President Rakhmonov in December 2002 expressed the desire to diversify Tajikistan's external relations. Tajikistan's behaviour in 2002 and up to mid-2004 indicated that it was consciously trying to defend its national interests and for this purpose was taking a tougher attitude towards Russia. When Rakhmonov started to make explicit references to Tajikistan's national interests this followed a line of thinking of much earlier date which previously had not had chance to be transformed into actual policy. This policy combined a open door policy with consciously balancing the Russian factor.

Tajikistan did not make a choice between Russia and the United States. It remained a close ally of Russia in the military field and an active member of the Collective Security Treaty Organization after September 2001. At the same time, it started to develop security cooperation with the USA and other NATO countries under the rubrics of combating terrorism and the drug trade. Cooperation with Western countries mainly took the form of them training and equipping Tajik border troops and anti-terror units. Tajikistan was thus integrated into different emerging security arrangements, which partly overlapped, partly differed. The Tajik government also used the prospect of future security cooperation with the West to beef up its claims and demands in relation to Russia, as reflected in the negotiations on the withdrawal of the Russian border troops.

After the package of cooperation agreements between Tajikistan and Russia was signed in October 2004, Russia seemed to be in the ascendant again in Tajikistan. These agreements guaranteed Russia a military presence, even though Russia had to withdraw its border troops from Tajikistan by 2006. The huge Russian investments in the hydro-energy and aluminium sectors indicated a substantial Russian presence in Tajikistan's economic and thereby possibly even political life. Whether these investments would be transformed into political influence over Tajikistan's foreign policy was too early to tell. Tajikistan's interest in its diversified foreign partners did not seem to abate.

To get a fuller picture of the foreign engagement in Tajikistan we included the regional powers of China, Iran, Pakistan and India. Although their engagement in Tajikistan is still limited, they are clearly in the ascendant. This is true especially of China and Iran, which by 2005 had already started to invest in Tajikistan, while India and Pakistan were planning to. All four countries showed interest in importing Tajik electricity in the future and in helping Tajikistan to develop its infrastructure in order to create transport links between themselves and Tajikistan. This analysis of the foreign engagement in Tajikistan thus shows that it was not only a question of Russia and the USA engaging in Tajikistan and competing for influence; there were several other foreign actors, and together they made for a completely new configuration of power and balances in the region.

The Tajik government welcomed this development. Its open doors policy fitted into this new dynamic situation, which also made possible a policy of balancing Russia.

Whether the plans and projects for the export of electricity from Tajikistan and for roads and railways connecting Tajikistan to Iran, Pakistan and India ever will materialize depends on the domestic developments in Afghanistan. Afghanistan is a key country for Tajikistan's exports to the south, as Uzbekistan has always been for Tajik exports to Russia. The developments in Afghanistan and Uzbekistan are most relevant to Tajikistan's own security and development.

We therefore turn now to the developments in Afghanistan and Uzbekistan to see how Tajikistan responded to the challenges presented and the opportunities offered by these countries.

# 5

# AFGHANISTAN, UZBEKISTAN AND TAJIK POLICY

How did Tajikistan's policy towards the neighbours Afghanistan and Uzbekistan change after 2001? The developments in Afghanistan had constituted a major source of threats to Tajikistan's national security after independence. Soviet troops had withdrawn from Afghanistan in 1989, and by the time the Islamic Republic of Afghanistan was declared three years later, a full civil war was on its way with the breakdown of Afghan society and political and religious radicalization as the direct results. Uzbekistan was a partner of Tajikistan in its capacity as a member of the Central Asian Cooperation Organization (previously the Central Asian Economic Union, created in 1994), and until April 1999 as a signatory of the 1992 Collective Security Treaty; but for most of this period Uzbekistan also presented a threat to Tajikistan and interfered in its internal affairs. Tajikistan tried to balance the negative impacts from Afghanistan and Uzbekistan by close military–security cooperation with Russia.

The post-September 2001 developments changed this situation and opened up new opportunities for Tajikistan to solve its security problems. In Afghanistan the US–British invasion of October 2001 and the fall of the Taliban opened the way for a period of reconstruction, and relations between Tajikistan and Afghanistan improved. Relations with Uzbekistan, however, remained a problem for Tajikistan.

## Afghanistan: A Turn for the Better?

Developments after 11 September 2001 seemed to open new prospects for relations between Tajikistan and Afghanistan and gave Tajikistan an opportunity to act as a foreign policy actor in own capacity. The security priorities of more than 100 years of Russian rule had determined Tajik–Afghan relations. In Tsarist Russia and the Soviet Union the border with Afghanistan was regarded as extremely delicate and vulnerable. After the break-up of the Soviet Union the Tajik leadership had had no other policy choice than 'bandwagoning' with Russia in order to meet the threats from Afghanistan. Only an improved security situation in Afghanistan could bring new conditions for a more independent Tajik foreign policy. How did Tajikistan's policy and relations with Afghanistan develop after September 2001 in the field of security and economics?

## Tajikistan and Afghanistan before 2001

Sharing a common history as parts of the same empires for centuries until the end of the Samanid Empire, the territories that later became Tajikistan and Afghanistan have an extensive cultural heritage in common.[1] The Tajiks are the second-largest ethnic group in Afghanistan, constitute almost a quarter of the population (numbering 4.3 million in 1995), and are found in many parts of Afghanistan, although they are concentrated in Badakhshan, around Kabul and Herat, in Rohistan and in the Panjshir Valley. Afghan Badakhshan is home to 100,000 Pamiris (considered an ethnic subgroup of the Tajiks).[2] The Tajiks speak Dari and, as the British diplomat Sir Martin Ewans writes, 'Because Dari has become the main language of the cities [in Afghanistan], the Tajiks came to play an active role in the administration and affairs of the state despite having been mostly excluded from the Pushtoon-dominated officer corps and senior government echelons'.[3] Since an independent Afghan statehood came into being in the 18th century, the Pushtuns had dominated the political scene in Afghanistan, at the expense of other ethnic groups. As Afghanistan was located at the crossroads between East and West, North and South, its statehood was threatened and undermined by the interference of the big powers. When Soviet power was established in the former Bukhara Emirate in the 1920s as many as half a million people fled to Afghanistan, most of them Tajiks.

The situation in Afghanistan has an impact on Tajikistan as their common border extends for 1,309 kilometres (km).[4] In 1895 the Pyandzh/Amudarya River became the boundary between the Russian and British spheres of interest, and both empires did their best to keep Afghanistan a buffer country. Tsarist policy tried to isolate Russian Central Asia from its neighbours in the south. The Soviets continued this policy and made it their objective to cut Central Asia off from the Muslim world and its neighbours to the south, and Afghanistan maintained its status as a buffer state between British and Russian interests after the Soviets secured power in Central Asia.[5]

The Soviet invasion of December 1979 changed this situation, and the Soviet Union tried to make Afghanistan part of the Soviet world. The coups of 1973 and 1978 were intended to initiate a rapid modernization process in Afghanistan, where hitherto the great powers had done their best to preserve the existing economic and political conditions. During the 1970s, cooperation had developed between Afghanistan and the Tajikistan Soviet Socialist Republic (SSR). Tajikistan exported electricity and concrete for construction work, sent specialists on agricultural development, and of course sent Dari-speaking interpreters. The modernization process, which was supported by the Soviet Union, provoked strong domestic resistance from the traditionalists and Islamic fundamentalists in Afghan society. In February 1979 a wave of Islamist activity in Iran brought about an Islamic revolution and increased Russia's concern about the geopolitical situation in the wider region and its own position in an unstable Afghanistan. On 27 December 1979 Soviet troops invaded Afghanistan to secure Soviet influence in the country.

The popular resistance among the Afghans to the ten-year Soviet occupation and the armed resistance of the mujaheddin in Afghanistan against the Soviet intruders also influenced Tajik society. While the first Soviet soldiers sent to Afghanistan had been mostly Central Asians, this policy was soon changed and the Soviet troops included more people from distant parts of the Soviet Union. The mujaheddin in Afghanistan raised the issue of the role of Islam in society, which became an issue in Tajikistan and in Central Asia in general as President Gorbachev's perestroika allowed more of a political and religious debate to take place. In Tajikistan this debate became politicized when it blended with regional–political lines of division.

After the Soviets left Afghanistan in 1989 it took only three years before the pro-communist regime of Mohammad Najibullah was overthrown and the Islamic Republic of Afghanistan was proclaimed.

When Burhanuddin Rabbani, an Afghan ethnic-Tajik, took over as president of Afghanistan in 1992 he received the backing of Russia. However, rival Islamic factions continued their fight for power in Afghanistan and the country fragmented into a cluster of self-ruled and self-sustaining regions.[6] In Tajikistan the Islamist flank of the opposition to the Soviet communist system viewed Afghanistan as a source of inspiration.

After the break-up of the Soviet Union, Russia continued to carry responsibility for protecting the Tajik–Afghan border. The Soviet border troops became Russian border troops. For both Tsarist Russia and the Soviet Union it had always been a priority to keep Central Asia isolated from Afghanistan.

Russia remained passive with regard to Afghanistan after the 1989 withdrawal and did not wish to be drawn into the maelstrom there. After intruders from Afghanistan shot dead 25 Russian border guards at a border post along the Tajik–Afghan border in the summer of 1993, Russia drastically increased the number of its border troops and its military presence in Tajikistan. When the Taliban first appeared on the Afghan political scene in 1994, this produced no visible action plan either in Dushanbe or in Moscow, although both countries' governments were deeply concerned that turmoil in Afghanistan would influence the outcome of the civil war in Tajikistan.[7] When the civil war erupted in Tajikistan in 1992, the Islamic Republic of Afghanistan declared its neutrality but, as the civil war raged in Afghanistan itself, some Afghan factions supported the Tajik opposition. Tajik opposition leaders found refuge and were allowed bases on Afghan territory, and rival political factions in Afghanistan played the 'Tajik card' in their own favour.[8] When the Taliban went on their offensive in 1996 and rapidly conquered area after area, and in September the same year took Kabul, Moscow feared that close relations could develop between the Taliban and the leaders of the United Tajik Opposition (UTO) in exile in Afghanistan, and urgently took the following three steps.[9]

The first was to bring an end to the Tajik civil war. It was an urgent task to mend the weak link in the chain of Russia's border system in Central Asia—that is, Tajikistan. The advance of the Taliban was a crucial factor when Moscow changed its policy towards Tajikistan and made a serious effort to contribute to a political compromise in which a role for the UTO was recognized. The new Russian policy was an important factor in bringing about the peace agreement between the regime of President Emomali Rakhmonov and the Tajik opposition. In June 1996, Russian Foreign Minister Yevgenii Primakov held separate meetings for the first time not only with the head of the Tajik government delegation but also with the head of the UTO delegation, Said Abdullo Nuri. In late December 1996 an agreement was signed between Rakhmonov and Nuri in Khos Deh in Afghanistan on the creation of the Commission of National Reconciliation (CNR).[10] The General Peace Agreement followed in late June 1997.[11]

The second step was to increase Russian military and security cooperation with the Central Asian states and join forces against the Taliban threat. On 4 October 1996, Russian Prime Minister Viktor Chernomyrdin and Central Asian leaders met in Almaty, Kazakhstan, and later in Dushanbe to discuss the new situation presented by the Taliban offensive. Uzbekistan spoke in favour of active support for the troops of the ethnic-Uzbek commander Abdurrashid Dostum in Afghanistan, but Kyrgyzstan and Kazakhstan stated that they did not wish to become involved in Afghanistan's internal affairs. Turkmenistan did not attend the meeting and abstained from any joint measures, citing its neutrality and calling the issue an internal Afghan matter.[12] The Central Asian leaders declared their readiness to take measures if necessary but did not decide on any troop increases along the Tajik–Afghan border, in spite of demands from President Rakhmonov.

Although Primakov was concerned about the Taliban advance, and had warned of Islamic fundamentalism in a 1994 report of the Russian Foreign Intelligence Service, he declared that Russia would not give support to any party in the Afghan conflict.[13] The head of the Russian Federal Border Guard Service, Andrei Nikolaev, declared there was no need to increase the numbers of Russian border guards.[14] Russian Defence Minister Igor Rodionov stated that the numbers of troops of the 201st Motor Rifle Division were not to be increased.[15] Instead, with references to the Taliban threat, Russia tried to promote military integration with the Central Asian states and to introduce the sharing of the defence of the Commonwealth of Independent States (CIS) external borders. Yet the results were limited.

The third step was to contribute to the creation of a broad anti-Taliban coalition inside Afghanistan between forces which had previously been hostile to each other. Moscow managed to bring Dostum, who controlled four northern regions close to the Uzbek border, on board together with Rabbani (who remained the legitimate president in the eyes of the international community even after the Taliban victory) and the ethnic-Tajik commander, Ahmad Shah Massoud, who controlled regions along the Afghan–Tajik border. Both Dostum and Massoud became ministers in Rabbani's shadow government as the new alliance was formed in October 1996.

Thus, from the time of the Taliban advances in the autumn of 1996, Russia supported the anti-Taliban commanders—Dostum and Massoud—of the Northern Alliance led by Rabbani. Uzbekistan initiated active measures to fortify its southern frontier, and Russia's General Staff began to elaborate plans in cooperation with the Uzbek Defence Ministry for how to resist possible Taliban aggression against Central Asia. Massoud and the Tajik connection were important to Russia, as were Dostum and the Uzbek connection, for the transit of material support to the anti-Taliban coalition.

Tajikistan continued with its domestic conflict resolution. The CNR started work in September 1997. The UTO criticized the slow pace of the process and the Tajik government's resistance to implementing the agreement, but the process was under way and the Tajik refugees in Afghanistan were returning.

Over the next few years, Russia assisted Uzbekistan with equipping Dostum's forces. (Uzbekistan was not only a much larger and stronger state than Tajikistan; it was also internally more coherent.) Russia was not prepared to go in itself in order to stop the Taliban, and therefore followed a policy of maintaining a buffer zone along the southern border of the former Soviet Union, although now on the shrinking territories in northern Afghanistan.

1998 was a turning point, as the Taliban continued their advances up to the border with Uzbekistan and Tajikistan. With the Taliban's successes, the anti-Taliban coalition wavered and individual Central Asian states started to look after their own interests since they believed the Taliban had come to stay in power in Afghanistan. From this point on Tajikistan became a key ally of Russia in the resistance against the Taliban as Uzbekistan lost interest in supporting the anti-Taliban coalition. When the Taliban conquered ethnic Uzbek-dominated regions in Afghanistan up to the border with Uzbekistan, the Uzbek anti-Taliban resistance was broken. Local ethnic-Uzbek commanders surrendered to the Taliban, and in August Dostum once again fled the country when the Taliban conquered his stronghold of Mazar-e-Sharif, the capital of Afghanistan's northern Balkh province. Uzbekistan now joined Turkmenistan in claiming that the war in Afghanistan was of a domestic character and that the only real reason for concern was the possibility of an influx of refugees into the CIS countries.[16] Russia thereby lost the possibility of influencing events in Kabul with the help of Uzbekistan. Uzbekistan at the same time had become uninterested in following Russia on military and security issues, had started to withdraw from such cooperation within the CIS framework, and no longer wanted to be part of a Russian-led anti-Taliban coalition. Top-level Russian military and diplomatic representatives tried to convince Uzbekistan to continue cooperation on the anti-Taliban cause, but without result.[17]

Massoud, who now was left with a small strip of territory under his control in north-eastern Afghanistan, never abandoned the field. By the end of 1999 the Taliban authorities controlled more than 80 per cent of Afghan territory.

In this new constellation Tajikistan became important to Russia for the support of the remaining anti-Taliban resistance in Afghanistan—the forces of Massoud. Tajikistan allowed Massoud to use its territory for safe haven and the airport at Kulyab to be used for transit transports. As Uzbekistan became reluctant to allow transfers of weapons and supplies to Massoud across its territory, the route to Afghanistan via Kyrgyzstan and Tajikistan became more important. Against this background an incident that took place at the railway station in Osh, Kyrgyzstan, in 1998 becomes important. Kyrgyz officials from the Ministry of National Security made it publicly known that they had confiscated a train of 16 wagons loaded with weapons, military equipment and food intended for road transports down to Gorno-Badakhshan (in Tajikistan) and across the river to Massoud. The trail led back to Russia and Iran, which actively supported Massoud. The reason why Kyrgyzstan chose to make this transport public could only be connected with a change of mind on the part of the Kyrgyz leadership with regard to support for the anti-Taliban coalition.[18]

In 1998 the US administration again became engaged in the affairs of Afghanistan. After the terrorist attacks on the US embassies in Kenya and Tanzania that year, for which the USA suspected Osama bin Laden, President Bill Clinton ordered US military aircraft to bomb Afghan territory on 20 August 1998 in an effort to hit bin Laden's training camps outside Jalalabad.[19] From about this time the USA became interested in strengthening the Tajik–Afghan border, and the US Export Control and Border Security (EXBS) programme started. For the USA, Uzbekistan became the strategically most important country in the region, and the US administration therefore concentrated its efforts on Uzbekistan. Tajikistan, on the other hand, became a bulwark in the Russian-led cooperation against the Taliban. Tajikistan was domestically weak, however, and was accused by the Uzbek authorities of not being able to prevent Uzbek Islamists from penetrating Tajik territory: in August 1999, Uzbek Islamist fighters intruded into the Batken region in the Kyrgyz part of the Fergana Valley from Tajikistan on their way to Uzbekistan, and the newly appointed Russian Prime Minister, Vladimir Putin, intensified the Russian effort to create a collective response of the Central Asian countries.[20]

The situation in Afghanistan therefore had consequences for Tajikistan's security vis-à-vis Uzbekistan, since Afghanistan had become a haven for Islamist rebels from the whole region. When one year later, in August 2000, another intrusion by Uzbek Islamist fighters took place, and fighting followed in the Surkhandarya region in southern Uzbekistan, Uzbekistan closed its borders with Tajikistan.

The increasing crisis over Afghanistan did, however, result in intensified contacts between Russia and the US administration. In August 2000, the first of what were to become regular bilateral talks took place between the Russian first deputy foreign minister, Vyacheslav Trubnikov, and the US secretary of state, Richard Armitage. The joint declaration issued after the meeting stated that Moscow and Washington envisaged joint, even active, efforts to achieve a radical change in the situation in Afghanistan with the use of diplomatic, law enforcement and other measures to combat the international terrorism emanating from the country, and to enable the formation of a government with a broad base.[21] When Russia and the USA introduced and lobbied for a joint proposal on UN sanctions against Afghanistan in December 2000 (adopted on 21 December 2000 as Security Council Resolution 1333), this was the first time in the modern political history of Afghanistan that they had acted together and coordinated their policies on the Afghan question.[22] The '6+2' talks (consisting of Russia and the USA together with the six states bordering Afghanistan—Iran, China, Pakistan, Tajikistan, Turkmenistan and Uzbekistan) to discuss settling the situation in Afghanistan by bringing all sides in the civil war to the negotiating table had already been going on without success for almost two years.[23] What was remarkable about the US–Russian proposal to the UN Security Council was not only the introduction of sanctions against the Taliban but also the request for an alternative, broadly-based government. The Tajik government could feel satisfied that the warnings it had been making about the Taliban were now bearing fruit in the international community. Moreover, it was the Tajik flank of the anti-Taliban coalition that had survived.

In the spring of 2001 the prospects for an anti-Taliban coalition under Massoud seemed to be improving. Several leaders returned from exile (among them Dostum, who had spent his exile in Mashhad in Iran, Gulbuddin Hikmatyar, and Ismail Khan of Herat) and they all gathered behind the Northern Alliance under Massoud. Massoud received international attention and was invited to discussions in the European Parliament and talks with the French foreign minister in April 2001.

What kind of government would these different political forces in Afghanistan present if they were to join forces and replace the Taliban? Uzbekistan was again approaching cooperation in the anti-Taliban coalition but wanted a say in how the coalition was led. However, a victory against the Taliban would mean a victory first of all for the countries which had wholeheartedly supported the coalition under Massoud—that is, Russia, Iran and Tajikistan. This axis of powers favoured neither the USA nor Uzbekistan.

The prospects for the Northern Alliance seemed positive at this point, and there were rumours that Afghans in exile were preparing for a government-in-exile, but the fact remained that the Taliban were still in control of the country, and it was extremely difficult to mobilize support from within Afghanistan or from territories that were outside Massoud's control. The Taliban regime was weak but still controlled most of the territory. With the social fabric broken into pieces, there seemed to be no force within the Taliban-controlled areas able to bring change in Afghanistan.[24] Neither Russia nor the USA was willing to take the risk of invading. The situation in early autumn 2001 seemed to be at a political dead end, and it seemed as if Afghanistan would constitute a black hole for its neighbours for many years to come.

## The Situation Reversed after 11 September 2001

On 9 September 2001 Ahmad Shah Massoud was murdered. Two days later the terrorist attacks of 11 September on the World Trade Center in New York and the Pentagon in Washington, DC, took place, and the international situation around Afghanistan turned upside down after US and British aircraft on 7 October 2001 began bombing Afghanistan. The strategic initiative for developments in Afghanistan and the region passed to the US administration.

In the new situation immediately after Massoud's death, Russia and Tajikistan increased their preparations to secure a successor to lead the Northern Alliance. Senior Russian, Iranian, Uzbek and Tajik officials gathered in Dushanbe for an extraordinary meeting to discuss the situation now that Massoud was dead.[25] One week later the Russian chief of staff, Anatolii Kvashnin, met the new leader of the Northern Alliance, Qasim Muhammad Fahim, another ethnic-Tajik Afghan, in Dushanbe.[26]

When the USA began to support the Northern Alliance as the force on the ground to overthrow the Taliban regime, its support at first went mainly to the Uzbek part of the alliance under commander Dostum. Russia, on the other hand, continued its support for the Tajik section. When US bombing paved the way for Northern Alliance troops to advance, voices within the Russian military demanded that Russia radically increase its financial support for Fahim to enable him to expand his control. On 17 October, Putin discussed Russia's military interests in Afghanistan and the Central Asian states at a meeting with Russian generals.[27] The military argued that the most important task was to neutralize the growing US influence, and that the creation of US military bases in Central Asia threatened Russian interests in the region.

The strategy behind Operation Enduring Freedom (the name given to the US-led military operations in Afghanistan), initiated on 7 October 2001, involved air strikes, building alliances with anti-Taliban Afghan forces, deploying special operations units to improve the capabilities of the opposition forces, and creating a system of sensors and strike aircraft to execute precision strikes on Taliban military formations.[28] In late October, US efforts concentrated on capturing the city of Mazar-e-Sharif in the north of the country in order to split the Taliban forces. On 9 November the city fell; the Northern Alliance forces took control of northern Afghanistan and the major east–west and north–south highways, and turned their attention to Kabul in the south.[29] President George W. Bush promised, and the Northern Alliance leaders agreed, that the Northern Alliance would not enter Kabul until agreement had been reached on a temporary government. However, on 12 November the Northern Alliance captured Kabul.

Disagreements over the composition of a new Afghan government to replace the Taliban regime surfaced at an early stage. Putin stated that a new government should be open to all ethnic groups but reiterated that former President Burhanuddin Rabbani was the legitimate leader of Afghanistan. On 22 October a meeting took place between the Russian and Tajik presidents together with Afghan representatives led by Rabbani. The different interests of the USA, Russia and the neighbouring states with regard to the composition of a new Afghan government became evident when the USA and Pakistan claimed that a new government should be open to moderate members of the Taliban, while Russia, Rabbani and Tajikistan explicitly ruled out Taliban participation of any kind.[30] An agreement to keep the Taliban out of a future Afghan government was later reached at a meeting in Dushanbe between the representatives of a Russian–US working group, of Russian First Deputy Prime Minister Vyacheslav Trubnikov and US Deputy Secretary of State Richard Armitage. The following day, on 3 November, President Rakhmonov said that he was convinced that the political process in Afghanistan should be aimed at creating a government with representatives of all nations and ethnic groups in Afghanistan but not including the Taliban.[31] The same day Rakhmonov and US Secretary of Defense Donald Rumsfeld agreed that Tajikistan would open its airspace and territory for US military on missions in Afghanistan.

The agreements on a future Afghan government were not clear, and the capture of Kabul by the Northern Alliance on 12 November therefore shifted the balance of power on the ground. General Fahim moved quickly to create a political–military fait accompli and appointed his people to all senior posts, thereby excluding Pushtuns and Hazaras.[32] On 17 November, Rabbani returned to Kabul and reasserted his status as head of state. At the UN-sponsored Bonn meeting in December 2001, where representatives from four Afghan factions participated, an interim administration under the ethnic Pushtun Hamid Karzai was appointed. On 22 December 2001 the interim administration under Karzai took power.

The Tajik faction of the Northern Alliance at first dominated the Karzai administration. Panjshiri Tajiks held the posts of minister of defence, minister of the interior and minister of foreign affairs (Muhammad Fahim, Yunus Qanooni, and Abdullah Abdullah, respectively) and provided 36 of the initial 38 generals.[33] The Northern Alliance allotted 17 of 30 cabinet positions but the intention was to widen the ethnic composition of the government.

The Bonn Agreement established a political process: a *loya jirga* (grand national council) was to be convened within six months to form a transitional government that would oversee the writing of a new constitution. A permanent government was to be selected within two years.

In spite of its old contacts with Rabbani, Russia supported the temporary administration of Karzai. Although he was a Pushtun, there was a risk that the Tajik dominance of the temporary administration would distance other minorities, in particular the Pushtun. The USA was now the major actor in Afghanistan in setting the agenda and priorities, and it now extended its contacts in Tajikistan as well.

The USA was slow to initiate any development projects in Afghanistan. In June 2003 President Bush adopted a new programme for Afghanistan, 'Accelerating Success', which was intended to break the deadlock in the country, bring change to the domestic power constellation, and speed up visible economic development before the situation in the country went out of control.

The US new policy came at a time when instability and rivalry between warlords seemed to be throwing Afghanistan back into factionalism.[34] In August 2003, however, Karzai managed to strengthen his control somewhat when he appointed a first deputy defence minister to balance Defence Minister Fahim. When the new US programme for Afghanistan was publicly launched in September 2003, large amounts of money were allocated to Afghanistan from the US budget.[35] The Constitutional Loya Jirga met in December 2003 and in January 2004 ratified a new constitution. It provided for a broader ethnic/regional base in order to bring back Pushtuns and Hazaras into the government and administration.

On 9 October 2004 presidential elections took place in Afghanistan and Hamid Karzai was elected despite accusations by his opponents of election fraud. On 23 December he announced his government. None of Karzai's three main ethnic rivals—Yunus Qanooni of the Tajiks, Karzai's chief rival; Mohammad Mohaqqeq, a Hazara; and Abdurrashid Dostum of the Uzbeks—was represented in the new government, although their ethnic groups were. Only five ministers remained from the previous government. The powerful posts of defence, the interior and finance went to ethnic Pushtuns. Of the three Panjshiri Tajiks in Karzai's last government, only Abdullah Abdullah kept his post as foreign minister. Fahim, the former defence minister, was not only removed from his government post but also dismissed from the army.[36]

Preparing for the parliamentary elections in 2005, most observers expected that the warlords would mobilize along ethnic dividing lines. The ethnic-Tajiks especially were reported to be dissatisfied at having been pushed aside by Karzai.[37] Karzai did his best to broaden the government. On 1 March 2005 Dostum was appointed military adviser to the commander-in-chief, that is, to Karzai.[38] This seemed to be part of a strategy to reduce the influence of the ethnic Tajiks in the government by balancing the warlords of different ethnic groups.

## A New Pattern of Relations in the Making?

Although the situation in Afghanistan did not normalize quickly, the post-2001 developments meant a new trajectory for Tajik–Afghan relations. Government-to-government contacts were now established with the new Afghan leadership. For the first time the Tajik government was able to take initiatives of its own outside the strict security framework that the Russians had constructed to keep Afghanistan at arm's length from the Central Asians.

For Tajikistan great opportunities to contribute to the reconstruction of society and the economy in Afghanistan opened up. In late January 2002 Hamid Karzai visited Dushanbe as the head of the temporary Afghan administration, and a joint communiqué was issued on future cooperation between the countries. The Afghan infrastructure was in ruins, but neighbouring Tajikistan could assist in the building of roads and bridges and in different kinds of construction work in Afghanistan, export electricity, and expand trade. Tajikistan saw itself in the role of a middleman. The financing for all projects was expected to come from international contributors and donors.[39] In early February 2002 the Tajik government had discussions with representatives of the diplomatic missions and international organizations in Tajikistan about how Tajikistan could contribute in the reconstruction of the Afghan society and economy. However, both the Tajik government and the international organizations were cautious about taking action before the security situation in Afghanistan stabilized.

In autumn 2002 Tajikistan sent an ambassador to Afghanistan, and later that year a Tajik consul-general was appointed to Mazar-e-Sharif. On 4 September 2002 President Rakhmonov received the credentials of the Afghan ambassador to Tajikistan, who was a long-standing associate of Massoud. In his speech on this occasion Rakhmonov stated that Tajikistan in its diplomatic work aimed at increased international assistance and support for post-conflict reconstruction in Afghanistan. He noted that work had already started to restore the electricity transmission line from Tajikistan to the northern provinces of Afghanistan and construct bridges across the River Pyandzh. He indicated plans for the building of roads via Afghanistan linking Tajikistan with Iran and Pakistan.[40]

There were therefore visions, both short- and medium-term, of returning to the export of electricity and construction material, as in Soviet times, and of encouraging cross-border trade and expanding trade between the countries. There were also grand visions of the construction of roads and railways to connect Tajikistan to the ocean and enable it to reach out to the world. In February 2003 Afghan Foreign Minister Abdullah announced that regional cooperation was to be a major focus of Afghanistan's foreign policy.[41]

The export of electricity from Tajikistan to Afghanistan was an important step. A protocol signed in March 2002 specified that the transmission line from Kolkhozabad–Geran–Karadam in Tajikistan to Sherkhon–Kunduz in north-east Afghanistan would be the first to be restored.[42] In April 2003 Tajikistan started to deliver electricity to Kunduz. The protocol also provided for the power transmission to be extended to Taloqan.[43] However, increased exports of electricity depended on two new transmission lines to Afghanistan being constructed, and also on when construction work on the Rogun and Sangtuda hydro-power complexes would be completed (see chapter 4).[44] When Russia signed agreements in October 2004 on investing in the expansion of hydro-energy in Tajikistan, the prospects for Tajik electricity exports to Afghanistan increased. Russian and Tajik interests overlapped on this issue.

In December 2002 the commander of Kunduz in north-east Afghanistan visited Tajikistan and the parties agreed that Tajikistan would not only to provide electricity to Kunduz but also reduce its tariffs on Afghan goods such as cotton and dried fruit in transit across Tajikistan. Tajikistan offered scholarships for Afghan students in technical subjects and pledged to build bridges across the River Pyandzh.[45] The export of construction material, in particular concrete from the huge Dushanbe factory, which had been working at very low capacity since the early 1990s, was discussed. There were numerous obstacles to bilateral trade, however. First, there were substantial mental obstacles in the mutual perceptions of the two countries. The Afghan ambassador to Tajikistan explained why the immediate prospects for trade seemed bleak despite official declarations of goodwill by referring to each country's perceptions of the other. The Tajiks viewed Afghanistan as a country still at war, without laws and regulations, and thus too insecure for business and investment. The perception of Tajikistan among several people in the Afghan leadership, he continued, was that communism still ruled in Tajikistan, or at least that the risk remained that the communists would come back to power. Afghan businessmen found Tajikistan very corrupt and thought the legal basis for trade was weak. The ambassador also mentioned a certain passivity among Tajik businessmen and a tendency for them to demand excessive prices for goods and services, which made them less competitive than their Pakistani and Iranian counterparts. 'Businessmen from Pakistan and Iran do business when it only brings them a few kopeks. But Tajik businessmen do not want to waste their energy if they are not guaranteed huge profits', he said. He warned that if the Tajiks continued as onlookers on the Afghan market, this niche would soon be filled by others.[46]

By 2004 the situation seemed to be changing. On 13 September 2004 the ministers of economic affairs of the two countries signed a five-year trade agreement, and in early November the same year an agreement was signed to open up border trade at three points along the Tajik–Afghan border in Gorno-Badakhshan—at Iskashim, Khorog and Darvaz.[47]

Afghanistan's natural gas resources offered prospects for joint Tajik–Afghan exploitation of those resources and the export of Afghan gas to Tajikistan in future, thereby reducing Tajikistan's dependence on gas imported from Uzbekistan.[48] In 2004 the Tajik government suggested renewed talks on the construction of a 120-km gas pipeline from the Shebergan field in Afghanistan, near Mazar-e-Sharif, to Kolkhozabad in Tajikistan. Afghanistan had previously exported gas to Tajikistan, but since 1989 the resources in the north of Afghanistan had not been tapped at all. However, the importing of gas from Afghanistan was a project for the distant future and to be realized only after the planned gas pipeline from Turkmenistan to Pakistan across Afghanistan has been built. The planned Turkmen–Afghan–Pakistan gas pipeline would also possibly allow Tajikistan to buy Turkmen gas in future without the gas having to transit across Uzbekistan.[49]

Several countries were eager to help Tajikistan play this role in regional cooperation. Russia, which itself hoped to find a future of economic exchange with Afghanistan, encouraged Tajikistan to plan to export electricity. Iran, with a vision of connecting the Farsi-speaking countries of Tajikistan, Afghanistan and Iran, concentrated on assisting in the construction of roads between the three countries, and in 2003 signed an agreement with both Afghanistan and Tajikistan on a project that was to cost 180 million USD.[50] US companies announced plans to build an 80-km railway line from the Uzbek town of Termez on the Amudarya through Khairaton to Mazar-e-Sharif in Afghanistan.[51] There were plans for roads from Termez to Mazar-e-Sharif and further down to Herat and into Iran, and from Mazar-e-Sharif to the east into Pakistan. If Tajikistan were to link up with these roads in future, this would help it reach the ocean in both Iran and Pakistan. A ferry at Nizhnii Pyandzh and five small crossings in Tajik Gorno-Badakhshan opened in 2002. In June 2004 the USA started the construction of a first large bridge across the Pyandzh, connecting Tajikistan and Afghanistan at Nizhnii Pyandzh. In September 2004 a trilateral meeting of the Tajik and Afghan presidents and the Pakistani prime minister, held in Dushanbe, discussed plans for the transit of Tajik electricity to Pakistan.[52] The economic sphere thus provided broad prospects for

Tajikistan's cooperation with Afghanistan as well as other states to the south, and held out the promise of Tajikistan gaining an exit to the sea in future.

A complicating factor in the development of relations between Tajikistan and Afghanistan was the drastic increase of drug production in Afghanistan after 2001 and of drug trafficking from Afghanistan across Central Asia. This 'soft' security threat from Afghanistan also secured the continued interest and concern of the international community in the development of the Central Asian countries and opened new prospects for wider international cooperation as Russia, the West and the regional powers all had a common interest in suppressing this lucrative but destructive business.

In spite of the ongoing reconstruction of Afghanistan and the Western military presence in the country, the laboratories producing heroin in the northern and north-western parts of Afghanistan continued their work. According to UN reports the production of opium in Afghanistan reached a peak in 2004 and accounted for some 86 per cent of world production. Tajikistan is one of the major countries for the transit of drugs from Afghanistan. During 2004, 6.7 tons of drugs (of which about 4.5 tons was heroin) were confiscated in Tajikistan. The increased production in Afghanistan was a serious threat to Tajikistan, and the new situation demanded greater and broader international cooperation. The UN Office on Drugs and Crime cooperated closely with Tajik colleagues and encouraged contacts with Afghan colleagues, and the new Afghan administration under Hamid Karzai improved the conditions for Tajik–Afghan cooperation in the fight against the drug trade.

The security situations of Tajikistan and Afghanistan became linked through the international cooperation that was developing. Vladimir Putin suggested that Afghanistan be associated with the Central Asian Cooperation Organization (of which Tajikistan was a member; Russia became a member in 2004).[53] The North Atlantic Treaty Organization (NATO), in Afghanistan on its first out-of-area mission, developed cooperation with Tajikistan. Thus, a new kind of security cooperation was emerging across the Pyandzh/Amudarya, undermining the tradition that the river separates the countries.

## Uzbekistan: A Turn for the Worse?

The post-September 2001 situation improved the external conditions for relations between Tajikistan and Uzbekistan. The fall of the Taliban reduced the external threat to both, and the larger US engagement targeted them both for cooperation. Moreover, the two countries were not only former Soviet republics with the heritage of a joint economic and transport infrastructure; they also shared a common cultural heritage to such a degree that it had been difficult to define them as separate states from the point of ethnic composition or language.[54] There is not only a large Uzbek minority in Tajikistan but also a substantial Tajik minority in Uzbekistan. According to official Uzbek statistics there are slightly over 1 million Tajiks in Uzbekistan, or about 4 per cent of the population. The unofficial figure is over 6 million Tajiks. They are concentrated in the Surkhandarya, Samarkand and Bukhara regions.[55]

After independence the relations between the two countries were marked by tension and suspicion. Then the new international situation in the region after September 2001 created new conditions for Tajikistan's policy towards and relations with Uzbekistan. How did its policy and relations with Uzbekistan change in the security and economic fields?

*Tajikistan and Uzbekistan before 2001*

There is much to lead one to expect that these two states would live as natural partners and allies. In theory Uzbekistan could be expected to be the natural ally of Tajikistan in the security sphere, since Uzbekistan is the potential regional power with the largest population and the strongest army among the Central Asian states. It could be expected to be an ally in the economic sphere since it is more industrialized, and northern Tajikistan was integrated into the economic processes in Uzbekistan long ago. Instead, friction and tensions characterized their relations.

While most of present-day Tajikistan, together with most of present-day Uzbekistan, once belonged to the Bukhara Emirate, which was formally a formally independent state entity until it was incorporated in the Soviet Union in the 1920s, parts of northern Tajikistan belonged to the Kokand Khanate. The latter included the whole of the Fergana Valley, and was a political unit from the late 16th century until it was swallowed by Russia in the late 19th century. The mountainous parts of present-day Tajikistan consisted of small independent fiefdoms until they were conquered by the Bukhara Emirate in the 1880s. Thus, there were no state entities based on ethnicity.

In contrast, the history of Tajik–Uzbek relations of the 20th century is closely connected with the nation- and state-building efforts. For a long time the issue of the existence of a Tajik nation was squeezed between the ideologies of pan-Turkism (oriented towards Turkey), which dominated the reformist movements of Tsarist Russia, and pan-Islamism (oriented towards Afghanistan), which dominated the official Bukhara Emirate.[56] The existence of a Farsi-speaking Tajik nation was therefore ignored. Bolshevik policy at first ignored aspirations for the creation of a Tajik state entity, and the Bolshevik division of Central Asia in the 1920s into national–administrative units had profound consequences for the Tajik nation. The Tajiks had to enter the political struggle to have their national identity and right to a territory recognized. The major opponents at the time were the supporters of the reformist pan-Turkic Jadidi movement, and the Jadidis built on the concept of the Sarts which Tsarist ethnographers used to classify the sedentary population. The Sarts were defined as a cross between the Tajiks (of Iranian descent) and the Uzbeks (of Turkic descent). The term 'Sart' was used as a definitional term until the Bolsheviks divided the region.[57]

The way in which the Tajik Autonomous Soviet Socialist Republic (ASSR) was created in 1924, subordinated to the Uzbekistan Socialist Republic, left deep traces in the memory and mind of the Tajiks. In April 1918 an Autonomous Turkestan Republic (ATR) had been organized on the territory of what was then Russian Turkestan (which did not include the Bukhara Emirate). During these early years the policy of the young Soviet regime wavered with regard to Central Asia. As early as 1918 some Russian ideologists advocated establishing ethnically-based administrative units there, in contrast to the ethnically heterogeneous entities based on tribes stretching throughout the whole region.[58] In 1918 in Tashkent a Turkestan Commissariat for Nationalities Affairs was established, directly responsible to Moscow, and in 1918–19 a series of departments for nationality affairs opened. During the years that followed there was an intense political struggle between those from the region who wanted to maintain the ethnically heterogeneous communality based on traditional bonds, such as those of the tribe, clan or region—to whom any separation of people along ethnic divides seemed wrong—and those which advocated a division along ethnographic lines.[59]

In 1920 the Bolshevik government decided to counter pan-Turkism by breaking up the ATR and dividing it into administrative units based on ethnographic divisions. This was reflected in Lenin's instructions to the Turkestan Commission in January 1920.[60] In 1923, as part of a strong reaction against the division of the region, demands were raised for an 'autonomous Fargana'.[61] Even so, in 1924 an administrative division into ethnic units was carried out.

At the time of the creation of Uzbekistan, 'Uzbek' was not a natural unifying concept for what later became Uzbekistan. As the scholar Edward A. Allworth writes, 'Instituting the name *Uzbek* as a defining concept in twentieth-century Soviet affairs could not have happened without determined Russian insistence on ethnic segregation'.[62] To Moscow the concept of Turkestan had become a threat since such a large territorial unit could call into question the centralized rule of the Bolsheviks and could aspire to independence for Central Asia.

While Moscow used ethnic divisions to fight both pan-Turkism and pan-Islamism, the Tajiks had problems defending their national specificity. Disregard of Tajik interests was noticed as early as 1919, when branches for nationality affairs under the People's Commissariat of the ATR were set up for the different Turkic-speaking peoples but not for the Persian-speaking Tajiks. Moreover, when the Central Committee of the Turkestan Communist Party established three national departments—Uzbek, Kyrgyz and Turkman—in late 1920, there was no Tajik department.[63] This was indicative of the dominant view at the time.

An intense debate followed on the issue of whether a Tajik language, nation and identity existed at all, and the defenders of the Tajiks had difficulty making their voices heard. Most intellectuals from the Tajik cities of Bukhara and Samarkand followed the trends of the time and believed that only a common Turkic identity and the use of the Turkic Uzbek language would lead to social progress and development. Although the Tajik language had been the language of culture and literature over the centuries, as well as being the language of state administration in the Bukhara Emirate up to September 1920, it now had to give place to the Uzbek language.[64] No journals in the Tajik language existed. As the issue of the existence of the Tajiks became politicized, the censuses of the 1920s were manipulated in order to define the Tajiks in such a way as to produce figures on the ethnic Tajiks that would be as low as possible. Many Tajiks were forced to declare themselves Uzbeks and Uzbek-speaking, writes the Tajik scholar Rakhim Masov.[65] Scholars like Allworth also point out how easy it was to manipulate the locals, since people did not identify in terms such as 'Tajik' or 'Uzbek'.

Although it can be said that the Tajiks in the end benefited from Moscow's policy of creating ethnically-based units, they were disadvantaged with regard to the territory the new Tajik Soviet state entity was assigned. When the borders of the proposed Tajikistan ASSR were discussed in 1924 its territory was limited to the eastern part of the former Bukhara Emirate. It did not include either the Tajik cultural centres of Bukhara and Samarkand or the larger cities of today's northern Tajikistan.

The Tajiks reacted strongly, and several leading Tajik communists came out in defence of what could be called Tajik national interests. As early as September 1924 the chairman of the Eastern Bukhara Central Executive Committee demanded that the Tajiks, like the Uzbeks, be given the right to constitute a Soviet republic of their own, and that Ura-Tyube, Khujand, Kanibadam, Isfara, Sokh, Rishtan and Uch-Kurgan (in the north of present-day Tajikistan) be transferred to the Tajik republic.[66] In May 1924 the first secretary of the Central Committee of the Communist Party of Uzbekistan, A. Ikromov, confessed that the attitude of the Uzbeks towards the 'small minorities', as he called the Tajiks, had been chauvinist. His frank admission was made possible by a previous statement by Stalin to similar effect. Others, like the Bukhara poet Sadriddin Aini, took a more serious and honest stance: Aini opposed efforts by Turkic-speakers to sustain the old Tajik–Sart–Uzbek symbiosis in Central Asia.[67] Nevertheless, when the Central Committee of the Russian Communist Party (Bolsheviks) RKP(b) decided in October 2004 to establish the Tajikistan ASSR, it included only the eastern part of former Bukhara Emirate and the mountainous districts of the Zerafshan Valley, including the cities of Penjikent and Ura-Tyube, among others.[68]

The Tajikistan ASSR had a hard time under the Uzbek authorities. Uzbek disregard of Tajik interests was demonstrated in the lack of Tajik schools and the way the Tajik language was ignored. Demands for Tajikistan to be given a status equal to Uzbekistan's therefore intensified. So did the requests that territories with a dense Tajik population be transferred to the Tajikistan ASSR from the Uzbek SSR. In 1929 a territorial demand was raised, that the Surkhandarya region be transferred to the Tajikistan ASSR—a request which was turned down.[69]

In October 1929 the Tajikistan ASSR finally became the Tajikistan SSR, on a par with the Soviet Socialist Republic of Uzbekistan. Moreover, Khujand was now transferred to Tajikistan, although Bukhara and Samarkand remained outside it. As a result of the drawing of borders in the 1920s, concentrations of Tajiks were left outside Tajikistan, in Samarkand and Bukhara, in the mountainous areas outside Tashkent, in the Fergana Valley, and in Jizzak province, Surkhandarya and Kashkadarya.[70]

Tajik historians of today point to the injustice done to the Tajiks during the early years of Soviet power as Tajiks and Tajik interests were systematically disregarded when borders were drawn and state entities within the Soviet Union created. They point to the historical injustice of Tajik cultural centres not being included in Tajikistan but being given to Uzbekistan thanks to the manipulation of population statistics during the 1920s.[71] Tajik historians such as Rakhim Masov blame individual politicians of Tajik ethnic descent who were heavily influenced by pan-Turkism for the injustices done to the Tajiks at the time. Yet some of these politicians changed their views during the late 1920s and became defenders of the claims for a separate Tajikistan SSR, to include Bukhara, Samarkand, Khujand, the Surkhandarya Valley and the Kashkadarya Valley.[72]

From the mid-1960s, growing Uzbek nationalism in Uzbekistan struck against the Tajik culture and language. Official support for the Tajiks was reduced and schools were closed, which caused tension in Bukhara and Samarkand and nearby rural areas.[73] In the late 1980s tension between Uzbeks and Tajiks in Uzbekistan increased, and in 1988 demonstrations in Samarkand and Bukhara demanded that territories with Tajik majority populations be united with Tajikistan. The Uzbekistan SSR authorities did their best to prevent all such efforts to organize Tajiks. Neil Melvin writes that 'Efforts by Tajiks to expand Tajik-language education, publishing and television have been largely thwarted by the government. The Tajiks also appear to have been marginalized from the new areas of economic activity in the country, with Tajik run markets having a lower status than those run by Europeans and Uzbeks. Tajiks also lack significant formal political representation at the highest level'.[74]

Uzbekistan had a favoured position during Soviet times. With Tashkent as the administrative centre in the region ever since Tsarist Russia first conquered Central Asia in the 1860s, it became the most industrialized and modern of the Central Asian republics. It maintained a 'big brother' attitude towards Tajikistan during the Soviet era, and was encouraged to do so as Moscow to a great extent relied on Uzbekistan.

After the break-up of the Soviet Union, Uzbekistan was an important ally to Russia. It was the strongest power in Central Asia. In the turbulence that followed, Uzbekistan played a central role in Russia's gaining control of Tajikistan and in bringing Rakhmonov to power in 1992.[75] It acted as Russia's regional policeman in Tajikistan, but also looked after its own interests. It provided logistical supplies, military training and air support to the Tajik paramilitary pro-communist factions. Uzbek units participated actively in the civil war in Tajikistan, and the Uzbek air force bombed opposition strongholds in Garm and Gorno-Badakhshan. However, Uzbekistan's strength also made it a potential competitor for influence in the region, which Russia sought to contain.

Uzbek President Islam Karimov was extremely concerned about the threat from 'Islamic fundamentalism' and about the toppling in September 1992 of his counterpart in Tajikistan, President Rakhmon Nabiev, by a coalition of secular and Islamic forces. He was also concerned about the position of the large Uzbek minority in the Leninabad region of Tajikistan. Uzbekistan therefore abandoned its support for Rakhmonov when in 1993 he initiated a process of 'kulyabization' of senior administrative and political posts in Tajikistan, thereby squeezing out those from all other regions, including Leninabad, from senior positions and replacing them with people from his own home region, Kulyab.

As Uzbekistan distanced itself from Rakhmonov after 1993 it could no longer play the role of Moscow's 'arm' in Tajikistan. Instead it became a rival to Russia in Central Asia. Trying to influence the Tajik domestic scene, Uzbekistan put Tajikistan under pressure and exploited the latter's economic and energy dependence. It also gave support to local warlords, particularly the rebel commander Makhmud Khudoberdiev, in their revolts against Rakhmonov. Uzbekistan was highly sceptical about the power-sharing arrangement of the Tajik General Peace Agreement of 1997 and about representatives of the UTO's Islamist flank being given seats in the Tajik government. In particular it opposed the Minister for Emergency Situations, Mirzo Ziyo, who had had Juma Namangani, the leader of the Islamic Movement of Uzbekistan (IMU), among his men when he was a UTO commander during the civil war, and had married a relative of Namangani.

The deterioration in relations between Russia and Uzbekistan after 1993–94 was followed by an increasingly pronounced Uzbek policy of increasing its independence in relation to Russia. In 1996 President Karimov visited the USA, and in September that year the Uzbek defence minister declared that his country did not intend to participate any further in CIS peacekeeping missions, and withdrew its troops from the CIS peacekeeping force in Tajikistan.[76] In 1998 Russia tried to intensify its efforts to improve relations with Uzbekistan.[77] As mentioned above, when Dostum in 1998 withdrew from fighting against the Taliban in Afghanistan and went into exile, Uzbekistan did not want to continue with Russia in the anti-Taliban alliance. Russia's and Uzbekistan's interests had started to diverge seriously.

Growing tensions within Uzbek society between the regime and its domestic critics—first and foremost radical Islamists—added a source of tension to the region as a whole. Karimov had already clamped down on the opposition in 1992–93 when opposition parties such as Erk and Birlik were banned. From the mid-1990s, suppression of the opposition increased. Uzbekistan also continued to influence the domestic life of its neighbours, all of which had large Uzbek minority groups in their populations.

In May 1998, when the 1991 law on 'freedom of conscience and religious organizations' was revised, the Uzbek authorities imposed new restrictions on religious groups. By then the tensions between the heads of several mosques in the Fergana Valley and the state authorities had sharpened. In December 1997 the authorities despatched elite troops to the town of Namangan following a murder, when an official was decapitated.[78] In March 1998 the former imam of the Tokhtabal mosque in Tashkent was arrested together with another imam accused of promoting Wahhabism. President Karimov followed up, speaking in harsh terms against the Wahhabites, whom he accused of turning Uzbekistan into a second Tajikistan, and stating that 'such people must be shot in the head. If necessary, I'll shoot them myself, if you lack the resolve'.[79]

In October 1998 the trial started of 15 men from Andijan, accused of being Wahhabites, on charges of terrorism, possession of arms and drugs, robbery and extortion. On the same day the trial opened in Tashkent of five men also accused of Wahhabism. These people were sentenced in January 1999 to prison terms of between two and 12 years.[80] On 16 February 1999 car bombs exploded in central Tashkent, targeting government buildings. Several people were killed and more than 100 wounded. The IMU and its leaders, Juma Namangani and Takhir Yuldashev, were immediately held responsible, but the repression that followed also targeted members of the moderate opposition who were far removed from the extremism of the IMU. After the Tashkent bombings, Uzbekistan closed its border with Tajikistan and alleged that there was a Tajik connection to the bombings.[81]

The February 1999 bombings demonstrated that Uzbekistan was vulnerable and already the target of extremists. Although deeply concerned, President Karimov did not turn to Russia for assistance. Instead he criticized Russia's large military presence in Central Asia, first and foremost in Tajikistan.

In August 1999 Uzbek Islamic fighters from the IMU intruded into the Batken region in Kyrgyzstan en route to Uzbekistan, and the threat from Islamic extremism seemed to have increased seriously. From Afghanistan, the IMU declared that it had launched a jihad to topple the Karimov regime and capture the Fergana Valley.[82] Thus the Batken events brought a new element into the security situation in Central Asia. For the first time radical Islamists from the region resorted to weapons in direct fighting with Central Asian military and interior troops.

The incursions increased tensions between the Central Asian states. The Uzbek government accused both the Tajik and the Kyrgyz governments of passivity. Tajikistan was accused of not taking measures to prevent Islamic fighters from maintaining camps on Tajik territory. Several IMU fighters had participated in the Tajik civil war on the side of the UTO. Uzbekistan now took measures, and Uzbek aircraft bombed villages on the Tajik side of the border, which led to protests from the Tajik government.[83] The IMU was an Uzbek movement, and the internal problems of Uzbekistan thus became a cause of instability to the neighbouring countries.

Tajikistan and Uzbekistan were both vulnerable. The former accused the latter of supporting the rebellious ethnic-Uzbek Khudoberdiev. The Uzbeks accused the Tajiks of allowing the Uzbek IMU fighters to hide on Tajik territory. For Tajikistan in this situation the close alliance with Russia was a defence against possible Uzbek pressure and interference.

*Dependence on Uzbek Infrastructure*

At the time of the break-up of the Soviet Union, Tajikistan's dependence on Uzbekistan was reflected in statistics. Uzbekistan was a major trade partner and supplier of gas. The north of Tajikistan was more closely integrated into the Uzbek economy than with the rest of Tajikistan. The Soviet infrastructure which the two countries inherited made Tajikistan dependent on Uzbekistan for exit routes since roads, railways and electricity grids run across Uzbek territory. Highly vulnerable because of this dependence, Tajikistan suffered seriously as soon Uzbekistan took unilateral measures to defend its security.

Economically, geographically and politically, the Fergana Valley long formed a natural unit set apart from the rest of Central Asia. The kinship and ethnic ties between its different parts were always strong. Today the Fergana Valley is shared between three countries. Of a total population of more than 10 million in the valley, almost three-quarters are Uzbeks. About 60 per cent of the territory is located in Uzbekistan, 25 per cent in Tajikistan and 15 per cent in Kyrgyzstan.[84]

During Soviet times Khujand was a hub in the region's web of railways and bus routes, but this is no longer the case. Today the natural trade in goods and services has to cross state borders.

For railways, there are three exits from Tajikistan which run across Uzbekistan, one in the north and two in the south. In the north a major Fergana railway connection enters Tajikistan from Uzbekistan in the west (Bekabad) and passes through the cities of Nau, Gafurov and Kanibadam, with one branch going down to Isfara and another branch re-entering Uzbekistan to the east (to Besharyk and Kokand). As a result of measures taken by Uzbekistan at the border, the 109 km of railway in the Sogd region stand practically idle.[85] As an illustration, in 2004 once a week a train left Andijan in Uzbek Fergana and passed through Khujand on its way to Russia but never stopped there for passengers,[86] and once a week another train started from Khujand bound for Russia through Uzbekistan but with only Tajik passengers. While the Leninabad railway station just outside Khujand was once called the 'Gateway to the Fergana', since it connected several railway lines, it no longer maintains that position. The other two railways leave Tajikistan to the west of Turzunzade, where the aluminium plant is located, and in the very south connecting to the Uzbek town of Termez. No other railway routes out of Tajikistan exist, and Tajikistan is thus fully dependent on Uzbekistan in this regard. There is no railway connecting Khujand in the north with Dushanbe in the south except one that runs across Uzbekistan.

In a similar way there are obstacles to road exits into Uzbekistan. In Soviet times the main highway of the Fergana Valley ran through the *avtovokzal* (bus terminal) of the town of Gafurov, next to the Leninabad railway station, and there were always buses full of people travelling in different directions of the Fergana. National regulations and intergovernmental tension changed all this. Nowadays Kyrgyz buses and drivers come to Gafurov full of people but Tajik drivers seldom go in the other direction since they have to pay higher costs than the Kyrgyz drivers at the Uzbek border stations on their way to Kyrgyzstan.[87] It is difficult to reach agreements regarding road freight. The road in the Sogd region and the Tajik towns of Isfara and Chorku runs to the Kyrgyz town of Isfana. It continues to Osh in Kyrgyzstan but on its way turns in and out of Uzbek territory and Uzbek exclaves on Kyrgyz territory.

The highway across northern Tajikistan was used by Uzbekistan to connect Tashkent with the Fergana Valley. In order to be independent of Tajikistan for these connections, Uzbekistan started a huge road project which was completed in 2002.[88] The highway along the Kamchikskii Pass runs up in the mountains on the narrow strip of Uzbek territory between Kyrgyzstan and Tajikistan. This highway is strategically very important to Uzbekistan and is strongly protected by border guards on the surrounding mountains and by military at the entrances to the two tunnels. Uzbekistan fears terrorists trespassing into the country. The new road makes it easier for Uzbekistan to block Tajikistan.

Tajikistan's dependence on Uzbek roads becomes more pronounced in the light of the fact that Tajikistan has hitherto lacked an all-year-round road connecting its south with the northern part of the country. The road connecting north and south Tajikistan was blocked by snow every winter from November until May at the Anzob pass in the Zerafshan range.[89] When the Uzbek authorities from time to time closed the border station to the west of Penjikent, the town had to live isolated through the hardships of winter.

The problems at the borders are several. First, each state has its border posts and checking routines.[90] Second, the new transit regulations introduced after independence mean high tariffs for international transit. Third, freight transport across borders involves a struggle with bureaucracies since several ministries have to give permission for transit, with both lengthy procedures and high costs as the result. On top of that, unilateral measures by one government aimed at defending its national security or economy have serious consequences for the neighbours. Uzbekistan has repeatedly taken unilateral measures to defend its security. In 1999 it closed crossing posts on the border with Tajikistan, started to introduce visa regulations, and increased tariffs and taxes on goods in transit. In the same year the Uzbek authorities started laying mines along the border with Tajikistan and Kyrgyzstan in the Fergana Valley. Since the borders were neither delimited nor demarcated, this resulted in civilians being killed by mines. Along the Tajik–Uzbek border there have also been incidents of people being shot by border guards.[91] From 1999, the Uzbek regime's fear of its domestic opposition—both the violent and the non-violent—contributed to the closing of borders. Radical Islamism, extremism and terrorism are thus dangerous triggers of a deterioration of relations as governments react to the threats they perceive from terrorists.

Border disputes between Tajikistan and Uzbekistan are a special aspect of the border problem. As already mentioned, the borders between Tajikistan and Uzbekistan were questioned from the very beginning. Since the break-up of the Soviet Union territorial problems have resurfaced, although both governments agree to the Soviet demarcations. The Tajik government has made no 'historical claims' on territory, although for many Tajiks the inclusion in Uzbekistan of Samarkand, Bukhara and some other historic cities of the Zerafshan Valley was a great injustice. Requests for border revisions can be heard in both countries, for example, unofficial Tajik claims to the Surkhandarya region in Uzbekistan to the south-west of Dushanbe.[92] The Uzbeks, on the other hand, recall that Khujand, Isfara and Kanibadam were not included in the Tajik ASSR in 1924 but included only in 1929, when Tajikistan became a soviet socialist republic.[93]

There is another aspect connected with borders, which concerns water and the distribution of water. The large Qayroqqum reservoir and the hydro-power stations in the Sogd region connected to the Syrdarya influence the water level along the river as it enters Uzbekistan. The amount of water the Tajiks release from the reservoir influences the level of the river in Uzbekistan.

Central Asia's water comes from the Amudarya and Syrdarya, which spring from the Pamir and the Tian Shan mountains and cross several countries until they reach the Aral Sea. Dams were built in Soviet time to store the water in reservoirs and use it for agriculture or hydroelectricity. Over 90 per cent of the available water is used for irrigation. The networks are old and inefficient, and half of the water never reaches the fields. In Soviet times the system worked reasonably well (apart from the drying up of the Aral Sea). Independence resulted in the end of centralized management, but the Central Asian states set up an Interstate Commission on Water Coordination for the joint management of water resources. The members meet every year to agree on the way water resources are to be shared; the currency is electricity and the mode of exchange barter. Downstream countries agree with upstream countries on the amount of hydro-power they will buy during the summer months when water is released. In the winter, power travels the other way in the form of gas, coal or electricity.[94]

Eighty per cent of Central Asia's water comes from Tajikistan and Kyrgyzstan, but these states are allowed to withdraw less than 15 per cent of the water, and have to restrict their generation of hydro-power in the winter in order to store water for the summer. They complain that they are not paid by the downstream countries to operate and maintain dams and reservoirs. The downstream countries, on the other hand, consider that they are overcharged for the hydroelectric power.[95] They accuse the upstream countries of releasing more water than agreed in order to generate electricity, thereby causing flooding in the winter and risking a shortage of water for irrigation in the summer. During the 1990s Tajikistan caused fewer problems in this regard since its electricity production went down as a consequence of the civil war.

The tension between Tajikistan and Uzbekistan that already existed at the time of the break-up of the Soviet Union increased during the 1990s, and relations between them deteriorated, especially after 1999.

*Developments after September 2001*

Tensions increased between Tajikistan and Uzbekistan in the immediate aftermath of the 11 September 2001 terrorist attacks. Uzbekistan closed its border to normal traffic and introduced strict regulations and high charges for transit.[96] For Tajikistan the costs were considerable: freight traffic was stopped at the Uzbek border and the high costs for transit through Uzbekistan were damaging Tajikistan's exports.[97] The stricter visa regime introduced by Uzbekistan created effective barriers to the transit of people, including shuttle traders and local merchants. Formally, Tajiks could enter Uzbekistan, but it was difficult and expensive to get a visa, there were various taxes on goods, and the procedure at the border crossing points was humiliating. As an immediate post-11 September reaction, on 25 September 2001 Kazakhstan suspended passenger train services from Tajikistan to Moscow via Kazakhstan.[98] Added to these problems were the unresolved issues between Tajikistan and Uzbekistan in the areas of gas supply, customs regulations for transit shipments, and water use. Uzbekistan repeatedly cut off the supply of gas to Tajikistan (as it also did to Kyrgyzstan and Kazakhstan), demanding immediate payment of Tajikistan's debt for its gas. Uzbek landmines in the Fergana Valley along the borders with Tajikistan and Kyrgyzstan continued to cause fatalities. By early 2002 almost 100 Tajik civilians had been killed or injured.[99] Most were women and children gathering firewood along the border or shepherds pasturing cattle in the area.

The fall of the Taliban in November improved the general security situation in Central Asia. Tension between Tajikistan and Uzbekistan abated when the external threat declined, but did not disappear.

Instability in Afghanistan continued but now seemed to be following a different trajectory, thereby giving Central Asia a chance to develop. The new increased Western engagement had become a factor for stability in Central Asia.

The overthrow of the Taliban regime contributed to remove IMU fighters from the scene, at least temporarily. In November 2001, Juma Namangani, leader of the IMU, was reported killed in combat in northern Afghanistan. As most of the IMU members had fought on the side of the Taliban, the organization went underground. In spring 2002 the Russian media reported from time to time that groups of IMU fighters were illegally entering Gorno-Badakhshan and Tavildara, in the heart of Tajikistan, from Afghanistan, but this was never confirmed. The Uzbek authorities, meanwhile, continued to refer to the threat from the IMU when defending their policy towards Tajikistan.

International developments after September 2001 initiated a process of normalization of bilateral relations between Tajikistan and Uzbekistan. Their two presidents met in Tashkent on 27–28 December on the eve of the summit meeting of the Central Asian Economic Community. The two leaders decided that more than 25 border crossing points were to be opened, fees paid at the border by those travelling in cars and trucks were to be reduced, and 10 per cent of the Tajik debt to Uzbekistan was to be written off. Their meeting restarted the work of the existing but inactive Tajik–Uzbek Intergovernmental Commission and, on 12 February 2002, several agreements were signed when Tajik Prime Minister Akil Akilov visited Tashkent.[100] According to comments in the Tajik press during spring 2002, the US presence made Karimov more willing to make agreements with Tajikistan. Thus, the USA was perceived as partly a regulator of bilateral relations in the region by providing incentives to both governments with which it had contacts.

The process of normalization proceeded slowly. Severe disappointment with its slow progress was reflected in an article in March 2002 in the Tajik newspaper *Biznes i politika* accusing certain circles in Uzbekistan of hegemonic ambitions in Central Asia and calling Uzbekistan's mining of the border and harsh treatment of Tajik transit passengers 'a kind of terrorism with regional means and on a regional scale'.[101] By August 2002 about 70 per cent of Tajikistan's border with Uzbekistan had been delineated[102] and by early October 2002 an agreement had been signed demarcating the 1,050 km-long border, apart from four disputed areas.[103] Four other areas in Sogd remained in dispute between Tajikistan and Uzbekistan after the agreement was signed. In August the prime ministers also signed agreements on rail transport, television broadcasting, Tajikistan's debt to Uzbekistan, and the functioning of border checkpoints.[104] Not until June 2004 did Uzbekistan announce at the Organization for Security and Co-operation in Europe (OSCE) Permanent Council in Vienna that it was to start de-mining the border with both Tajikistan and Kyrgyzstan.[105] This was a welcome decision, since Uzbekistan had denied the existence of mines for years and refused to discuss them. Yet, again, the process of de-mining was delayed.

In spite of signs pointing to a normalization of relations between the two countries, the problems at the border continued. To the Uzbek authorities' fear of threats to national security and anxiety about the stability of the regime were added the implications of their economic policy. In efforts to make the Uzbek currency convertible, the borders to neighbouring countries were more or less closed to prevent uncontrolled exports. On 1 November 2004 Uzbekistan further restricted the possibilities for Tajik citizens to receive an Uzbek visa for transit through Uzbekistan to Russia by rail.[106]

The unresolved issues between Tajikistan and Uzbekistan created several kinds of obstacle to Tajikistan's development. The electricity grids from Soviet times are a special aspect of Tajikistan's dependence on Uzbek infrastructure. Tajikistan is both an exporter and an importer of electricity in relation to Uzbekistan.[107] In 2003 it exported 550 million kilowatt an hour (kWh) to southern Uzbekistan while importing 234 million kWh into northern Tajikistan, which experiences power shortages in winter.[108] Tajikistan is also an exporter to Kyrgyzstan and Kazakhstan, although Tajik customers themselves often suffer from lack of electricity and from time to time have had to put up with only a few hours' supply of electricity a day.

In 2003, as plans started to take shape for the construction work on the Sangtuda hydro-energy complex which would make Tajikistan a large electricity exporter in the future, the Russian state electricity monopoly, the Joint Stock Company Unified Electric Systems (RAO UES), started to import cheap Tajik electricity into southern Russia.[109] A second agreement was made for 2004, which was to be a test case for whether Uzbekistan would allow the export of Tajik electricity to other countries, which requires transit across Uzbekistan. In February 2004 representatives of Russia's UES and the Tajik Energy Ministry initialled an agreement for Tajikistan to supply Russia with electricity from the Nurek hydro-power station during the summer to southern regions of Russia. Tajikistan had supplied about 190 million kWh to southern Russia over a period of slightly more than a month for the first time the previous summer, in 2003.[110] The company had intentions to increase this volume eightfold for 2004, from 190 million kWh to up to 1.4 billion. As the Russian media reported, '[Tajikistan's] entry onto new electricity markets of the Eurasian Economic Community opens up major new prospects not only for more investment but also for the growth of Tajikistan's economic potential as a whole'.[111] However, in

2004 no such electricity transmissions took place since the Uzbek authorities, referring to an 'overloading of the grid', did not allow them.[112]

In February 2005 Russia and Tajikistan again signed an agreement on Russian imports of Tajik electricity. Anatolii Chubais, the director of UES, said, 'I understand all problems for Tajikistan with neighbouring states but at the same time I want to say that this project has a future'. He also made clear that he was prepared to proceed with importing Tajik electricity through the Uzbek extension as well as the one across Kyrgyzstan and Kazakhstan.[113]

A more serious aspect of the controversy was that Tajikistan's plans for the future export of energy, after Sangtuda and Rogun start operating in the future, to Iran and Russia across Uzbek territory may be threatened if agreement cannot be reached with Uzbekistan.[114] The agreement between Tajikistan, Uzbekistan and the Asian Development Bank in March 2004 on a project to modernize the ageing regional power transmission system inherited from Soviet times gave hope of a solution to this problem.[115] The major economic interests behind the Russian energy investments could also be viewed as a guarantee that some kind of compromise would be found with Uzbekistan.

To reduce its dependence on the Uzbek power grid, in March 2004 the Tajik government initiated work on a new 54-km power line running from Kanibadam in northern Tajikistan to Batken in southern Kyrgyzstan, which opened in June 2005. The line, which opened in June 2005, bypasses Uzbek territory and provides the Sogd region with electricity from the Aygul-Tash power station in the Batken region.[116] It does not solve all problems mentioned above, but it pointed in the direction of the Tajik government working towards alternatives to the Uzbek power grids. To reduce dependence with regard to road transit across Uzbekistan as well, Tajikistan started a search for alternatives. In December 2003 the Tajik and Kyrgyz authorities agreed to reconstruct the road from Dushanbe running through Garm and Jirgatal into Karamyk in Kyrgyzstan, and then roads in Kyrgyzstan—parts of Kyrgyzstan's Osh region—and thus to reach back into the north of Tajikistan.[117] In 2005 a new stretch of the road opened, bypassing the Uzbek exclave of Sokh on Kyrgyz territory. Thus, problems in relations with Uzbekistan obliged the Tajik government to look for alternative solutions, circumventing Uzbekistan by building roads and grids in other directions.

The tense domestic scene in Uzbekistan continued to throw a shadow over relations between Uzbekistan and Tajikistan. After the US–British bombings of Afghanistan started in October 2001, and the leader of the IMU, Juma Namangani, died in northern Afghanistan in November that year, the IMU was silent and passive for a time. Then came the outbreaks of terrorist acts in Bukhara and Tashkent in March–April 2004, followed by a series of bombings on 30 July the same year.

To this should be added discontent with the religious situation, especially in the Fergana Valley. Persecution and the authorities' strict control over religious life were intended to prevent uncontrolled political activities emanating from the mosques, but these measures rather raised the anger of ordinary religious people, who were not allowed even to teach their children the Koran. The legislation in Tajikistan is not very different from that of Uzbekistan, but the Uzbek authorities have been much more sedulous in the way they follow the law and are notorious for the way in which they do so. Adult religious education is available only in the madrasas—colleges for Islamic instruction—of which there are only ten currently functioning in Uzbekistan. Adults who work in secular professions and schoolchildren are not allowed a religious education.[118] The state authorities regularly close down mosques or dismiss imams whom they suspect of being linked to the radical Islamist organization Hizb-ut-Tahrir. In several cases people attract the term 'Wahhabite' or are labelled supporters of Hizb-ut-Tahrir merely for being interested in religious studies or being critical of the often corrupt official clergy. The large demonstrations that took place in several cities of the Fergana Valley in November 2004 were related to new regulations for the bazaar trade, but discontent with the religious situation was also being expressed.

President Karimov's repression of the political and religious opposition since the early 1990s has resulted in the previously mainly secular opposition becoming radicalized and channelled into religiously dressed forms of expression. After September 2001 the religious–political underground opposition continued to be the dominant one. The Karimov regime showed no intention of initiating serious reform of governance which might ease the situation. Instead, under the guise of the fight against terrorism, Karimov strengthened the system of repression, and a further spiral of political violence was the result. Uzbekistan, with a record of terrorism that did not exist in any other Central Asian country, developed into a threat to the security of its neighbours, especially Tajikistan. Quite apart from the direct measures taken by the Uzbek authorities against Tajikistan, the tense domestic situation in Uzbekistan was nourishing radical Islamism, the ideas of which were spreading to both Tajikistan and Kyrgyzstan.

Uzbekistan's suspicion of Tajikistan and the regime's fear due to the deteriorating security situation were reflected in a reduction in the volume of Tajik–Uzbek trade from the year 2000. During the second half of the 1990s, Uzbekistan's trade with Tajikistan had expanded. The decline after 2000 can be explained first of all by the unilateral security measures taken by the Uzbek regime as the security situation in the country deteriorated. Although the security situation improved after the fall of the Taliban, and as the reconstruction process in Afghanistan started, trade between Tajikistan and Uzbekistan did not recover. Instead a drastic reduction in the official trade statistics was apparent (see table 5.1). The decline in trade was not stopped by declarations of goodwill by the Tajik and Uzbek governments. Bilateral relations thus remained frozen solid.

**Table 5.1: Uzbekistan's Share of Tajikistan's Trade Turnover**

|                        | 1991 | 1997 | 1998 | 1999 | 2000 | 2001 | 2002 | 2003 | 2004 |
|------------------------|------|------|------|------|------|------|------|------|------|
| Share of trade turnover | 8.0  | 29.0 | 26.9 | 32.9 | 19.4 | 17.7 | 14.1 | 11.9 |      |
| Share of total exports | 6.1  | 23.1 | 21.0 | 26.2 | 12.5 | 13.3 | 9.9  | 8.4  | 7.2  |
| Share of imports       | 9.9  | 34.8 | 31.9 | 39.8 | 27.5 | 21.9 | 18.4 | 15.1 | 12.3 |

Source: *Vneshneekonomicheskaya deyatelnost' Respubliki Tadzhikistan: Statisticheskii sbornik* (Dushanbe: Gosudarstvennyi komitet statistiki Respubliki Tadzhikista (Goskomstat), 2004), pp. 27–30. Figures for 1991 are from *Ezhegodnik Respubliki Tadzhikistan 2003* (Dushanbe: Goskomstat, 2003), pp. 264–65.

## Conclusions

Developments after September 2001 resulted in a major strategic reconfiguration in Afghanistan. In spite of the remaining instability in the country, the fact that the political process continued, elections were carried out and development projects were initiated gradually changed the Afghan domestic scene. Three circumstances contributed to open up completely new prospects for Tajikistan—the USA's engagement, its encouragement of regional development between Afghanistan and the neighbours, and the interest of regional powers in developing the transport infrastructure. The Tajik government actively sought a role for Tajikistan in the reconstruction of Afghanistan. As the situation in Afghanistan slowly improved, the outlines of a stronger Tajik emphasis on relations with countries to its south took shape.

The US factor did not have any direct impact on Uzbekistan in the sense of influencing Uzbekistan to normalize its relations with Tajikistan and promote regional development. As Neil MacFarlane writes, the USA did not seem to make much of an effort to encourage regional cooperation but instead developed bilateral relations with each of the

Central Asian states.[119] Yet the US factor did constitute a constraint on Uzbekistan's behaviour towards Tajikistan.

The Tajik government tried to improve relations with Uzbekistan after September 2001 but not very successfully. The failure resulted in a Tajik search for ways of circumventing the need for transit across Uzbek territory. In its policy towards Uzbekistan, Tajikistan kept a low profile, although taking initiatives for issue-oriented regional cooperation within the Central Asian Cooperation Organization (as the Central Asian Economic Union was renamed in early 2002) on issues relevant to both countries, among them those of water and the environment. The issue of water distribution was especially important since the large hydro-power complexes would influence the flow of the water of the Pyandzh/Amudarya. For Tajikistan its close relationship with Russia and its membership in the Russian-led Collective Security Treaty Organization continued to be a security guarantee against Uzbekistan. As the USA engaged in Uzbekistan and Tajikistan, indirectly it also became a guarantor of security in the region.

# PART III

# THE DETERMINANTS OF
# TAJIKISTAN'S FOREIGN POLICY

# 6

# EFFORTS TO STRENGTHEN THE REGIME

A major driving force behind the Tajik government's foreign policy after September 2001 was the desire to consolidate the state, strengthen national security, and develop the country economically. President Rakhmonov's 'open door policy' was coined in late 2002, and in early 2003 he used the concept of 'national interests' for the first time. The Tajik government pursued what seemed to be a conscious strategy of extending contacts with new partners in line with the national interests as they now evolved. As Deputy Foreign Minister Abdunabi Sattorzoda said, while the Russian government hesitated over how to act in the immediate aftermath of 11 September 2001, the Tajik government very soon understood that the new international situation would benefit Tajikistan.[1]

Consolidating the country was also, and to a great extent, a matter of consolidating the regime. The government had to extend its control over the territory as by the autumn of 2001 there were still 'white spots' in the sense that rebellious warlords controlled large pockets of Tajik territory. President Rakhmonov's hold on power was still in question. Recognition by the international community of his regime and personal power therefore strengthened his hand. The fact that Tajikistan had never wavered in its resistance to the Taliban throughout their rule in Afghanistan gave Rakhmonov political credibility in the eyes of the USA and its allies undertaking operations in Afghanistan. The issues of anti-terrorism and anti-extremism were already high on the Tajik political agenda, and Tajikistan became a willing partner of the US-led anti-terror coalition. As the salience of the drug trafficking issue increased on the agenda of international cooperation, Rakhmonov declared himself a determined partner in the international efforts to combat it.

Consolidating the regime also meant satisfying the material interests of people in high-ranking posts, and it is here that the problem of corruption comes in: corruption is a deeply rooted illness of Tajik society and it is difficult to find a cure as long as drug trafficking provides opportunities for enrichment.

The optimism that arose among Western observers after September 2001 as Western governments were to engage in the development of Central Asia was soon replaced by disappointment with the meagre results. Martha Brill Olcott wrote in early 2003, 'Years after the beginning of the war on terrorism, many of the hopes for a new beginning in Central Asia appear to remain unfulfilled'.[2] Olcott wrote that there had been hopes of economic reform and take-off, reform of governance and democratization; Western governments and international organizations engaging in projects in and financial support for these countries had tried to encourage economic and political reform, but the result was halting economic reform—almost stagnation—centralization and a strong trend towards authoritarianism. The Central Asian presidents preferred a kind of 'authoritarian modernization' strategy, Olcott wrote, and, like several other foreign observers and domestic Central Asian critics, she feared that plain authoritarianism was on the way. However, at first this did not seem entirely true with regard to Tajikistan. It was different from other Central Asian states because, in contrast to the latter, in Tajikistan there were signs of movement towards democratic reform. Tajikistan had always had a relatively more pluralistic tradition than Uzbekistan. The political compromise that ended the civil war created a political system which allowed an Islamic political party (the Islamic Revival Party, IRP) to exist and guaranteed Tajik society a greater degree of freedom than the rest of Central Asia enjoyed. In 2002–2003 independent news agencies, newspapers, and radio and television stations were set up.

Tajikistan's increased international cooperation after September 2001 resulted in government reforms and introduced a dynamic of change in Tajik society. Requirements for economic and governance reform were embedded in the international development assistance programmes. Numerous non-governmental organizations (NGOs) disseminated knowledge of Tajik laws and citizens' rights, and the values of democracy and human rights. Nonetheless, as the president consolidated his position, authoritarian tendencies were soon apparent in Tajikistan as well. The regime, which on the one hand had an interest in introducing reforms, on the other hand feared the political implications of these dynamics for society and for its own capacity to maintain power. The disturbances in Kyrgyzstan in spring 2002 and the overthrow of President Askar Akaev there in 2005 illustrated the worst fears of the Tajik regime. Akaev had been unable to control both the general domestic discontent, which erupted in demonstrations and public disturbances, and the rivalries between clans and regions. The situation sent shivers down the spines of all the Central Asian presidents.

The years after September 2001 will here be roughly divided into three periods: a first period of 2001–2002, when the regime stabilized, government control over the territory extended, and a cautious policy of reform was introduced; a second period of 2003–2004, up to the parliamentary elections in early 2005, when the regime started to take measures in preparation for those elections; and a third period, from early 2005, when the regime was acting against a background of the popular uprising in Kyrgyzstan and the takeover of power by the opposition there in March 2005.

There is a basic assumption here that a government will form a foreign policy that is in the interests of the regime and will pursue this policy as long as it finds it instrumental for its overall strategic interest of staying at power. A loosening of its control over the domestic scene— for example, in a situation of infighting between factions of the regime, or of a prolonged 'tug-of-war' between the regime and groups of discontented citizens—may undermine the regime's capacity and force it to rethink its foreign policy in order to ensure a continued hold of power. Thus, if the vulnerability of the regime increases, it may be forced to seek international support where otherwise it would have chosen not to do so.

This chapter looks at the efforts of the regime to maintain power. Chapter 7 examines the dynamics of the domestic scene in greater depth, and the concluding chapter discusses the possible implications for foreign policy of developments on the Tajik domestic scene.

## Stabilization and Expectations of Reform: 2001–2002

The Tajik government responded eagerly to the US proposals that it participate in a US-led international anti-terrorist coalition. The fight against international terrorism became the main heading under which international cooperation was to develop. This was an issue which fitted the external security concerns of the Tajik government as well as its domestic security agenda.

The new international attention and assistance to Tajikistan strengthened Rakhmonov and the regime and contributed to confirm the stabilization of society and political life that had followed the 1997 General Peace Agreement. This stabilization was welcome. For the regime it was a serious challenge to break the power of the remaining local warlords who refused to comply with the political compromise and power-sharing arrangement of the General Peace Agreement or to recognize the authority of the government. Success for the regime in this regard was a precondition for any further post-war reconstruction and economic development in the country, and the developments after September 2001 helped to strengthen government control over the country.

Extending the central government's actual control over the country, the president tried to consolidate his own narrow power base—the Kulyab district—and secure the imbalance of power between the regions that was the result. He tried to strengthen an arrangement which would prevent the regions from becoming political actors in confrontation with the central government or with each other. At the same time, consolidating central control was of course a precondition if reforms were to have any effect.

The strengthening of the regime after September 2001 thus, on the one hand, confirmed and further developed the regional imbalance that had been created as a result of the power shift after Rakhmonov came to power in 1992. On the other hand, it also resulted in a further shrinking of the president's own regional base of support as he favoured people who were descended not only from his home district, Kulyab, but even from his birthplace, the small town of Dangara in Kulyab district, when appointing top officials. The power-sharing arrangement of the General Peace Agreement, which prescribed a 30 per cent quota of administrative posts for members of the United Tajik Opposition (UTO), had at first somewhat softened Rakhmonov's narrow, regional recruiting. After the 2000 parliamentary elections, however, many of those who had been appointed from the former opposition were ousted. As a result of the president's appointment policy the Leninabadis withdrew from politics, Pamir fell back into obscurity, the Karategins sidelined, and the Kulyabis became frustrated.

Rakhmonov had carried out an administrative reorganization of the country in 1999, which created five administrative units: (a) the Khatlon region (Kurgan-Tyube and Kulyab were made into one region); (b) the 'districts directly under republican subordination' including districts to the west of Dushanbe (the Hissar district) and former strongholds of the opposition to the east of Dushanbe such as Tavildara, Garm and Karategin; (c) the city of Dushanbe; (d) the Sogd region (former Leninabad region); and finally (e) the Gorno-Badakhshan autonomous region (GBAO). With only limited central budget funds to pay for a proper 'carrot and stick policy', the president's leverage over the regions through the purse remained limited. When Rakhmonov reinforced his power after 2001, it became easier for him to exercise the rights over the regions and districts which the constitution gave him. The 'power vertical' given by the constitution includes his right to appoint the heads of the executive bodies (*hukumat*) at all state administrative levels (national, regional and district).[3] Rakhmonov also took to regularly reshuffling local administrative leaders through his appointments policy in order to prevent them developing strong local identification, bonds or networks.

The clan system in Tajikistan roughly follows the administrative borders in the country, although the 1999 administrative units brought together several clans—the Khujandi (in Sogd region), the Kulyabi and the Kurgan-Tyubi (in Khatlon region), the Hissari and Karategini in the districts under republican subordination, and the Pamiri (or Gorno-Badakhshani). Dushanbe, the capital, was a mix of people but was dominated by the state administration, and therefore the Kulyabi clan. In a system with a fixed clan constellation like Tajikistan's under Rakhmonov, developments with regard to clans and to groupings within clans in the form of loyalties to a smaller territorial unit or to a leader or group of leaders are important for the president to control.

Clans and sub-clans provide a network that is usually invisible to the outside observer, but they play a crucial role in the political and social life of the country. The concept of clan as defined by the American expert Kathleen Collins constitutes 'an informal social institution in which actual or notional kinship based on blood or marriage forms the central bond among members'.[4] In Tajikistan the clan (*avlod*) has been described as being based on unilineal descent (patrilineal or matrilineal) or ideas of territorial exclusiveness, clan solidarity, leadership, and the prestige of a leader or group of leaders.[5] The informal ties and networks of clan life reduce the high transaction costs of making deals in an environment where impersonal institutions are weak or absent and stable expectations are difficult to form. Clan adherence implies a social responsibility for poor families and is a kind of informal social welfare institution when official structures do not function. For the regime, however, the clans constitute a potential threat, as they form networks of political loyalties and thus may provide the power base for political opponents or rivals to the president.

Behind the formal political structures there are thus the invisible politics of clans (the 'power horizontal'). By strengthening central government control over the regions (the 'power vertical'), Rakhmonov tried to control the balance between clans. The Tajik scholar Saodat Olimova writes that the central government tries to control the situation by blocking any independence of administrative–territorial units and to prevent the clans from strengthening their positions in the districts.[6] It can be assumed that, as society stabilizes and political structures at the local level strengthen and become more important as arenas for political bargaining, they also become important targets for the clans to penetrate.

Rakhmonov is both an arbitrator between the clans and at the top of a clan pyramid.[7] This strong position has become intolerable to the people around him who once helped him to power. The concentration of power in the president's hands and the fact that he decides the allocation of all administrative resources have led people in his entourage as well as the leaders of other regional elites to try repeatedly to take power. Those who have sufficient financial resources, political support and enough loyal men under arms have tried to challenge the power of the president.

The constitution of 1994 and the 1999 amendments give great power to the presidency. International organizations engaging in Tajikistan repeatedly point to the need to carry through the separation between the three branches of state power—the executive, the legislature and the judiciary—which is embodied in the constitution but is constantly violated, in order to create a system of checks and balances. The constitution makes the president the head of state, head of government, guarantor of the constitution, supreme commander, and head of the Security Council. He also controls the judiciary by virtue of his right to propose the judges of the Constitutional Court, the Supreme Economic Court and the Supreme Court, the procurator-general and the military procurator.[8] Given the weakness of the political structures, the president controls all branches of the state.

Developments after 2001 helped Tajikistan to undertake economic reforms. The privatization of small and medium-sized business intensified. Reforms of governance were discussed with assistance from international organizations and experts, although there was a reluctance to take on structural reform. Independent media developed after 2001 as independent news agencies, radio and television stations, and new newspapers and journals were started. The public debate became more outspoken, although most participants were careful not to overstep the line of what could be expected to be permitted, or to create a confrontational situation. Memories of the civil war were still vivid.

In this sense, some positive developments took place up to mid-2003. Meanwhile, it was obvious that the president was doing his best to marginalize his political opponents of the former UTO, and in particular its Islamic flank—the IRP.

When the anti-terrorist campaign started in autumn 2001, the IRP feared that Rakhmonov would exploit the anti-terrorist agenda for domestic purposes and use it as a pretext to clamp down on the party, accuse it of indirectly supporting terrorism, and ban it. During the spring of 2002 Rakhmonov called for mobilization against the threats of terrorism and extremism.[9] In a speech in September 2002 on the 11th anniversary of Tajikistan's independence, he stated that the 'fight against terrorism and religious extremism' was 'one of the top priorities for Tajikistan'.[10] In spring 2002 rumours began to circulate in Dushanbe that mosques were to be closed down in an intensified campaign to register all mosques and increase state control over them. In summer 2002 the president initiated a campaign against radical Islam which resulted in the dismissal of several imams but also targeted the IRP.

The worst fears of the IRP—that the authorities would ban the party—did not materialize, but the IRP became a target when the government tried to increase its control over political and religious life in the republic. The campaign took off in summer 2002. It started in the Isfara district in the Sogd region, close to the border with Kyrgyzstan.

The Isfara district had long been a religious stronghold, and the IRP had strong support there. In the 2000 parliamentary elections in the small town of Chorku the IRP received as much as 93 per cent of the vote. Chorku, however, was not only a stronghold of the IRP; it had also developed into a bastion of radical Islamism. A town of 25,000 inhabitants with a high rate of unemployment and great social discontent and frustration, it became a radical stronghold. Many young men returning from studies at madrasas abroad who had no opportunity to find work after their return contributed to uphold strong religious and social control in the town, and demanded that all women in town wear the hijab, that girls and boys be separated in school, that no civil weddings should take place, and that no alcohol should be available.[11]

In summer 2002 the Isfara district attracted particular attention from the government. In early July 2002 the Tajik Security Council held a special meeting in the town of Isfara behind closed doors. It was attended by the president, the secretary of the Security Council, the ministers of all the security departments and the chairman of the Sogd region.[12] A few days later, on 10 July, President Rakhmonov, in Isfara, urged the citizens there not to give in to calls by extremist religious figures.[13] He said that he had chosen Isfara specially as the venue for meeting the public because two residents of the Isfara district were detained at the US military base in Guantanamo, Cuba. He complained that there were more mosques than schools in the district. There were, he said, only 82 schools for 200,000 people but 192 mosques, although the law stipulated one mosque per 15,000 people. He called this an 'alarm signal'.[14] He also brought up the issue of the return soon of more than 1,500 young Tajik citizens, children of former refugees from the Tajik civil war, including 60 from the Isfara district, who were studying at foreign religious educational establishments, particularly in Saudi Arabia, Iran and Pakistan, where they 'learned Wahhabism', adding that 'if every graduate of these educational establishments propagates Wahhabism, then this will lead to religious dissent and discord, which may cause the destabilization of the situation in the country'.[15]

While Rakhmonov was without doubt pointing to a serious problem—how to socialize these young radical Islamists into society and help them find a place in life—he linked this issue to the IRP. In July 2002 he accused some IRP members of 'indoctrinating people in the spirit of extremism, which may lead to a split of society'. He specifically cited the activities of IRP members in Isfara district,[16] and claimed that eight clerics in the mosques were IRP members, which was, he said, a 'flagrant violation of the law'.[17] He accused the IRP of engaging in activities similar to those of Hizb-ut-Tahrir[18] and the Islamic Movement of Uzbekistan (IMU), and implied that the Tajik nationals at Guantanamo Bay had ties to the IRP. His comments were the harshest criticism he had so far levelled at the IRP since the 1997 peace agreement.

The IRP leader, Said Abdullo Nuri, rejected all accusations against the party on 1 August 2002. 'We [the IRP] have always acted and will always act only within the framework of laws of the country.' He dismissed any suggestion that the IRP had connections to the Tajik detainees at Guantanamo, and stated that opinions expressed by IRP-affiliated imams in Isfara did not represent the official position of the party. It would be wrong to accuse the party when 'it is the fault of its individual members' and to blow those people's presence in the party out of all proportion for political ends.[19]

As a result of the campaign, the Isfara town prosecutor reported in November 2002, 63 imams were investigated and charged, and four criminal cases were opened against 14 people on suspicion of involvement in Hizb-ut-Tahrir. Ten grand mosques and 144 ordinary mosques were refused legal authorization to continue their activities.[20]

These incidents illustrated how complex the domestic situation in Tajikistan was after 11 September 2001. The general security situation had improved, and the political situation had stabilized. Nevertheless, the political attack on the IRP illustrated the risk of the regime trying to exploit the post-September 2001 international situation by using the 'anti-terrorist' label to legitimize action to weaken and remove its opponents.

### Tightening the Rope: 2003–2005

In 2003 the president began to take measures to secure the extension of his rule after the parliamentary and presidential elections which were to follow in early 2005 and late 2006. President Islam Karimov in Uzbekistan had set a precedent when, in a referendum of January 2002, he extended his term of office to seven years. The term of office of the Tajik president had already been extended to seven years in the 1999 amendment to the constitution, but was limited to one term in office. In 1999, Rakhmonov had been heavily criticized by the UTO for extending the term that the parties had agreed on in 1997. Now he proposed the introduction of a second term of office.

In the spring of 2002 the Tajik media published reflections on how the rule of Rakhmonov could be extended. In May 2002 the weekly

*Ozodi va inkishof* flew a 'kite' with an article entitled 'Shah or president?' written by a close associate of Rakhmonov. The author suggested the introduction of a constitutional monarchy and the election of Rakhmonov to this post, referring to the tradition of a shah during and after the reign of the Samanids in the 9th and 10th centuries.[21] When the 1994 constitution was adopted, he said, it had not been possible to raise the issue of introducing a shah, since the government and the parliament were dominated by former Communist Party bureaucrats, but now, after more than ten years with Rakhmonov, it was time to hold a referendum to decide on the post of a shah as the head of state, and to have Rakhmonov elected shah simultaneously with the referendum.[22]

A referendum on constitutional amendments was held on 22 June 2003. The package of questions put to the voters included the right of the president to stand for two seven-year terms (which could take President Rakhmonov up to 2020). The initial draft of the amendments had also included a proposal to change the text in the constitution on political parties: it suggested deleting the clause which explicitly allowed religious parties to exist. This the critics, naturally, interpreted as an assault on the General Peace Agreement, and above all on the IRP. After heavy criticism the president agreed not to try to change this paragraph. If the amendment had been adopted, the status of the IRP would have been gravely undermined. This episode seemed to further indicate that the regime had plans to wipe out the IRP.

The opposition parties were loud in their criticism of the amendments. Shortly before the referendum the Democratic Party (DP) boycotted the vote, claiming that it would be rigged. Its chairman, Makhmadruzi Iskandarov, accused Rakhmonov of violating the 1997 General Peace Agreement by extending the presidency with a second term in office. After the referendum he criticized the outcome and claimed that it was invalid since according to his party's estimates voter turnout was only 20 per cent.[23]

Under political pressure from the regime, the IRP backed down from confronting the government on the issue of the referendum. When Iskandarov announced on 16 June 2003, just a week before the referendum, that his party was calling on its members to boycott the referendum, and refused to send observers to the polling stations, IRP chairman Nuri had already backed down. On 9 June he announced that the IRP did not intend to support any statement that was hostile to the referendum since opposition to the referendum could lead to confrontation and instability. '[I]ll-considered actions could lead to a new confrontation.' At the same time he stressed that this did not mean that the IRP was in favour of the referendum.[24] Observers interpreted the IRP's backing down as a consequence of the authorities' increased pressure on it and the arrest of one of its deputy chairmen, the regional head of the IRP in Sogd, Shamsiddin Shamsiddinov. Nuri, under pressure, wanted to soften the position of the party. Shamsiddinov was accused of organizing an armed criminal group during the Tajik civil war, illegally crossing the border, possession of illegal weapons, polygamy and murder, and was sentenced half a year later to 16 years in prison. A second senior IRP member, Qosim Rahimov, was arrested in July 2003 and later sentenced for rape of minors.[25] The IRP viewed the arrests and sentences as the regime's efforts to discredit the IRP politically in the eyes of the voters for the forthcoming elections.

The accusations against Shamsiddinov were related to the burning issue of amnesty for former fighters. Although a law of 1998 gives amnesty to former fighters for acts during the civil war (except those who committed seriously violent crimes), according to the opposition the authorities were now persecuting and harassing these people, accusing them of illegal possession of arms or other illegal activities, and individual officials were trying to frighten and blackmail them.

The amnesty law was part of the political compromise behind the General Peace Agreement. The UTO at the time submitted a list of 5,377 former combatants who were to be pardoned as part of their integration into the state and military structures.[26] Shamsiddinov, a former commander of the opposition and a former director of the Tajik Anti-Drug Agency (under the terms of the 30 per cent quota after the peace agreement), was accused of crimes committed during the civil war. As IRP chairman Nuri said, many contemporary politicians had been leaders of armed groups at the time of the peace agreement, and thus would all be under the threat of such accusations. Among the possible targets for such accusations Nuri mentioned Rakhmonov himself and Makhmadsaid Ubaidulloyev, the mayor of Dushanbe, from the government side, as well as Hodji Akhbar Turajonzoda (the first deputy prime minister and a former leader of the Islamic flank of the UTO).[27]

Although the IRP considered that the way the authorities were implementing the amnesty law was a clear violation of the peace agreement, it chose to keep a low profile. In November 2003 as many as 35 members of the UTO were imprisoned, accused of murdering civilians and Tajik and Russian soldiers during the civil war. The amnesty law had become an inflammatory political issue and the regime used it to intimidate members of the former opposition.

By the end of 2003 Rakhmonov faced a frightening scenario. The Georgian 'Rose Revolution' had resulted in the ousting of President Eduard Shevardnadze in November 2003 after thousands of people took to the streets, and two months later, in January 2004, Mikheil Saakhashvili was elected president of Georgia. The Tajik leadership followed events in Georgia carefully. In contrast to Kyrgyzstan's President Akaev, who commented loudly on the events in Georgia,

Rakhmonov only stated that this was an internal affair of Georgia. Presidential adviser Sukhrob Sharipov, on the other hand, blamed Russia for what had happened in Georgia and accused President Putin of *gruboe vmeshatel'stvo* (gross interference) in its internal affairs. According to Sharipov, Moscow never forgave Shevardnadze for turning away from Russia when Russia did not deliver assistance as promised.[28]

The Georgian scenario was especially frightening for the Tajik leadership, which had entered a pre-election period. The deputy chairman of the IRP, Hikmatullo Saifullozoda, warned that 'Currently, the hard life in Tajikistan, the concentration of power especially during the last years, and people who wish to change the situation … all these factors can pave the way for confrontation in the next Tajik elections'.[29] In late November 2003 an anonymous leaflet was circulated in Dushanbe, entitled 'How to carry out a velvet revolution in Tajikistan?', which drew up a scenario under which Rakhmonov could be removed from power.[30] Amid a wave of rumours of the kind that accompanies any such unexpected events, rumours spread in Dushanbe that the mayor, Ubaidulloyev, was behind the document.[31] Ubaidulloyev was known to be a long-term rival of Rakhmonov for power. He was hardly a liberal and was not to be expected to support the ideas of a Georgian scenario, but the rumours hinted that there were individuals at the top who in a struggle for power had an interest in meddling in muddy waters.

Rakhmonov now went into action to silence his most outspoken opponents. Among them, Iskandarov, the chairman of the Democratic Party, was a central figure. On 28 November 2003 he was dismissed as head of Tajikgaz, a post he had been assigned in 2001 under the General Peace Agreement's 30 per cent quota for distributing top posts. A former UTO commander, Iskandarov had first served briefly (as part of the 30 per cent quota) as chairman of the State Committee on Emergency Situations and became chairman of the DP in 1999. His close friend Salamsho Muhabbatov, another former commander of the UTO and former head of Tajikneft, was also dismissed.[32]

Iskandarov was accused of shortcomings in the company's performance and an investigation started immediately into his role and responsibility. The reasons for his dismissal were unclear, but the fact that he had been detained twice by the police at the beginning of the year, when two of his bodyguards were arrested, proved that something had been in the making for a long time.

The political reasons for getting him off the scene were obvious, and financial misconduct could not be excluded. Another reason could be Rakhmonov's plans to privatize large companies, including the large monopolies of the energy sector, and his desire therefore to have his own people in charge of the energy companies. In December 2003

Rakhmonov signed a strategic plan on the restructuring of monopolies and major enterprises in 2003–2007, and ordered the de-monopolization, restructuring and denationalization of the whole of Tajikistan's energy sector. Several reasons seemed plausible, but the most probable seemed to be Rakhmonov's wish to remove Iskandarov from the political scene.

Waiting for the results of the investigation, in early December 2003 Iskandarov went back to his home district, Tajikabad in Rasht, together with his comrade-in-arms from the civil war, Muhabbatov. Their four-month stay in the mountains raised concerns in Dushanbe that an armed uprising was in preparation. As part of the political game, Iskandarov was obviously using the uncertainty of the situation as a bargaining chip. As a former commander of the opposition and born in Tajikabad, he remained a leader of influence in the Rasht Valley. The very fact that he had a regional basis of support, and that it was believed that people were not only loyal to him but prepared to take up arms for him, made him a crucial political actor. Moreover, he was economically independent as a businessman with his business mainly in Russia. Thus, Iskandarov was a person the president could not ignore.

In the early spring of 2004, in a remarkable move, Rakhmonov also tried to get rid of his long-term comrade-in-arms, Gaffor Mirzoev, the head of the Presidential Guard, by dismissing him from his post on 26 January 2004, replacing him with Colonel Rajab Rakhmonaliev, a native of Dangara. Mirzoev (or *Sedoi*, 'the grey-haired', as he was called) and Rakhmonov had kept step with each other during their careers, which started in Kulyab. In 1991 Mirzoev became deputy commander of the special brigade of the Ministry of Interior Affairs, and thereafter took an active part in the civil war as a commander of the People's Front. After Rakhmonov came to power the special brigade was transformed into the Presidential Guard and as such prevented revolts and coup attempts against Rakhmonov. As head of the Guard, Mirzoev had 3,000 men under his command. In the post-war period he had also engaged in business and de facto controlled the only casino in Dushanbe, the meat combine in the city, a tourist company and the national asset, the aluminium factory in Turzunzade.[33] It had been expected for some time that Rakhmonov would take measures against Mirzoev sooner or later. He was in too strong a position not to be a danger to the president, and in 2003 the authorities had closed the casino he controlled and handed over companies under his control to foreign investors. (For the time being, Rakhmonov only managed to transfer him to another top state position.)

For Mirzoev the dismissal was unexpected, and he did not accept it. He declared that if he left he would do so together with 200 of his most loyal men and all the weapons he had bought for the Presidential Guard, which he considered his personal property,[34] but denied that he would take to arms. Alarmed by this strong reaction, Rakhmonov retreated, and on 30 January offered Mirzoev the post of head of the Tajik Anti-Drug Agency. The agency is important not only because its task is to fight the most lucrative business in Tajikistan—the drug trade. It is also a prestigious body since it cooperates with the United Nations and the UN funding for joint projects on fighting drug trafficking.

Rakhmonov feared Iskandarov and Mirzoev forming an alliance against him. Repeatedly during spring 2004 he tried to call Iskandarov back to Dushanbe. Iskandarov returned in April 2004, and had what he himself described as a frank seven-hour conversation face to face with the president. Iskandarov raised his criticism and demands, and was given the impression that the president was to take measures in line with Iskandarov's requests.

One important issue Iskandarov brought up with Rakhmonov during their talk was the 1998 law on amnesty for fighters from the civil war. Iskandarov demanded that the law be properly implemented.[35] This was a burning issue since a majority of those of the opposition who fell under the terms of the amnesty were still in prison or under investigation.[36]

Another burning issue he discussed with Rakhmonov was the draft election law. In general, not only the election law but the construction and composition of the parliament were in need of reform if Tajikistan was to live up to democratic standards. The weak legislature was no counterweight to the strong presidency. The writing of the Tajik constitution was inspired by the Russian constitution of 1993, and thus prescribed a similar relationship between the president and the legislature. However, while the Russian 1993 constitution streamlined a parliament which had disobeyed the president, in Tajikistan the parliament (the Majlisi Oli) and its two chambers (the upper chamber or Senate, the Majlisi Milli, and the lower chamber, the Majlisi Namoyandagon) were fully subordinated to the president from the very beginning. Their servility was helped by the fact that, of the 33 senators, the president appointed eight directly, and indirectly he appointed many of the remaining 25, who were often heads of local administrations and thus already appointed by the president.[37] Of the 63 deputies in the lower chamber, 22 are elected according to a party-list proportional system, with a 5 per cent threshold to avoid the proliferation of small parties (to gain a seat, a party must receive a minimum of 5 per cent of the total vote), and 41 are elected according to majority vote in single-mandate constituencies. The Tajik parliament thus retained many of the characteristics of a Soviet parliament, and presented to the public a façade of unity. The media seldom reported any disagreements or disputes in the parliamentary debates, although clashes of interests sometimes did take place in the chambers. Its weakness undermined the parliament's legitimacy and authority.

The government focused on reform of the election law, and in spring 2002 it started work on preparing a revision of the law. The political parties, together with the Organization for Security and Co-operation in Europe (OSCE), pursued a dialogue on how the law could be amended. All opposition parties were looking forward to a revision in the hope that it would give a better chance for free and transparent elections. The by-elections to the national parliament that had taken place after the 2000 parliamentary election and local elections illustrated that there were some opportunities for the parties to stand for election. Candidates from non-ruling political parties participated in many constituencies. With the support of the OSCE and other international organizations and NGOs, the opposition claimed their right to register candidates. At the same time these elections also clearly demonstrated the weakness in the existing laws and regulations, the lack of knowledge of these laws and regulations among state representatives and party activists, and last but not least an entrenched suspicion on the part of the authorities, in particular the local authorities, of all non-government-supported candidates.[38]

During seven months of discussions in 2003 more than 80 amendments were discussed in a working group consisting of representatives from the parliament and the political parties. After that the draft lay idle for over five months, and was not introduced to the parliament in session. A crucial point of the government draft of the election law was the introduction of a registration fee. For political parties this fee amounted to 33,000 times the minimum wage, and for candidates standing in the single-mandate constituencies it was 3,500 US dollars (USD)—equivalent to 1,500 times the minimum wage.[39] These registration fees were incredibly high and clearly meant to prevent the non-ruling political parties, whose finances were weak, from registering.

An alternative proposal was written by a group of parliamentarians from the Communist Party and the Islamic Revival Party, and included conditions for guaranteeing free and independent elections, for ensuring that the election commissions' documentation was correct, and for preventing the authorities intervening in the election process. The most important demands were that the political parties be represented on the election committees, that the parties provide the observers with a copy of the protocols, and that the practice of filling in the protocols in pencil instead of ink be ended. The communists also suggested that 50 per cent of all seats be elected from party lists, instead of one-third as at present.

In spite of fierce criticism from the opposition in summer 2004, the parliament adopted the government draft on 16 June. The opposition parties hoped that the president would refrain at the last minute from signing the law and send it back to the chambers instead. Rakhmonov's declaration in May to the OSCE Chairman-in-Office for Central Asia that all amendments to the election law approved by the UN and the OSCE would be taken into consideration when the new law was adopted was used by the opposition as an argument for calling on the president to refuse to sign the bill and return it to parliament.[40] Five opposition parties published a statement in the Tajik newspaper *Ruzi-i Nav* on 1 July appealing to the president to veto the bill and incorporate the proposals put forward by the opposition.[41] Nevertheless, the president signed the new election law in the form in which it had passed the two chambers and without considering any of the changes proposed by the opposition.[42] Only the deposit for the registration of candidates to the national parliament was reduced, but it still remained extremely high for Tajik conditions.[43] The introduction of a registration fee hundreds of times larger than the official minimum wage reduced the number of candidates wishing to stand for election.

In the discussions of the draft electoral law, Iskandarov was one of its most outspoken critics. He had waited several months for the president to fulfil the promises he claimed Rakhmonov had made him during their conversation back in April. Waiting for the investigation into his case to be concluded, he was in a kind of limbo,[44] but this did not prevent him from participating in all political events in Dushanbe, where he was met with respect by both friends and enemies, and doing his best to influence the outcome of the bill. Iskandarov was still a person to be reckoned with, even if the president obviously did not intend to fulfil any of his promises. The investigation of his case so far had not come up with any evidence against him.

In early August 2004 the rope seemed to tighten around him. Iskandarov was called to the prosecutor's office and left for Russia. The day after he left, on 27 August, an armed attack took place against the militia station and the prosecutor's office in Tajikabad. The Tajik authorities arrested two people for the attack, both of them close to Iskandarov—a relative and adviser, the former UTO commander, Erbek Ibragimov (nicknamed 'Sheikh'), and a bodyguard and driver of Iskandarov—and found a large cache of weapons. Similar attacks on militia personnel were reported in Raushan and Draband. A former commander of the UTO, Akhmadbek Safarov, in an interview in the Democratic Party journal *Adolat*, explained the Tajikabad attack as revenge against the police from the side of the former UTO fighters who had been released under the amnesty but were still, together with their families, under investigation by the authorities.[45]

Earlier the same month, on 6 August 2004, Mirzoev was arrested.[46] He was now accused of a murder back in 1998 in a case which had previously been considered as suicide, of illegal possession of a huge depot of weapons, and of unlawful business activities. Two days after his arrest the prosecutor-general announced that the authorities had enough evidence against him to be able to detain him. On 9 August he lost his position as director of the Anti-Drug Agency. Arrests of his closest subordinates at the agency followed. The authorities feared that Mirzoev's arrest could result in a violent reaction and took preventive measures. Government security forces were put on high alert on 6 August and all vehicular traffic into and out of Dushanbe was closely monitored.[47]

Different theories appeared to explain why Rakhmonov had turned against Mirzoev. There were various possible reasons for his removal. He had long been suspected of being involved in the drug trafficking to Russia.[48] In Dushanbe he was considered by many to be making a profit out of both drugs and business. Another theory was that Rakhmonov wanted to get rid of former civil war commanders in a demonstration of strength and resolution before the international community.[49] A third major factor seemed to be a struggle for control of the economic assets of the country. Mirzoev controlled the aluminium factory, which came under Rakhmonov's plan for the privatization of large companies.

At about the time Mirzoev was dismissed from the Presidential Guard, in January 2004, in an interview with Russian journalist Arkadii Dubnov, Iskandarov had said that he and Mirzoev had 'close contacts'.[50] Iskandarov was sceptical about the accusations that Mirzoev was keeping illegal weapons, and said that the existence of these weapons had long been well known since they had once been meant for Afghanistan. Iskandarov later demanded that Mirzoev get an open trial.[51] What Iskandarov and Mirzoev seemed to have in common was a growing frustration with Rakhmonov's rule.

By December 2004 Rakhmonov had added to the list of accusations against Mirzoev. He was accused of 'preparing an armed coup and the seizure of power', of responsibility for a series of explosions in Dushanbe in 2003 (eight explosions, some of which were close to the Interior Ministry, the Security Ministry and the Prosecutor-General's Office), and of circulating anti-government leaflets in 2003.[52]

In early October 2004 the prosecutor general started legal proceedings against Iskandarov. On 9 December he was arrested in Moscow following a request by the Tajik authorities. According to the Russian Interior Ministry, the Tajik Prosecutor-General's Office put Iskandarov on the international wanted list on suspicion of committing serious crimes, including terrorist acts and setting up an illegal armed formation. On 11 December the Tajik prosecutor-general detailed the charges against him. They now included terrorism, the illegal storage of weapons, attempted murder, large-scale embezzlement of state funds, and abuse of office. He was held responsible for the attack in Tajikabad, although by then he had left the country.[53] He was accused of ordering his driver, before setting off for Moscow, to 'start the war' and to head an armed band hiding in the mountains.[54] The arrest of Iskandarov made it impossible for him to stand in the parliamentary elections. In January 2005 the procurator-general announced that Iskandarov was barred from standing.[55]

The authorities had managed to get rid of a fierce opposition leader and well-known public figure.

During the following months the legal cases against Mirzoev and Iskandarov developed further. On 3 April 2005 Iskandarov was suddenly freed from prison in Moscow by the Russian prosecutor-general, who stated that he had no legal ground to detain him, especially after Iskandarov had pleaded for political asylum in Russia. However, after he was freed, Iskandarov was kidnapped by the Tajik security service, and after ten days the Tajik prosecutor-general announced that he was in an isolation detention camp in Dushanbe.

Rakhmonov was thus taking action against some of the most important contenders for power in time for the upcoming elections. He had turned against his allies in 2003–2004, when several cases were reactivated and the Tajik authorities succeeded in having these people extradited from Russia, where they had been arrested. Among them was Jakub Salimov, who was appointed minister of interior affairs in 1992, then became head of the Customs Committee, and was ambassador to Turkey until 1997 when he fled the country after being accused of preparing a military coup together with the rebel commander Makhmud Khudoberdiev. In 2003 he was arrested in Moscow at the request of the Tajik authorities.[56] Salimov, who was known to be thoroughly corrupt and deeply involved in the drug trade, was born in Kulyab and grew up with Gaffor Mirzoev.[57] He had supporters in Tajikistan, and as soon as he was transferred to Dushanbe speculation started as to whether or not he would be freed as part of a bargain between different power groups. In April 2004 a letter in support, signed by more than 1,600 people, was sent to Rakhmonov, calling all allegations against Salimov for involvement in a coup 'baseless'. In November 2004 Salimov's trial started behind closed doors.

Parallel to these events, the previous media freedoms which Tajikistan had developed during 2002 and 2003 were eroded. Not much remained by the time the parliamentary elections took place on 27 February 2005. In late January the country's only remaining independent newspaper, *Neru-i Sukhan*, was closed down.

By early 2005 President Rakhmonov thus seemed to be safe in the saddle. He had removed the major contenders for power and was keeping up regular reshuffles of people in the top positions at ministry level and in the regions, moving them from one post to another.

Sometimes a minister was removed from the political scene in Dushanbe or in the country by being appointed ambassador to Turkmenistan or some other politically distant place. Rakhmonov had by then already introduced a yearly rotation of ministers and regional leaders after his annual speech in January. He replaced his appointees in what seemed to be an effort to prevent political alliances being established, whether on a regional or on a national scale.[58]

As Tajik commentators said, when a minister is appointed ambassador to a foreign country, in the Tajik context this is most often interpreted as a sign that the president wants the person out of sight and influence.[59] Deputy Prime Minister Kozidavlat Koimdodov, who had helped Rakhmonov to power in 1992, was appointed ambassador to Turkmenistan in January 2005.[60] His was not the only case. In mid-December 2003 Rakhmonov in a sudden move dismissed the head of the presidential administration, Shukhrat Sultanov, who was sent to Turkey as ambassador.[61] Tajik commentators concluded that the dismissals and appointments since early 2004 demonstrated that Rakhmonov intended to cleanse the state apparatus and the power ministries of former commanders of the People's Front, who had helped him to power and had been his allies since his very first years in power.[62] The way the Taraqqiyot Party was denied registration and was harassed before the 2005 parliamentary elections is another example of how Rakhmonov prevented former allies acting against him politically.[63]

The political struggle at the top thus intensified during 2004. The looming elections explain why the president took different kinds of measure to secure his hold on power, but there are two other possible explanations which help us to understand what actually took place as the president turned against his former allies.

The first is the increasing frustration with Rakhmonov's appointment policy, which was increasingly resulting in appointments of people whose origins were in Dangara. There was an especially strong reaction among the Kulyabis, who had helped Rakhmonov to power and now could no longer tolerate his extending and increasing his personal power. Salimov, Mirzoev, Koimdodov and Sulton Kuvvatov (leader of the Taraqqiyot Party) are all from Kulyab. None of them has entirely clean hands, and this was used against them after they started to challenge the president politically. Kuvvatov was well respected among the population in the south of the country, and therefore his party had to be discredited.

Second, the increased political struggle was related to the forthcoming privatization of large and medium-sized state companies. Tajik observers pointed to the role the forthcoming privatization of large companies played in the arrests of Rakhmonov's old guard. The president wanted a new administration that would be better suited to the task of privatization of large state companies like the aluminium factory

(TadAZ), the Nurek and Sangtuda hydro-power stations, the Dushanbe airport and the Sharki Ozod publishing house.[64] In early December 2003 Rakhmonov signed a strategic plan for 2003–2007 on the privatization of medium-sized and large companies and the restructuring of the huge energy monopolies.[65] The first target was the electricity sector, the national Barq-i Tojik ('Tajikistan's Electricity')—the country's main energy monopoly. It was to be restructured into an open joint-stock company and comprise all the country's functioning hydroelectric power plants, including the biggest heating and power stations in Dushanbe and the southern town of Yovon.[66] Other companies were to follow.

The jewel in the crown was the huge aluminium factory. Intense struggles for control of it had taken place in the 1990s, even involving the use of armed force by Khudoberdiev. In 2004, when Mirzoev had been in control for several years, the struggle around the aluminium factory again flared up. Not only was the factory waiting to be privatized. Its privatization was planned for 2005–2006, and the Russian companies RusAl and SUAL declared their interests in it.[67] The aluminium factory is the third-largest company of its kind in the whole of the Commonwealth of Independent States (CIS), with a production capacity of 600,000 tonnes of aluminium a year. And with this the intrigues within Rakhmonov's court intensified.

Mirzoev, who had actual control of the aluminium factory until he was arrested, had close links with the mayor of Dushanbe and speaker of the upper chamber of the parliament, Makhmadsaid Ubaidulloyev.[68] Ubaidulloyev in turn had close contacts with the mayor of Moscow, Yurii Luzhkov, and was reported to be a middleman in contacts with the Russian aluminium oligarch Oleg Deripaska. When Deripaska's plans for investing in Tajikistan started to take form, his contacts with Mirzoev contributed to Rakhmonov taking control of the situation by removing Mirzoev and making an agreement with Deripaska himself concerning investment in the aluminium sector. All events concerning the factory, as well as the Tajik company Anzol, which was the middleman in Tajik aluminium exports abroad (to the Netherlands), reflected the power struggle at the top during 2004–2005.[69] Rakhmonov feared Mirzoev's association with Ubaidulloyev as well as with Deripaska because it would strengthen Mirzoev.

Rakhmonov had thus removed the major competitors for power from among his own ranks and from the opposition, and had done all he could to disarm the opposition parties in time before the parliamentary elections. Taken together, these events formed the pattern of a regime acting out of fear that discontent and frustration among the population and within the establishment would create alliances that would threaten a continuation of Rakhmonov's rule. The regime took all possible measures to prevent this happening.

## 2005: Into the Shadow of the Kyrgyz Revolution

In preparing for the parliamentary elections, the regime took measures not only against the IRP and the Democratic Party but also against other political parties. The tiny Socialist Party was split and the authorities refused the critical flank under Mirhusein Narziev, who cooperated with the opposition parties, official registration, and thus denied Narziev the right to stand for election in early 2005. The Social Democratic Party (SDP) was left in peace, although its leader, Rahmatullo Zoirov, was an articulate critic of Rakhmonov's policy. Still, the Social Democrats were newcomers and so far without popular support.

Elections to the lower house of the national parliament and to the local parliaments took place on 27 February 2005, and elections to the upper house on 24 March 2005. In all the elected assemblies the president secured dominance for his party, the People's Democratic Party (PDP). Although Tajikistan had not banned any foreign-financed NGOs, election officials warned on 14 January that any candidate found to be receiving financial support from foreign organizations or individuals would be barred from taking part in the elections.

The outcome of the February 2005 parliamentary elections gave the PDP 74.9 per cent of the votes, the Communist Party (CP) 13.6 per cent, and the IRP 8.9 per cent. Other parties received less than 3 per cent. After the distribution of the mandates from the party-list vote and the single-mandate constituency vote, the PDP received 52 seats (17+32+3 in the second round), the CP four (three + one), the IRP two (both party-list seats), and five independents won seats who in all likelihood would ally themselves with the PDP.[70] The PDP thus took a solid majority of the 63 seats in the lower chamber and the chairs of all the committees. Thus, in the 2005 parliament the president had stronger support than in the previous parliament, elected in 2000.

When the parliamentary elections in Tajikistan were taking place, the revolutionary events in Kyrgyzstan were already under way. In the south of Kyrgyzstan, in Osh and Jalalabad, large demonstrations took to the streets in anger at the falsification of the election results. The unrest spread to Bishkek and resulted in the fall of the Akaev regime. In the comparatively more open Kyrgyz political system, with fairly far-reaching media freedoms and debate, and numerous NGOs, the opposition had long been building up its organization.

Rakhmonov made no official comment on the events in Kyrgyzstan, but he was alarmed, and turned to President Putin to ensure that he had Russian support. On 6 April 2005 Rakhmonov unexpectedly left for Sochi to meet Putin. His meeting was linked to a three-hour conversation on Kyrgyzstan that he had had the day before in Dushanbe with Russian Defence Minister Sergei Ivanov.[71] Although Putin declared his support for Tajikistan, Russia seemed to be moving towards a shift of emphasis in its Central Asia policy, from giving full support to the ruling group to a more sophisticated approach of waiting on the sidelines. This was the bitter lesson learned after the presidential elections in Ukraine in November 2004, when Putin burned his fingers by openly supporting one candidate during the election campaign. In Kyrgyzstan Moscow had learned that it was more in its interest to maintain a low profile during the overturn of a regime in order to have good relations with the new leaders.

On 6 April, the day Rakhmonov met Putin, the Russian prosecutor-general had already freed Iskandarov from arrest in Moscow. Nevertheless, Rakhmonov was guaranteed Moscow's continued support. On 15 April Iskandarov was reported to have disappeared, and on 26 April the Tajik prosecutor-general announced that Iskandarov was in Dushanbe and under arrest. It was obvious that this operation by the Tajik Security Service could not have taken place without the assistance of their colleagues in Moscow and the silent approval of the Kremlin.

On 17 May 2005 events were set in motion in Uzbekistan by a group of armed men breaking into the prison in Andijan and freeing more than 20 prisoners, local businessmen and persons accused by the authorities of being radical Islamists. Thereafter followed a meeting on the central square in Andijan, with slogans against President Karimov and demands for democracy and human rights. The military and interior troops surrounded the city and by dusk had moved into the city to dissolve the demonstration by shooting straight into the crowds.

Most important with regard to the official Tajik reaction to the events in Andijan were the statements made by the first deputy leader of the ruling PDP, Abdumajid Davlatov, and the secretary of the Tajik National Security Council, Amirkul Azimov. Commenting on what had happened in Andijan, Davlatov emphasized that these activities were run by 'extremists' who wanted to destabilize the situation in the whole region by force, and praised the tough measures taken by the Uzbek president to stabilize the situation. Azimov was even more outspoken in support of President Karimov. He said that 'the Uzbek authorities took adequate measures to suppress the riot' and branded these measures 'timely and correct', adding that if the Tajik authorities had 'demonstrated firmness and applied harsh measures to suppress the riot of a mob of extremists' 13 years before, when the huge demonstrations started in Dushanbe, they would have prevented the bloody five-year long civil war which claimed 150,000 lives.[72]

There was therefore no doubt that if a similar event were to take place in Tajikistan at any time in the future, the president would not hesitate to take tough measures to stop it. However, his strategy, as it seemed during the years 2002–2005, was to act early against anyone who could pose a threat to the stability in the country or to his personal power.

## Conclusions

The desire to consolidate the state and the regime was a driving force behind Tajik policy, including its foreign policy, after September 2001. While the international support for the Tajik regime was to contribute to legitimize and consolidate the rule of Rakhmonov, the international economic aid and assistance was to give economic development the chance to take off. For almost two years there were hopes for serious economic and political reforms. As Rakhmonov took measures to get rid of potential rivals at the top in order to secure a continuation of his hold of power, he also increased his control of the political life in the country. From mid-2003 a phase followed which here is called 'tightening the rope'. Rakhmonov had the constitution amended and the new election law made it more difficult for opposition parties to be elected. He had the freedom of the media limited, and the space for free political debate shrank substantially. He took measures to marginalize his opponents in the UTO—first the Islamic Revival Party, and then the Democratic Party. He also began to outmanoeuvre former friends and allies among his closest entourage, accusing them of corruption, of financial misconduct, and of preparing a coup in a campaign that looked like a way of removing potential rivals for power.

By 2005 Rakhmonov seemed invincible as all major contenders for power had been removed and the opposition parties were reduced to insignificance. Nothing like the unrest in Kyrgyzstan and Uzbekistan seemed possible in Tajikistan. Not only was there still war-fatigue and a fear of confrontation and conflict as a result of the civil war; there was also a different political atmosphere. In Dushanbe in 2005 independent-minded people had become much more cautious in their statements (although Tajikistan was still far from any comparison with Uzbekistan). The change in the air was felt when a member of the Tajik National Security Council expressed sympathy for Karimov's tough measures in crushing the revolt in Andijan.

It did not seem likely that the power struggle at the top would trigger any sizeable support among the population. Although codes of loyalty towards former commanders remained, another civil war would not be their choice. The most influential actors from the civil war had been given a slice of the cake in post-Soviet Tajikistan. With large villas and incomes from business in restaurants, construction work and not least drug trafficking, they would defend their personal interests by all means possible; but they would hardly find substantial groups of supporters among the population. Tajik society was tired of war and everyone wanted to live a normal and quite life. The repair and construction work going on in Dushanbe as well as the small businesses along the roads in the country expressed new hope for the future. The president, however, continued to take measures to further secure his hold of power.

In this struggle to consolidate power there were 'windows of opportunity' for external actors to use. The government's desire to attract foreign donors and investors provides such windows. So does Rakhmonov's concern to secure his rule and remove contenders for power. As Rakhmonov feared that former allies were able to strengthen their positions thanks to future Russian investment in the aluminium sector, he immediately acted to remove both Mirzoev and his allies, in order to take control himself over the aluminium factory and be the one to benefit from the deal with the Russians.

In the opinion of many Tajik commentators the president considers Russia to be the guarantor of his regime and the only power to provide military force to support him in case of domestic turmoil in Tajikistan. The question then naturally comes up whether there are dynamics on the domestic scene that may threaten the regime in the future.

To this question we turn in the next chapter.

# THE DYNAMICS ON THE DOMESTIC SCENE

To what extent are there domestic dynamics on the Tajik political scene which may influence foreign policy making, whether directly or indirectly? This chapter discusses the dynamics of protest from within society. In a long-term perspective domestic trends and currents may influence the foreign-policy orientation of the state. In the short- and medium-term perspective it is most often a question of how the government responds to the challenge of domestic protest. Is it able to adapt and take measures, or will a wave of spontaneous or organized domestic unrest force the government to look for external support in order to stay in power?

One major assumption made here is that the ability of the government to respond to challenges and demands from society determines not only the course of events in the country but also the capacity of the state to pursue a foreign policy of its own.

Tajikistan was one of the poorest republics of the Soviet Union and has remained one of the poorest post-Soviet republics. Yet since the civil war its economic development has been positive, and Tajikistan now shows several positive indicators of macroeconomic growth. The annual real growth rate since 2000 has averaged 9.7 per cent, but the economy is still only about 50 per cent of its size in 1989.[1] As a result of this macroeconomic growth and money transfers from Tajik migrant workers in Russia, poverty has been reduced. According to estimates of the International Monetary Fund, the percentage of the population living below the poverty line was as high as 83 per cent in 1999, but was down to 68 per cent in 2003.[2] The poverty line was defined as 2.15 US dollars (USD) a day, allowing for certain regional specifics.

This economic growth is not, however, reflected in improvements of the standard of living of the individual citizen. There are numerous problems in society which affect daily life. Discontent and economic frustration are spreading among the population as people perceive the spread of corruption and the widening gap between rich and poor, as well as between regions. The decisive question is how the population responds to the problems politically. Organized protest can be expected to be difficult to develop for some time to come, not only because democratic rights in the country are very restricted but also because such a large number of men at their most productive age are working in Russia as migrant labour. In a traditional society, women will hardly be the first to take to the streets. Where will popular discontent go? Who can articulate the discontent of the population? Will its expression take the form of spontaneous outbursts or of individual protests?

In this chapter, three possible directions of protest will be dealt with—secular-political, religious-secular, and ethnic-national. To this picture of protest should be added the discontent and frustration at the top of society, among circles around the president. The reasons for their protests, frustration and demands may be related to an ongoing struggle for personal power at the top, but the behaviour of these people and the response by the regime may add to the dynamics of protest in society.

The major challenge for the regime is how to respond to the discontent within the population, whether among the elite or among broader groups. The way it responds will reflect its capacity to change and adapt to new conditions. In the post-September 2001 situation the Tajik leadership declared its intention to develop international cooperation and undertake economic and political reforms. A domestic reform programme was a precondition for attracting donors and investors and receiving international aid, assistance and credits. Tajikistan declared its interest in participating in the US-led anti-terror coalition and in far-reaching reform. Thus, Tajikistan took on international obligations to undertake a democratization of its society and political system.

## Secular–Political Protest

Although the Tajik political parties were still very weak in September 2001, they became stronger as organizations during the following year. They existed under the protection of international organizations, in particular the Organization for Security and Co-operation in Europe (OSCE). They were much better known to the citizens of the capital and other large cities than to the rural population who had neither electricity nor newspapers.

The Tajik constitution prescribes a multiparty system. By the beginning of 2002 there were five political parties registered. Except for the ruling People's Democratic Party (PDP) and the Communist Party (CP), there were the Islamic Revival Party (IRP), the Democratic Party (DP) and the Socialist Party (SP). Three parties were represented in parliament after the 2000 parliamentary elections—the PDP, the CP and the IRP. Neither the DP nor the Socialist Party passed the 5 per cent threshold. In December 2002 a sixth party was allowed to register—the Social Democratic Party (SDP) under Rahmatullo Zoirov, a presidential adviser on legal issues. He had tried three times to register before he finally succeeded. After the June 2003 referendum on amendments to the constitution, of which he was highly critical, he left his post as presidential adviser.

The political parties other than the ruling party were all weak and worked under difficult conditions. Apart from the CP, which had maintained at least the skeleton of its organization from Soviet times, the local organizations of all the parties were generally undeveloped. Personal ties, kinship relations and regional affiliation continued to be more important to people than party affiliation. There also was a general caution about creating tensions in society: the experience of the civil war was still vivid in people's minds, preventing the growth of the political parties. The PDP pursued an active policy of co-opting people from the Communist Party and the former United Tajik Opposition (UTO). Thus, although formally a multiparty system existed, in reality the opposition parties had serious problems in surviving.

The Tajik political parties cannot be classified into the traditional categories of right and left. They have regional bases but no clearly defined social base. They have a general ideological platform but most of them have not developed party programmes or demands corresponding to the economic, social and political requirements of different social groups.

The three parties introduced below constitute the core of the opposition—the DP, the IRP and the latecomer, the SDP. The IRP and the DP were parts of the former UTO of the civil war period.

The *Democratic Party* was created in August 1990 but banned three years later in June 1993, together with the other opposition parties at the time. It was not allowed to operate again until the ban on opposition parties was lifted in August 1999. The party suffered from splits from the very beginning. As the Tajik scholar Saodat Olimova writes,

> From the very beginning, the DPT represented an extreme diversity of interests within the party. It consisted of a few liberal democrats, nationalists, representatives of counter-elite groupings of an ethno-regional character, and representatives of other ethnic groups (mostly ethnic Russians). The only factor, which united its members, was their place among the intelligentsia. The heterogeneity of the DPT had caused a considerable inner-party struggle already in the initial stages of its formation.[3]

As a party of the former UTO, it had its strong regional bases in the eastern and central areas of republican subordination and the city of Dushanbe.[4] In the 2000 parliamentary elections, the DP won 18.5 per cent of the votes in the Garm region.

Makhmadruzi Iskandarov became the Democratic Party chairman in 1999. During the years 1999–2002 the DP kept a low profile. Under the 30 per cent quota of the General Peace Agreement many party members were included in the government and in top administrative posts. Iskandarov himself became the director of the state gas monopoly Tajikgaz. As he became more outspoken in his criticism of the president's policy, in 2003, the public image of the party changed and its support among the population increased, according to independent public opinion surveys.[5] As the Sharq independent research institute has shown, support for both the IRP and the DP doubled between December 2001 and May 2004, although from low levels.[6]

When Iskandarov called for a boycott of the referendum in June 2003 he also strongly criticized the government's policy with regard to its ineffective economic reforms, its weak social policy, and the widespread corruption. One month after the referendum the Democratic Party held its congress and Iskandarov drew up the guidelines for the party during the period up to the parliamentary and presidential elections. It was evident that he and the party intended to take on a high profile as an opposition party. He accused the government of being incapable of handling the situation due to its narrow clan interests and the prevailing corruption. 'As a consequence there are high unemployment, unsolved questions concerning labour migration, a fall in the level of education and health care and lots of other socio-economic problems. If the situation doesn't change in the near future, Tajikistan will face a social and demographic catastrophe.'[7]

The *Social Democratic Party*, which was not registered until December 2002, was created in March 1998 under the name Tajikistan's Party of Justice and Progress. It is led by two lawyers and constitutional experts, Rahmatullo Zoirov and Shokirjon Khakimov. As mentioned above, the party leader, Zoirov, was a presidential adviser on legal issues from 2001 until he left in protest at the referendum in June 2003. Neither Zoirov nor Khakimov has a regional support base of his own but the party receives support especially from the Sogd region and Gorno-Badakhshan, both which are weakly represented in the government decision-making structures.

The *Islamic Revival Party* belongs to the secular–political opposition, although it is an Islamic political party. Its programme and guidelines confirm that the IRP respects the secular Tajik constitution, democratic and human rights, and the separation between government and religious affairs. The IRP is an offspring of the June 1990 Congress of the Soviet

Union Muslims, which took place in Astrakhan, Russia, and in which delegates from Tajikistan participated. The Islamic All-Union Renaissance Party was constituted during the Congress, and in December 1991 the Islamic Revival Party of Tajikistan was registered.

The roots of the IRP go further back, however—to the underground youth organization that was started in 1978 and led by Said Abdullo Nuri. This was mainly a study group of young people engaged in studying and spreading the views of Sheikh Hasan Banno, the brothers Said Kutb and Muhammad Kutb, Said Havvo and Abul'alo Mavdudi. When interviewed in 1991 the then party leaders, Muhammadsharif Himmatzoda and Davlat Usmonov, emphasized that the party's objective was the creation of a constitutional and democratic statehood with a government that would enjoy the trust of the nation. The government would consist of representatives from various political forces based on the multiparty system currently being formed. Thus, the party was striving to participate legally in the political processes of the country as a parliamentary party, and recognized that a long-term educational campaign was needed to revive Islam in Tajikistan.[8]

The party then became radicalized during the early 1990s, and the goal of an Islamic state became more pronounced. Yet the IRP was pragmatic enough to enter a political compromise in the 1997 General Peace Agreement, and thereby declared its respect for the secular constitutional system of Tajikistan and for its president. The ban on the party that had been introduced in 1993 was lifted in 1999.

The outcome of the 2000 parliamentary election was a disappointment and unbelievable for most IRP members. They had expected greater support from voters and were critical of a leadership which they considered was too prepared to give in to the Rakhmonov regime. However, the IRP remained the most important opposition party. As mentioned in the previous chapter, it exists under strong pressure from the authorities, and it feared for its very survival as Rakhmonov intensified an anti-terrorist campaign after September 2001.

The IRP has been facing a dilemma since the 2000 elections, and tensions within the party are increasing. On the one hand the party needs to modernize and become more of a proper political party in order to expand its support among the population. On the other hand many of its grass-roots supporters have a more traditional and conservative view of an Islamic party and believe that if the party members are all true believers this will guarantee them political support. Others want to bring Islamic values into government affairs. Among the IRP's grass roots, there have always been voices that are more in favour of a stronger influence for Islam on state affairs than the party leadership wants.[9] Since the party respects the secular constitution of Tajikistan and its strict separation of religious and government affairs, they know that the party cannot develop too far in such a direction. One minority in the party, led by the first deputy chairman, Muhiddin Kabiri, wants to blend European political ideas of democracy and a market economy with Islamic values, but these modernists are meeting resistance from within the party. The different factions within the IRP have continued to be divided over the issues of the party's objectives and methods.[10] After 2001 tension increased in the party.

Party leader Nuri, himself also a religious leader, understood the important role of Kabiri for the future for the party. Kabiri has a university education, is independent-minded, and adopts the manners and dress of the contemporary world. Nuri acts a broker trying to bridge the factions and keep them together. As the tension between factions in the party increased, in September 2003 at the party congress Nuri even threatened to resign as party chairman, but was persuaded to stay.[11]

Kabiri's intentions are to modernize the party and transform it into a more fully-fledged, modern political party similar to the Christian Democratic Party of Germany, where religious values are the basis of party policy while the party at the same time respects the secular political system prescribed by the constitution. 'Our party is not religious', Kabiri stated in an interview, 'because its activities are based on secular legislation. However, the basis of our ideology is religious values. For this reason there is confusion in interpretation. The task of maintaining religious values does not necessarily conflict with the building up of the secular state'.[12]

The regional basis of support for the IRP was reflected in the results of the 2000 and 2005 parliamentary elections. It had support in the districts to the east and north-east of Dushanbe, in the Faizabad, Kafarnihan and Garm districts where the opposition had been strong since the war; to the south of Dushanbe in Vakhsh and Kabodiyon; and in the Isfara district in the Fergana Valley. Moreover the party managed to establish branches in districts which had previously been closed to it, for example in Kulyab to the south-east of Dushanbe. It successfully established the image of an opposition party in regions such as Sogd and Gorno-Badakhshan which had no voice, or only a minimal voice, in the Tajik policy-making structures.

In 2004–2005 tensions increased within the party over its future direction. When in spring 2004 the independent journalist and former IRP press secretary Sulton Khamadov was appointed editor-in-chief of the IRP newspaper *Nadzhot* (Salvation) this seemed to be a victory for the reformists/modernists. Khamadov had the mixed background of a former Soviet Committee of State Security (KGB) officer who joined the IRP, fled to Afghanistan during the civil war, where he had responsibility for a camp of Tajik refugees, returned to Tajikistan, was press secretary of the party, and then left this position, as well as his membership in the party, but remained close to it. He was a good journalist with ideas for improving the paper. His appointment as editor-in-chief had reflected the IRP leadership's intention to restore the popularity the party's printed organ had had before. Upon being appointed, he stated that 'We will cover the most pressing problems of our society. The main focus will be given to the human rights issues, problems of official corruption, illegal actions by authorities, etc.'.[13] During his time as editor-in-chief the paper became more interesting, and its circulation increased.

Khamadov's editorial policy included publishing articles on politically sensitive topics, among them the role of women in society, and showing pictures of active modern women dancing or with their heads uncovered, which gave rise to great controversy. As Khamadov came up against resistance among the party conservatives, they soon found the opportunity to strike against him. In one issue of *Nadzhot* Khamadov wrote of Kabiri as the IRP chairman while the latter was only acting chairman as Nuri was on holiday. In July 2004 the conservatives demanded his dismissal, and for the sake of peace between the factions Nuri accepted this. Khamadov immediately withdrew in order not to provoke the conservatives to turn against the modernizers in the party leadership.

The treatment of Khamadov illustrated the dilemma of the party. If the IRP wants to broaden its support it has to change. Yet change exactly is what the conservatives fear. Nuri, who bases his leadership on compromise and coalition-building, avoids taking measures against the conservatives.

### Emerging Cooperation between the Opposition Parties?

In April 2004 the IRP together with the SDP and the Socialist Party created a pre-election coalition called For Fair and Transparent Elections. Kabiri became its chairman. Although the coalition was not able to influence the government, the work and the experience of cooperation provided a basis for future cooperation among the opposition parties and in future election contests.

Although the opposition parties became more outspoken in their criticism of the president's and the government's policy towards mid-2003, they had difficulty joining forces even for tactical purposes. They were not able to do so in time for the June referendum. Instead each party was manoeuvring, trying to defend its interests.

The pressure on the opposition parties from the side of the authorities was heavy before the June 2003 referendum on amendments to the constitution. At a press conference of four political parties on 16 June 2003, a week before the referendum, when the Democratic Party chairman, Iskandarov, made his call for a boycott of the referendum and declared that he refused to send party observers to the polling stations, the other opposition parties did not join him. The leader of the Social Democratic Party, Rahmatullo Zoirov, declared that he saw no point in boycotting the referendum. On the other hand, he saw no point in participating, since, as he said, the outcome of the referendum was decided in advance. The leader of the Socialist Party, Mirhusein Narziev, stated that his party would participate in the referendum but that he personally planned to vote against. The IRP argued strongly against any revision of the constitution but did not take part in the press conference. The party was under especially heavy pressure from the authorities as one of its deputy chairmen, Shamsiddin Shamsiddinov, had been arrested a week before. Nuri therefore wanted to soften the position of the party, and on 9 June he announced that the IRP did not intend to support any statement hostile to the referendum, since opposition to the referendum could lead to confrontation and instability in society.

In November 2003 the Democratic Party and the Social Democratic Party initiated cooperation in order to prepare the revision of the draft of the election law. Iskandarov was dismissed from his post as director of Tajikgaz, left Dushanbe in early December and did not return until April 2004, when he had his conversation with the president (see chapter 6). As a result of this conversation with the president, the DP did not join the coalition For Fair and Transparent Elections set up the same month: instead Iskandarov waited for the president to keep his promises on changes in the draft bill.[14] The coalition therefore initially consisted of the IRP, the Social Democrats and the Socialist Party, and the DP only joined later.[15] Yet the democratic parties did act in unison in trying to influence the revision of the draft of the new election law.

The coalition was overtaken by the following events.

First, the parliamentary debate on the two drafts of the election law (see chapter 6) took place on 3–5 June 2004. All the comments and requests made by the opposition parties (and the OSCE)—that all registered parties be represented in the election committees; that election bulletins be published; that the procedure of counting the votes should be transparent and take place in the presence of independent observers; and that ink be used instead of pencil when the election protocols were filled in—were ignored when parliament voted on the bill on 16 June, and the president signed the law in July.

Second, the Social Democratic Party faced particular trouble after it allowed the unregistered Taraqqiyot (Progress) Party under Sulton Kuvvatov to include its candidates on the SDP party lists. The SDP announced that it would allow five candidates of Taraqqiyot to stand on its party list.[16] Kuvvatov, who was to stand for election in Kulyab, was taken off the Social Democrats' list in January 2005 by the minister for security and the prosecutor general, who accused the party of serious crime.[17] Legal proceedings were soon started against the deputy chairman of Taraqqiyot.

Third, immediately after the first round of the February 2005 parliamentary elections, the opposition parties announced that they accepted the election outcome in Dushanbe, but a week later four party leaders (Shodi Shabdolov of the CP, Zoirov of the SDP, Kabiri of the IRP and the first deputy chairman of the DP, Valiev) signed a joint declaration demanding that the elections in Dushanbe be annulled. If they were not annulled they threatened to leave the Social Council (nominally an advisory body of a kind, where all registered political parties meet under the chairmanship of the president).[18] After the elections the authorities' pressure on the opposition parties intensified, and two members of the SDP in Sogd were taken to court.

The campaign before the February 2005 parliamentary elections took place in an atmosphere of reduced political freedom. By then all independent newspapers had been closed for different reasons, as had independent radio and local television channels. In spite of all the difficulties, during the campaign up to 27 February 2005 the opposition parties were activated. The party leaders complained that candidates had problems registering and that those that had registered were intimidated and blackmailed by the authorities.

When the demonstrations in Kyrgyzstan started in early March 2005, the opposition leaders spoke out in support of the Kyrgyz opposition. The IRP chairman of the Sogd region warned that similar events could happen in Tajikistan as well if the authorities violated the election law.[19] SDP leader Zoirov first clearly expressed his support for the opposition taking power in Kyrgyzstan, welcoming this as a democratic development. He compared the Kyrgyz situation with that in Tajikistan, where the opposition was much weaker, but did not exclude a repetition in Tajikistan of the events in Georgia and Ukraine.[20] At the end of March 2005 he warned that the Kyrgyz opposition was diverse and 'infiltrated by many negative forces, which were bringing to naught all its achievements'.[21] Being so outspoken, Zoirov soon became a target of the government press, and the newspaper of the presidential administration, *Dzhumkhuriat*, accused him of being the personal agent of Islam Karimov and thus an official of the Uzbek security service.[22]

By spring 2005 the secular–political opposition was beaten, and the leaders of these parties were under strong pressure from the authorities.

## Religious–Political Protest

After 2001 the revival of Islamic values in Tajik society continued. The revival as such had no clear political message. It only had a potential to be exploited politically depending on who were to articulate political demands.

As popular discontent increased and frustration with the corruption of the secular Rakhmonov regime spread, Islam seemed to many to provide an alternative. To these people a state based on sharia law would mean the cleansing of the state and government structures from all corrupt elements. Yet the IRP was not able to exploit these ideas. Instead radical political interpretations of Islam were spreading. In 2005 the question whether the hijab should be allowed in Tajik schools had become an inflammatory political issue. In the streets of Dushanbe the hijab way of tying the scarf was to be seen more often than a year before, when hardly any hijabs could be seen. The traditional Tajik way of wearing a scarf was still predominant, but it was obvious that the hijab was becoming the latest fashion. Wearing a hijab was clearly a demonstration of an Islamic identity that previously had not been felt necessary.

### The Heritage

Islam's powerful role in Tajik society is partly linked to the strong traditionalism of society. In Soviet times traditionalism became a reaction to forced modernization and industrialization. As Saodat Olimova writes: 'The modernization and industrialization were perceived by the people in Tajikistan as something alien and unnecessary. New values clashed with traditional values and were therefore rejected. A large part of the population responded by preserving its traditional system of values'.[23] This process of a return to traditionalism intensified in the 1990s in reaction to the breakdown of society and social norms during the civil war, the post-civil war reconstruction, and the transition of post-communist society. The trend towards traditionalism is nourishing political Islam.

Tajikistan has no tradition of a religiously-based political system, but it does have a tradition of political–religious discourse. The Fergana Valley, the greater part of which belonged to the Kokand Khanate and was incorporated into Russian Turkestan in the 1870s, has coloured the religious life of Tajikistan to a great extent. The clergy often played the role of political leaders, especially in revolts against Russian rule. When riots developed against Russian rule the clergy were often among the leaders. As the presence of Russian soldiers and administrators increased, native protests followed. In the Fergana Valley a widely respected leader of the Naqshbandi order, the Sufi ishan Madali (Muhammad Ali or Dukchi Ishan), led a very violent uprising. The founder of a madrasa, two mosques and a library in Margelan, he organized and led 2,000 men in an attack in May 1898 on the cities of Andijan, Osh and Margelan as a holy war against the Russians.[24] The Basmachi movement, which fought the Soviet power into the 1930s, had a stronghold in Tajikistan.

The Russian conquerors and Tsarist officials were extremely cautious about interfering deeply with Islam. The Bolsheviks, by contrast, did their best to control it. An important step in this direction was taken when in June 1922 Moscow passed a law requiring religious societies to register with the state and provide lists of their clergy.[25] The law on religious associations of the Russian Soviet Federated Socialist Republic of 1929 became the model for similar legislation in all Soviet republics, and later in the independent states on former Soviet territory as well. It regulated the activities of religious associations, the obligation to register, the way they were to be organized, the right to have buildings of their own and hold ceremonies and meetings, and restrictions on that right, and last but not least it banned the teaching of religion in any place or context beyond the official and special theological courses offered.[26] The direct attack on Islam in Central Asia began in 1923 by a slow but systematic confiscation of *waqf* land and properties,[27] restrictions on and the destruction of the Islamic courts, and restrictions on the Muslim school system. By 1927 the Communist Party was in a strong enough position to launch a frontal assault to close the mosques, eliminate the clergy, and initiate sweeping changes in the traditional family structure and status of women, Shoshana Keller concludes.[28]

The reformist–modernists of Muhiddin Kabiri link the IRP back in history to the Jadidi movement of the late 19th century, although without the pan-Turkic leanings. As mentioned in chapter 2, Jadidism was a reformist movement in Tsarist Russia from the late 19th and early 20th century which worked to introduce both Western ideas about science and society and a modern reinterpretation of Islam. It was one of the many intellectual Islamic reform movements that swept the colonized Muslim world in the late 19th century. It started as a movement for educational reform but developed as an effort to modernize the Central Asian Muslim societies. The Jadidis played an important role in the break-up of the Bukhara Emirate.[29] They found inspiration from among others Akhmad Donish of the late 19th century as a Tajik Muslim reformer and a representative of the school of enlightenment.

Islam was severely suppressed during the 1930s and 1940s, with the physical elimination of clerics and the suppression of religious literature, and most mosques and madrasas were closed.[30] In 1943, however, the situation changed. In 1947 the mosque in Khujand, the Sheikh Mosleheddin Friday Mosque, reopened.[31] Under Khrushchev the Soviet Union sought to improve relations with Third World countries and used Central Asia as a 'show case' to show to Muslim countries around the world. Religious education started to develop in official institutes as well as unofficially in private homes. From the 1970s there was an Islamic revival, which expanded during Gorbachev's years of perestroika. This process accelerated after the break-up of the Soviet Union as the societies in Central Asia searched for their heritage, identity, norms and values.[32] There were dozens of private religious schools around Dushanbe alone. One of these unofficial schools was held in the Silk Factory quarter of Dushanbe in the private house of Muhammadjan Hindustani. Most leaders of Tajik traditional and political life were his students. Among them were Said Abdullo Nuri and Muhammadsharif Himmatzoda, who became political leaders of the IRP.

Domulla Hindustani (born Muhammadjan Rustamov, 1892–1989) was born in Kokand, was educated first from madrasas in India, and suffered years of repression by the Soviet authorities. He moved to Tajikistan and Dushanbe in 1947 and worked in the central mosque there.[33] From the late 1950s he organized illegal instruction (*hujra*) for small groups of believers in his mosque, and his works were disseminated all over the Fergana Valley, where he played a major role in the revival of Islam in the 1970s and 1980s. Hindustani wanted to increase the level of knowledge of Islam and Islamic scholarship by a discussion of both religious and social affairs. He educated a new generation of Islamic scholars and contributed to the Islamic revival.

The revived religious discussion also resulted in a split within Islam in Tajikistan in the 1960s and 1970s.[34] More radical voices wanted to reform local Islam in the sense of cleansing it from certain local, traditional ceremonies which were considered not to be connected to religion, connected for example with the worship of saints' graves and the funeral and wedding ceremonies. Yet such popular traditions had entered deeply into the rituals of Islam in the region. The majority of people defended the popular forms of Islam in everyday life, and efforts at reform encountered resistance.[35] While Hindustani upheld the traditional approach of not mixing religion with politics, some of his pupils wanted to develop political positions among the believers. His radical pupils, such as Rahmatullah-'allamah and Abduwal-qari Mirzaev from Andijan, who wanted to reform Islam and cleanse it of 'innovations', became 'Wahhabites'. Hindustani stood up strongly against what he labelled Wahhabites—the term he applied to all radical 'purifiers' of Islam. Hindustani thus introduced the term to Soviet territory, although in strict terms these people did not belong to the Wahhabite sect.[36] Thus, representatives of both traditional and political

Islam, as well as moderate and radical Islamism, can trace their heritage back to Hindustani.

In the 1970s Hindustani's pupils spread the radical message. Thus, when religious literature from Arab countries reached Central Asia in the mid-1980s it became a catalyst for ideas which already existed there. Under the influence of international events—in particular the 1979 Iranian Revolution—radical Islamist ideas spread in Central Asia. The Uzbek scholar Bakhtiar Babadzhanov writes:

> The armed struggle of the Afghan mujahiddin against the Soviet army and the Iranian revolution of 1979 proved profoundly symbolic for the Mujaddidiya. It is possible that under the influence of these events, the Mujaddidiya began to see the possible realization of their ideas only in the event that Islam (of course in a purified form) became the state religion, and the country where it would blossom would bear the name Musulmanabad ('Muslimbad').[37]

Representatives of the traditional Hanafite school of Islam opposed efforts to purify Islam. The radicals wanted to give Islam political status, and initially tried to achieve legalization by establishing domestic branches of the Party of Islamic Revival in the late 1980s and early 1990s. The Tajik and Uzbek parties of Islamic revival were examples of this. The split within Islam coloured the period during and after independence and increased tensions within the Muslim community, thereby adding to the other divisions of both a regional and a political character.

Independent Tajikistan maintained a secular state with guarantees of the freedom of religion. The law prescribes that religion is not to interfere in state affairs and the state authorities are not to interfere in religious affairs. The official Islamic structure is formally not part of the state. The state does, however, regulate religious life carefully in order to control it. The Tajik government maintains control over the official religious leadership and appointments to it, forbids it to issue resolutions (fatwas) and does not allow unregistered religious activities. The State Committee on Religious Affairs has the responsibility of upholding the regulation of religious life in the country.[38]

Tajik law forbids the Islamic clergy from joining a political party or using the mosques for political propaganda. The government fears that the clergy will start to preach political messages from the mosques. Yet by controlling religious activities the government is also provokeing the very trends it is seeking to prevent. When the clergy are too strictly controlled and perceived by believers as puppets of the government, this strengthens unofficial or informal religious leaders who remain outside state control and are not seldom more radical in their interpretation of

Islamic texts. Moreover, since the Sovet Uleima (the Council of Scholars, composed of 10–15 official religious leaders) has no power to issue fatwas, only Hizb-ut-Tahrir can take a clear stand (by distributing illegal leaflets) on many issues of concern to Islamic believers. Thus, the measures taken by the government are sometimes counterproductive. This is a dilemma which is difficult to resolve given the present authoritarian character of the regime.

The 1994 Law on Religion and Religious Organizations defines the rights of religious organizations, the form and content of their activities and their place in spiritual and social life.[39] Article 7 of the law defines religious organizations as religious societies and centres, *jomeas* (Friday mosques), monasteries, religious brotherhoods, missionary societies, spiritual educational institutions, and associations of several religious organizations. All religious organizations have to be officially registered and receive authorization from the State Committee on Religious Affairs.[40] In September 2001 there were more than 3,000 ordinary mosques registered as *panjvaqta—pyatikratnye* in Russian—which means places for praying five times a day, and 241 *jomeas*, where the imam is allowed to read a *hutba*, or sermon, on Fridays. There were also 58 registered non-Islamic religious organizations, most of them Christian, and ten unregistered non-Islamic organizations.[41]

Formally, the regular worshippers at a mosque elect the imam. In practice, the elections follow the Soviet tradition, which in this case means that the *hukumat* (local government) together with the local representative of the State Committee on Religious Affairs suggests a candidate and has an unofficial but deciding vote. As a result, the heads of the mosques are appointed not because of their qualifications or authority on religious issues but on the basis of their relations with the state authorities. The state authorities appoint the heads of the *jomeas* after consultation with the Sovet Uleima. The state security organs keep control of the Friday lectures given by the clergy (*imamkhatibs*).

In March 2002 President Rakhmonov launched a campaign to increase government control over religious institutions. Under the existing legislation all mosques are required to register, yet many small mosques remained unregistered. In a speech that month Rakhmonov emphasized that all mosques had to be registered.[42] This set off a countrywide campaign to get registered mosques to re-register, and non-registered mosques to register. This made it possible for local authorities to drastically reduce the number of mosques.[43] The authorities also initiated a nationwide campaign to check the imams' knowledge of religious issues as well as of the state laws on religious affairs.[44] However, places for praying that were not allowed to register often turned into unofficial *pyatikratnyi* mosques disguised as ordinary tea-houses. Such had been the practice in Soviet time, and so it continued.[45]

This also illustrates the risk the authorities run when taking measures to increase control over religious institutions—that of provoking the kind of religious–political opposition that they seek to prevent.

In this context the distinction between the concepts of 'political Islam' and 'Islamism' becomes important. While 'political Islam' relates only to the use of religion in a general political context, Islamism relates to political activities for the purpose of creating a society built on sharia and as an ultimate goal a theocratic state. Within Islamism there is a further important distinction—between 'moderate' and 'radical' Islamism.

Since the late 1990s Hizb-ut-Tahrir has been the fastest-growing organization in Tajikistan, Uzbekistan and Kyrgyzstan. At first it did not attract a great deal of attention because it did not advocate violence as a political means. Since then IRP leader Nuri has warned several times that Hizb-ut-Tahrir is a serious threat both to the IRP and to Tajikistan.[46] The organization was made illegal in Tajikistan in 2001. It was included on the Russian list of terrorist organizations presented by the Russian Federal Security Service (Federal'naya Sluzhba Bezopasnosti, FSB) in February 2003.[47]

Members of Hizb-ut-Tahrir are regularly arrested for carrying leaflets and printed materials. It draws its support mainly from young uneducated and unemployed men, but its ideas of creating an Islamic state based on sharia—a caliphate—across borders in Central Asia attract broader groups of the disaffected population. Although the organization does not provide solutions to specific problems, its general call for a caliphate is presented as the solution to many practical problems of direct concern to the individual: the caliphate will dissolve state borders, and sharia will eliminate corruption and social inequality.

Hizb-ut-Tahrir is an international organization with branches in many countries. There are local variations and the Central Asian branches differ from those in the Middle East. However, they share the same basic convictions, which can be summarized as follows: to fight the corruption and moral decay of the rulers, imperialism, colonialism, and the ideological influence of the West; to condemn and fight the ideas of the *kufr* (the infidel); to lead the *umma* (the world community of Muslims) into a struggle with the *kufr*, his systems and thought until Islam embraces the whole world; to condemn the concepts of democracy, pluralism, political compromise, the market economy and dialogue as instruments intended to cheat the Muslim population into subordination to the West and undermine the true faith by blurring the distinction between true and false; to oppose the secular state and the secularization of social and political life; to overthrow the governments and regimes of the *kufr* by mobilizing the population; and to create 'an Islamic society ... where all aspect of life in society are administered according to the rules of the Shari'ah, ... the Khilafah State ... in which Muslims appoint a Khaleefah ... he rules according to the Book of Allah ... and the Sunnah of the Messenger of Allah ... and on condition that he conveys Islam as a message to the world through *da'wah* and jihad'.[48]

The political programme of Hizb-ut-Tahrir draws on criticism of the serious economic and social conditions in the Central Asian countries— the corruption, injustice and social inequalities. By mobilizing the population against the ruling political and religious elite it aims to overthrow the governments and install a theocratic state led by a head of state who will rule by the 'true' interpretation of the Koran. The goal is to create a state where the leader runs both state affairs and religious affairs by being the source of the authoritative interpretation of sharia. Several experts have drawn a comparison between Hizb-ut-Tahrir and Leninist groups in the sense that both have a long-term vision of a paradisal society; a belief that they have a monopoly on the truth; an understanding of the party as the avant-garde; the idea that they have a special relation to the masses; and the organizational structure of an illegal and conspiratorial party.

The ideology of Hizb-ut-Tahrir has the same kind of attraction as all extremist ideologies in that it offers a consistent and closed system of thought with one general, simple solution to all problems. The organization is built on a structure of small cells (*halka*) of between five and seven people, which is typical of illegal parties.[49] Members are supposed to know only the other members of the same cell and the leader who prepares them ideologically for membership. In theory, the organization has a well-developed strategy with separate stages for mobilizing and preparing the population for a takeover of power.[50] Yet the reality of Hizb-ut-Tahrir in Central Asia still seems far from this description of such an organizational structure.

Although it is still a small organization in Tajikistan, Hizb-ut-Tahrir is growing rapidly as it becomes more attractive to a population that is discontented and frustrated with present conditions. The first legal cases against members were raised in 1999.[51] It spread from Uzbekistan and the Fergana Valley. Even though the organization had its support base in the north, it soon developed in other parts of Tajikistan as well.[52] More than 244 members were arrested in Tajikistan between 2000 and autumn 2002, and 165 were sentenced to prison terms.[53] In 2004 the prosecutor of Sogd explained the increase in the number of Hizb-ut-Tahrir members in northern Tajikistan by the movement of radicals to Tajikistan after the authorities in Uzbekistan clamped down on their activities. However, the organization then spread in the south of the country. According to an estimate made in 2004 by the prosecutor in Dushanbe, the number of Hizb-ut-Tahrir supporters in Tajikistan was then about 3,000. The Security Ministry stated in October 2003 that in

Dushanbe several private schools where the ideology of Hizb-ut-Tahrir had been taught had been closed. The sentences were severe. The average sentences for Hizb-ut-Tahrir members were between eight and 15 years in jail.

In April 2004 a new radical Islamist organization became known as the authorities arrested 20 people in the Isfara district, alleged to be members of a religious extremist organization called Bayat ('The Pledge' or 'The Vow' in Arabic). They were accused of setting up an illegal organization with the purpose of destabilizing the situation in the north of the country and persecuting members of other confessions (Christians). According to the prosecutor, Bayat had financial support from international radical Islamist organizations, among them al-Qaeda.[54] It had its base in Chorku in the Isfara district.

The question of how to prevent radical Islamism from spreading is increasingly pressing. Several efforts have been made to get the state authorities to choose methods other than repression. As Hodji Akhbar Turajonzoda, a former leader of the Islamic flank of the UTO, pointed out in 2004, the approach in fighting radical Islamism has to be complex. 'To use mainly force (*silovykh metodov bor'by*) leads to undesired results and increases the authority of the extremists in society.' Turajonzoda explains that 'Unfortunately, today the agitation work against Hizb-ut-Tahrir is monopolized by two forces: individual representatives of the so-called "official clergy", who have no authority in society, and people from the power structures. From such a struggle it is impossible to expect any serious results'. He continues,

> ... it is necessary to support in all ways the activity of respected representatives of the intelligentsia and Islamic clergy, independently of how 'official' their status is. It is also possible to use the potential of Sufi sheikhs and the Islamic Revival Party. It is very important that *siloviki* [people from the 'power structures'] and state officials do not appear at the centre of this struggle. People must be convinced that the measures taken are taken not in defence of the government but in order to maintain statehood, national unity and stability in society.[55]

The fact that the state authorities are preventing a free debate from developing within Islam is creating a serious problem. As a result of the state authorities' strict control of Muslim institutions of learning, mosques and clerics, the scholarly level of the clerics is generally low, and they are unable either to answer many of the questions of young people or to enter into a debate with the radicals. 'Young people do not find answers to their questions with these clerics', according to the Tajik scholar Rahnamo Rakhmullo. At the same time there is an interest in religion, and unofficial seminaries are developing. According to

Rakhmullo centres of religious education are developing especially in the north, in Isfara and Mastchah, but also in southern and central Tajikistan, for instance in Dushanbe, Kafarnihan (Vakhdat), Karategin and Faizabad, and in Kulyab and Kurgan-Tyube.[56] In a situation in which people do not have access to religious education, the radicals may find followers.

To sum up, the religious–political dimension has great potential to channel popular protest, and radical Islamism is on the increase.

### Ethnic–National Protest

The regime faces the task of strengthening a national identity and bridging regional divisions. Since independence it has made more pronounced efforts to create a state ideology which will unite the nation and override regional and clan divisions. Tajikistan is in the process of creating a national identity, and for this purpose focusing on the national culture, national history and national language.

In formulating a national heritage, the Central Asian regimes refer to different aspects and periods of what is to a great extent the common history of an area in which boundaries have shifted over the centuries. This process is necessary to consolidate the state, and an urgent task for a regime that is trying to consolidate its power. As Martha Brill Olcott writes, 'The leaders of each Central Asian nation are looking to the past to write national histories which affirm their claims to statehood . . . These efforts pose a potential security risk in themselves, because contemporary boundaries and reinterpreted historical ones in no way coincide'.[57]

With an extensive common heritage in an area where different ethnic groups, language groups and cultures have blended over the centuries, it may seem difficult to separate what belongs to one nation from what belongs to another. The very task of formulating a national heritage is by definition exclusionary rather than inclusive. What is specific to 'my' group has to be different from what characterizes 'the other' group. Thus, the ongoing nation- and state-building process is itself a major factor preparing the ground for an ethno-national form of protest in the future. As ethno-nationalism becomes more pronounced, it risks bringing tensions between the ethnic majority and national minorities in the country.

Like most other regimes on former Soviet territory, Tajikistan is formulating its national identity very much in ethnic terms. The Tajiks as an ethnic group constitute the core of the state, while other ethnic groups are national minorities, and their rights as such are guaranteed by the constitution. However, the very search for the national heritage and past brings with it the embryo of conflict, and risks creating tensions between Tajiks and Uzbeks in particular. Two aspects of the process of national identity-building are relevant in this regard: first, to separate what is 'Tajik' from what is 'Uzbek' and defend the Tajik heritage in relation to the historical Uzbek dominance; and, second, to trace the Tajiks back through history.

The present state ideology traces the first Tajik state to the Samanid Empire of the 9th and 10th centuries. The search for a national past has also gone even farther back in history, and the Tajik heritage has been traced back to the original inhabitants of Central Asia, the Indo-Iranian tribes of the Aryans. As Rakhmonov wrote in *The Tajiks in the Mirror of History*, 'The Tajiks are one of the oldest peoples on earth. They are the descendants of the Aryans who, in time immemorial, spread through Central Asia'.[58] He goes further, claiming that the earliest written texts by Indo-Europeans and Zarathustra belong to the Tajik heritage.[59] In September 2003 President Rakhmonov decided that 2006 would be celebrated as the Year of the Aryans.

Although numerous archaeological investigations have proved that southern Tajikistan has a long history, the way in which Tajik official historiography interprets this has been seen by scholars as an effort by the regime to strengthen the legitimacy of its narrow regional base. As Saodat Olimova writes, 'In the works of present-day Tajik historians and publicists a new political mythology of Tajikistan is being created, based on the idea that the purest and most true Tajiks are the representatives of the ruling Kulyab ethno-group, who can trace their lineage from the ancient population of Bactria—the direct descendents of the Aryans'.[60]

This is complicated, however, by the fact that the Uzbeks partly claim the same heritage. In the ongoing nation- and state-building process in Uzbekistan, the Uzbeks are also trying to trace their history back as far as possible. As *The Tajiks in the Mirror of History* states,

the progressive intellectuals in neighbouring and especially in Turkic speaking countries, being inspired with their newly gained independence and rebirth of national consciousness, turned their attention towards the ancient civilisations and history of their ancestors ... it quite often implies some unjustified historical claims in relation to the cultural achievements of other nationalities and an inflated opinion of one's own role in these historical processes. ... As a result of the turbulent events of the twentieth century, and especially of the last two decades, some countries are not only striving to re-establish and strengthen their frontiers in pursuit of today's geopolitical interests, they are also trying to revise history and draw some new demarcation lines dividing up ancient states and civilisations. Quite often it is being done at the expense of their neighbour. Some smaller and bigger nations when tracing their origins are ready to unjustly expand the

boundaries of their own culture and civilisation thus misappropriating the
historical and cultural heritage of their neighbours.[61]

This competition between Tajik and Uzbek claims on history makes it all
the more important for the Tajiks to point out the difference between
the Indo-European Tajiks and the Turkic Uzbeks. 'And what about
some Turkic nationalities and tribes who a millennium later conquered
the territories of what used to be Ancient Bactria, Sogdiana and
Khorezm and who nowadays, after being declared independent and
sovereign states make claims on the Aryan historical and cultural
heritage: do they really have any common roots with the Aryans who
originally settled on this land?'[62] The role of the Turkic tribes has been
discussed for years in Tajik scholarly works, and the Uzbek claims on
ancient history have been refuted.[63] Many of these works describe a
drama as Turkic tribes expanded towards the south in ancient times,
thus forcing the East Iranians further south, in a process that continued
into the 20th century. This perspective is reflected in the title of the
book by Tajik scholar Rakhim Masov, a member of the Tajik Academy
of Science—*The Tajiks: Ousting and Assimilation*—where the Turkic
Mongolians and their descendents are accused of genocide against the
Tajik nation.[64]

The accusations against the Uzbeks sometimes take on a racist
element, for instance, when another Tajik scholar, Khaknazar Nazarov,
writes,

> However, the efforts to refer the beginning of the history of one's people
> to the ancient past, and to be the hegemon in the region, had as a result
> that certain politicians and nationalistic scholars of Turkic-language
> countries questioned the results of research by major scholars and
> suggested their own views on the problem, for which there is no real
> proof. For example, contemporary Turkic people announced themselves
> the direct inheritors of the ancient East Iranian nomadic tribes of Turan,
> and referred the beginning of their history to the period when the sacred
> book of the ancient Iranians—the Avesta—was compiled. However, it is
> well known that they belong to the Mongolian race, the Huns are their
> antecedents, and the beginning of their recorded history is defined to the
> 3rd century BC.[65]

There is also, as these studies point out, the injustice that in the 1920s
Tajikistan was not given territories of historical–cultural significance with
a dense Tajik population, in particular Bukhara and Samarkand. This
Tajik discussion has been going on for a long time, but the Tajik
government raises no claims on these territories. From time to time
articles appear in the Tajik media claiming rights to parts of Uzbek
territory, for example, an article in August 2004 pleading that the

president ask for part of the Uzbek Surkhandarya region to be returned to Tajikistan.[66]

The evolving Tajik state ideology is based on ethno-nationalism. In speeches by the president and by top officials, among scholars and in the media, this ideology of national unity (*Vakhdat*) is strengthening. It builds on the idea of a unity and solidarity of ethnic Tajiks without regard to differing political views, social position and cultural diversity. This is complicating relations with the Uzbek national minority in Tajikistan. They constitute a large group, as Tajiks do in Uzbekistan.[67] The complex ethnic matrix of Central Asia, with large concentrations of ethnic groups spread over large territories, sometimes makes it difficult to talk in terms of minorities. These groups have lived there for many centuries as a kind of historical remnant as empires replaced each other. Moreover, the oasis cultures of the old Central Asian centres were always multi-ethnic. The Fergana Valley in particular presents a complicated mix.

The Uzbeks still make up a large group in Tajikistan, but there was a remarkable reduction in their share of the population between the population census of 1989 and that of 2000. In 2000 Uzbeks constituted 15.3 per cent of the population of Tajikistan: in 1989 it was 23.5 per cent.[68] The largest concentration of Uzbeks can be found in the north, in the Sogd region, which is part of the Fergana Valley, where their share fell from 31.1 per cent in 1989 to 19.1 per cent in 2000. Uzbeks also live along the border in the south-west of the country in Hissar, and in the Khatlon region in the south, especially around the towns of Shartuz and Kurgan-Tyube. The statistics show that in the Khatlon region between 1989 and 2000 the share of Uzbeks in the population fell from 24.4 per cent to 15.6 per cent; in the districts under republican subordination in the west and central parts of the country it fell from 21.6 per cent to 14.5 per cent; and in Dushanbe it fell from 10.6 per cent to 9.1 per cent. In Gorno-Badakhshan the small population of Uzbeks, 250 in 1989, was reduced to 22 in 2000.[69]

The Uzbeks' competence in the Tajik language is a highly relevant question, as the Tajik language is the state language and is gradually being introduced in state institutions. The 2003 statistical yearbook of Tajikistan gives a percentage of only 36.2 per cent of Uzbeks in the country who speak the Tajik language fluently.[70] This seems to reflect a situation of large groups of the Uzbeks living in isolated concentrations.

Laws on state languages were adopted in Central Asia as early as 1989–90 and were fairly relaxed compared to the language laws of the Baltic states. In Central Asia there were generous timetables for the laws to be implemented. Other languages were reduced to the status of languages of national minorities, whose right to their own language was guaranteed. Russian maintained its position as the language of the educated strata of society, although it soon lost its former dominant position among the population as a whole. In December 2001 Kyrgyzstan granted Russian the status of 'official language' after the state language, Kyrgyz.[71] When a similar suggestion was made in Tajikistan in the spring of 2002, this raised heated debate.[72] Opponents feared that if Russian were granted such a status the Uzbeks in Tajikistan would soon demand a similar status for the Uzbek language.

After 2002 the process of introducing the Tajik language as the working language in state institutions was intensified, but it was still extremely slow. Russian retained a strong hold and the number of officials who could speak and write the Tajik language was still limited. In his speech to the country on 20 March 2004, Rakhmonov reiterated that 'Representatives of the intelligentsia should set themselves the goal of knowing their own native·language and speaking it properly, that is to say communicating in their literary language, since the new generation ... will follow their example. Media plays a great role in this'.[73] In 2004 plans were worked out for implementing the law on the use of Tajik as the working language.[74] Other institutions like the Academy of Sciences were criticized for not implementing the language law.[75]

The nation- and state-building project in Tajikistan is taking place on a territory where in the past no particular attention was paid to either borders or ethnic descent.[76] In the post-Soviet Central Asia, national minorities have come under pressure from the state authorities, which represent the ethnic majority and its interests. This process has not yet gone far in Tajikistan but it is on its way. Intergovernmental tensions between Tajikistan and Uzbekistan add to the pressure on minority groups in these countries. As a result, minorities complain that their rights are violated, for example, Tajiks in Uzbekistan and Uzbeks in Tajikistan complain that they have no access to books in their own language or to schools that teach in their own language.[77] On several occasions people have demonstrated in Khujand and Dushanbe to draw attention to President Karimov's treatment of Tajiks living in Uzbekistan. Many of the demonstrators had recently returned from Uzbekistan.[78] The fact that the SDP leader, Zoirov, was accused of being an Uzbek in the aftermath of the events in Kyrgyzstan in 2005, as he gave his support to the Kyrgyz opposition, illustrates the Tajiks' suspicion of Uzbeks in Tajikistan.

As yet, the ethno-nationalist dimension of protest does not play a significant role, but there is a risk that this dimension might become important in the future if it is triggered by interstate tensions and exploited for political purposes by particular groups or by governments.

## Conclusions

This chapter has analysed the domestic determinants of Tajik foreign-policy making by raising the question whether the regime is vulnerable on the domestic scene or strong enough to be able to pursue the foreign policy it initiated after September 2001, and itself shape foreign policy. In general there seemed to be widespread support for the pragmatic 'open door' policy of the government which provided new opportunities for contacts and exchange with other countries. However, the high degree of 'autonomy' of the state in relation to society on domestic issues also holds true with regard to foreign policy. There are no channels by which voices from below can influence policy making.

This 'autonomy' of the state vis-à-vis society can at present be interpreted as a strength of the regime in the sense that the government can pursue its policy without being questioned from within the country. At the end of the day, however, this 'strength' may prove to be a major liability. There is growing discontent in Tajik society which sooner or later will find expression one way or another.

With an enormous black and grey economy, large differences are developing in the standards of living in Tajikistan. The way people look upon their own situation follows from the conditions under which they live as judged in relative rather than absolute terms. People perceive the widespread corruption, together with social and regional stratification, and popular discontent and frustration are rapidly building up. While in 2002 people had positive expectations for the future, the post-parliamentary election period after 2005 reflects more frustration. The outcome of the parliamentary elections showed that the regime would not listen to the voice of the people, and the outcome of the 2006 presidential election was already decided.

There are numerous problems in society which affect the daily life of the citizens. The decisive question is how the population responds to the problems politically. Who takes the lead in articulating demands, formulating a political agenda and drawing up a long-term vision for society? The Tajik economy is still lagging behind, and there is a possible breeding ground for protest and for extremist ideas.

Of the three directions of protest considered here (secular–political, religious–secular, and ethnic-national) the conclusion is that the secular–political dimension is the strongest. However, it is at present hamstrung and will most probably remain so, at least until the presidential election has taken place in December 2006. The religious–political dimension therefore has potential, especially since there is a general trend towards reinforcing traditional and Islamic values in society. Although Islamic values in no way contradict a development of democratic values, a revival of Islamic values may narrow the mental perspective and thus reduce the number of options for what is considered a possible way forward for the country in future.

The developments in Kyrgyzstan in 2002 and 2005 showed what might be a future scenario in Tajikistan as well. The events in Andijan, Uzbekistan, presented the frightening scenario of future bloodshed and violence as people took to the streets. The fact that the Tajik media reported on Andijan in detail can be explained by the concern many Tajiks felt as they recalled their own experience from the Tajik civil war.

In this context the destabilizing impact of the drug trade has to be mentioned. The drug trade is adding to the level of general corruption in society and increasing social divisions. The contest for market shares in the drug trade is colouring the struggle for political power at the top, and it may be feeding the desire at the top to exploit popular discontent as an instrument against rivals.

Although foreign policy was not a divisive issue among the political elite after 2001, and no strong opinion was expressed in favour of cooperation with any of the large powers, there were factions at the top which wished to extend relations with Russia or the United States to promote their own interests. Different opinions as to how far the government should rely on Russia or the West were reflected in the media. Some Tajik commentators even suspected a link between the new foreign policy and the dismissals of top officials on the domestic scene, although such links seemed indirect and complex.

It may seem logical to expect that a reform-minded government will opt for a Western-oriented foreign policy, and vice versa; close cooperation with Western countries will promote a reform-minded government. Yet such conclusions do not automatically follow. In politics decisions most often have to be taken more pragmatically.

As shown above, the Rakhmonov regime at present has the domestic situation in the country under control. Yet the dynamics of protest evolving among the population may be exploited by competing factions at the top in a struggle for power. To the picture of protest in the country must be added the discontent and frustration at the top of society, among circles around the president. These people may ride on the back of popular protests to promote their own interests. Thereby they add to the potential of popular protest. Rakhmonov is trying to prevent this situation by putting potential contenders for political power behind bars. The dynamics of popular protest will sooner or later come to the fore. The crucial question is how the regime will respond in such a situation.

It seems that any political faction that comes to power in the future will most probably continue trying to pursue the open door policy of Rakhmonov and develop cooperation with all big powers. However, in the short-term perspective it cannot be excluded that Rakhmonov will turn to Russia for help if his regime is seriously threatened. If domestic turmoil undermines the regime and it becomes more vulnerable in a prolonged 'tug-of-war' with the opposition, this situation may force the government to turn for foreign support and thereby undermine the previous foreign policy course.

# PART IV

# CONCLUSIONS

# Efforts to Strengthen the Regime

# 8

# CONCLUSIONS

This book has dealt with the development of Tajikistan's foreign policy during the first four years after the terrorist attacks of 11 September 2001 on New York and Washington. These years have been described as a formative period of Tajik foreign policy. Three sets of questions were raised: What change has there been in Tajik foreign policy? Why this change? and What are the possible implications of this change of foreign policy? This study has also touched upon the wider issue of a small state and a weak power, and its efforts to break away from an earlier 'foreign policy paradigm' to take active initiatives in order to improve its position in the international system.

## The Change of Tajik Foreign Policy

How to understand the change of Tajik foreign policy after 2001? Chapter 1 introduced Charles Hermann's definition of policy change. According to Hermann the level of most drastic foreign policy change involves the reorientation of the state towards world affairs and implies a basic shift in the understanding of its role and activities. A less drastic level relates to the way major problems and goals are defined, which means that the original problems or goals that policy previously addressed may be replaced or simply abandoned. A still lower level of policy change is programme change, that is, methods and means (instruments of statecraft) are changed while the purposes remain the same.

There was intense foreign policy activity in Tajikistan after 2001 as the government extended its external relations. In December 2002 President Rakhmonov termed his foreign policy an 'open door' policy. This defined a policy that was open to cooperation and exchange with all possible states in an effort, above all, to develop Tajikistan economically. The policy emanated from disillusionment with Russia's will to engage in Tajikistan economically, even though both countries are members of the

Eurasian Economic Community and have signed numerous declarations and decisions on economic cooperation and integration.

The major new development with regard to Tajikistan in the post-2001 situation was the USA's engagement in the country and Tajikistan's immediate preparedness to initiate cooperation. When, after 11 September, the US administration asked whether Tajik airports could be used during military operations in Afghanistan by the international coalition, the Tajik government immediately showed interest. As Deputy Foreign Minister Abdunabi Sattorzoda said in June 2005, while Russia had been hesitant about how to relate to the USA in the immediate aftermath of 11 September, the Tajik government immediately understood the new opportunities the situation might bring for Tajikistan's international cooperation. Tajikistan viewed the US strikes against Afghanistan as being in accord with its own interests, since the Taliban had been regarded as a threat to Tajikistan's national security ever since they appeared on the Afghan scene.[1]

The Tajik government now formulated its policy explicitly referring to the 'national interests'. The president used the term in an official context for the first time in early 2003.

Did these efforts include a desire to 'balance' Russia? They certainly did, Sattorzoda said in 2005: the 'open door' policy did not allow Tajikistan to develop relations with one country at the expense of relations with any other state. In his view Tajikistan's national interests included both a reduction of the 'Russian factor' in Tajikistan and a counterbalancing of this very factor.

However, to what extent was this a new orientation and to what extent was it only a stronger determination on the part of the government to carry out a policy that had existed previously and could now be implemented, as the external circumstances changed? As already mentioned, ideas about a more diversified foreign policy had existed within the government for several years. Nevertheless, these ideas only became official policy after 2001, and then they contributed to bring about the kind of conscious reorientation of foreign policy of which Hermann writes. Thus, it is not enough to say that the political purposes remained the same all the time and the post-2001 Tajik foreign policy was only a revision of means and methods. There was something more, and the fact that the Taliban regime had fallen and foreign powers were engaging in the Central Asian region contributed to an understanding that the situation had changed and major security threats and problems had to be redefined.

During the three years 2002–2004 Tajikistan demonstrated that it had learnt the art of diplomacy to play the interests of different countries off against each other. Without doubt the interest of Iran—encouraged by the Tajik government—in investing in the Sangtuda-1 power station helped Russia finally to decide to act and sign the agreements in October 2004 on huge Russian investments in the hydro-energy and aluminium sectors of Tajikistan. Moreover, Tajikistan used the interest of the USA and the European Union (EU) in contributing to strengthening the capacity of the Tajik border troops to bring about the agreement on the withdrawal of the Russian border troops from the Tajik–Afghan border. As Tajikistan counted on such assistance from the West, it was able to insist that the 1993 Tajik–Russian agreement on protection of the Tajik border, which actually prescribed Russian withdrawal after ten years, be implemented.

Tajikistan's security cooperation with the USA and the EU grew substantially during these years. Although it remained limited to capacity-building for border protection and combating drug trafficking, this cooperation was of crucial importance both for creating normal external conditions for Tajikistan and as a political factor supporting a more independent Tajik foreign policy. While the Tajik government was very willing to develop close cooperation with the United Nations Office on Drugs and Crime, this was interpreted in the outside world as proof of a willingness and capacity to tackle its own problems, which was more than could be said of the Uzbek and Turkmen regimes.

Tajikistan's relations with China developed during this period. The opening of the road which connects Tajik Gorno-Badakhshan with Chinese Xinjiang drastically improved the conditions for economic cooperation. With China's declaration in 2004 of its interest in developing cooperation with Central Asia, the great increase in the amounts of Chinese goods on the Tajik market seemed no coincidence. China's efforts to revitalize the Shanghai Cooperation Organization (SCO) also signalled its interest in playing more of a role in Central Asian security affairs in the future.

The turmoil in Afghanistan since the early 1990s had been a contributing factor to Tajikistan's close relations with Russia, and Russia constituted a security guarantor for Tajikistan vis-à-vis Afghanistan. As the situation in Afghanistan changed after the fall of the Taliban, and the USA became the dominant foreign actor in that country, Tajikistan's need for Russia's protection vis-à-vis Afghanistan disappeared. Afghanistan instead was developing into a key country for Tajikistan's external relations, and most of the latter's projects and plans for energy exports were built on transit across Afghanistan. As the USA supported regional cooperation between Afghanistan and its neighbours, the key for Tajikistan's future seemed to depend a great deal on the continued US presence and engagement in the region.

Tajikistan's relations with Uzbekistan remained on a low level and, although there were certain improvements in their bilateral relations during 2002, tensions between them continued. Tajikistan's policy was obviously to reduce its dependence on Uzbekistan by finding alternatives to the importing of Uzbek gas and transit across Uzbek territory. Since the USA became a major security partner of Uzbekistan after 2001, while Uzbekistan's security cooperation with Russia was almost nil, Russia could no longer act as a guarantor of Tajikistan's security vis-à-vis Uzbekistan.

Tajikistan's agreements with Russia, signed in October 2004, seemed at first to represent a change in its policy vis-à-vis Russia. The major Russian investments due to come to the Tajik hydro-energy and aluminium sectors seemed to indicate that Russia's political influence on Tajikistan would increase in the future. Many commentators considered that Russia had the upper hand in the negotiations with Tajikistan and had played the card of the Tajik migrant workers in Russia. If those young men were no longer to be allowed to come to Russia to work, the potential for domestic turmoil in Tajikistan would increase drastically. On the other hand Tajikistan had several cards to play in relation to Russia. In June 2005 the State Premium Prize of the Russian Federation, awarded to people who had made an honourable contribution to the Russian state, was given to three people for their work in developing the Okno space monitoring system, and it became obvious to all that this station, up in the mountains at Nurek in Tajikistan, had been one of the most important objects in the negotiations.

However, the 2004 agreements with Russia did not indicate a sudden turn of Tajik foreign policy towards closer relations with Russia. Whether such a turn would take place depended on several other factors, to which we will return.

Tajik policy after 2001 favoured a situation of different layers of security cooperation—with Russia, with the West, and with the SCO, in which China played a leading role. In the economic sphere Tajikistan did its best to attract foreign partners, and in this sphere the regional powers such as Iran, Pakistan and India played a role together with the Russian, Western and Chinese actors.

Tajikistan's great asset in the post-September 2001 situation was its geographical location next to Afghanistan. The Tajik government became aware that its assets were the interests of the large powers in two issues in particular—fighting terrorism and the illegal drug trade. These were major threats to Tajikistan's national security. By making them priority issues on its agenda for international cooperation, the Tajik government gained political credit within the international community. Thus, it also could attract international donors and partners for economic cooperation in the future.

## Why this Change?

What determined the change of policy? Chapter 1 introduced three theoretical approaches to understanding the change of Tajik policy which offer different explanations of what factors were most important.

The *regional system approach* looks at changes in the region, which follow, first of all, from the impact of the engagement of the big powers. We found that this approach explains a great deal. Developments after 11 September 2001 strengthened trends that were already present in the Central Asian region in general, such as the reduction of Russia's presence and influence, and the increase in the engagement of other foreign actors. The US factor in Tajikistan made the Tajik 'open door' policy possible since the US presence attracted other governments to become involved in Tajikistan. Although there was a competition for influence between the big powers and the regional powers, this had no negative impact in Tajikistan. Instead the improved relations between Russia and the USA, combined with the drastic increase in the US engagement as well as that of other Western and Asian countries on the global level, the new situation in Afghanistan and the prospects for Tajikistan's economic cooperation with Afghanistan all made regional powers such as Iran, Pakistan and India more interested in Tajikistan, which could now be accessible across Afghanistan in the not-too-distant future. Thus, changes in the regional system created the external conditions which made possible the shifts in Tajik foreign policy.

The *domestic consolidation approach* presents the regime's efforts to consolidate the state and the regime as major factors behind Tajikistan's new post-11 September 2001 foreign policy. Often, and especially after September 2001, it was clear that there was a certain built-in duality in these efforts. The new foreign policy was intended both to legitimize and strengthen the rule of President Rakhmonov through international recognition and international assistance, and to promote the economic development of the country. The two objectives overlapped to a great extent. Yet over the years a dilemma has become visible, as the survival of the regime and of the personal rule of the president has become a first priority, while reforms of governance, for example, which could be regarded as part of a consolidation process and as preconditions for economic development, are a second or third priority.

The regime was able to pursue its foreign policy autonomously of society in the sense that there were no organized interests or groups strong enough to have an influence on foreign policy making. There were professional and far-sighted analysts and advisers around the president at the time of September 2001 who helped him draw up the guidelines of a new foreign policy. There was general understanding of and support for the government's open door policy among different political factions, yet there were also—naturally—specific interests which wanted to give more emphasis to cooperation with Russia rather than the USA and European countries, and vice versa. Through all the twists and turns that led up to the October 2004 Tajik–Russian agreement on Russian investments there was an intense power struggle going on within Tajikistan in which both sides wanted to use the Russian connections.

*The societal approach* looked for domestic dynamics of protest as a factor behind shifts in foreign policy. As chapter 7 shows, foreign policy was not a political issue at the time and there were no organized interests from below in society trying to influence foreign policy decision making. The chapter concludes, however, that there is a potential for future popular protest finding its way in the secular–political and religious–political directions. The question was raised whether President Rakhmonov will turn towards Russia again as he needs Russia's support in maintaining power, especially against the background of the revolution in Kyrgyzstan and the violent events in Andijan, Uzbekistan.

The three approaches do not exclude but rather complement each other. Together they give a fuller understanding of why foreign policy change took place and why it may happen in the future. Discussing their relative weight in explaining Tajik policy change after September 2001, the regional system approach is the most important. The changes in the region created the external conditions for a diversified foreign policy. However, it was the interest of the regime, determined to a great extent by its efforts to maintain power, that led it to carry out the foreign policy change (the domestic consolidation approach).

However, if the narrow interests of the regime of political survival were the determining factor, what does this tell about the future? If the regime fears the 'Kyrgyz scenario', does this mean that it will turn to Russia again?

## The Foreign Policy of Small Powers

It is more or less received wisdom that a small power cannot influence the international system. A small power reacts rather than acts. The conclusion of this study is that a small power may take the chance and the opportunities that are offered by a sudden shift in the international situation, change its foreign policy, expand its external relations, reorient towards new partners, and thereby reinforce ongoing trends in a region.

The distinction between the external and internal factors behind the foreign policy of a state can never be clear-cut, as the introductory chapter makes clear. A state is vulnerable to the impact of its international environment, and its domestic scene is subject to influence from the outside. The involvement of big powers and their mutual relations have an impact on relations between the states of the region, and thereby on the conditions in which the individual state makes foreign policy. Thus, relations of rivalry or cooperation between the big powers colour the relations between the regional states. The big-power involvement may deepen already existing divides, or it may contribute to overcoming them. External support for one state in a region may shift the power balance between the states of the region by helping one of them develop. Thus engagement by external powers can set off a series of processes in the regional system. The pattern of suspicion and friendship often follows old dividing lines between the states in the region, and this is something the external powers cannot change easily, if indeed they can change it at all. The dynamics of interstate relations in the region have strength of their own. The domestic scenes of the individual states of the region also have their own dynamics which outside influence can change only with difficulty.

A crucial question for this study is whether the dynamics on the Central Asian regional scene contributed to improve the conditions for Tajikistan as a small power. As has already been pointed out, the accelerated foreign engagement in the sub-region as well as in the wider Central Asian region after September 2001 changed the geopolitical constellations. The fact that Russia accepted US military deployment (although competition between the external powers remained) was of crucial importance. Thus, the external engagement created the conditions necessary for a more independent Tajik foreign policy.

What assets can Tajikistan use after September 2001 to maintain international interest in the country? Maria Papadakis and Harvey Starr indicate an answer to this question:

> Small states can exert influence and leverage on a larger state by appealing to mutual interest. The power of persuasion may be substantial if a small state can convince a larger power that a particular action is also in the interest of the bigger state. This may especially be the case if the small state has something to offer the larger state such as a strategic location, a valuable commodity or a prestigious political association. In this sense, strength on the part of the small state emanates more from its relationship with the other state than by any raw measures of power.[2]

In the case of Tajikistan its location next to Afghanistan and its own ambitions to become a key transit country between former Soviet Central Asia and countries to the south (Afghanistan, Pakistan and Iran) make it especially interesting to external powers. The Tajik government is shaping a profile of the country as a bridge to the south.

Tajikistan's assets are also issue-based and related to its role in fighting the drug trade, terrorism and radical Islamists. The Tajik government is exploiting the country's proximity to Afghanistan and its vulnerability to these evils in order to attract international assistance, as these issues are of the utmost concern to the UN, the EU, the Collective Security Treaty Organization (CSTO), the SCO, NATO, and individual governments. The political credit the Tajik government currently enjoys in the eyes of the international community follows above all from its actions with regard to these threats. Thanks to Tajikistan's close cooperation with the UN Office on Drugs and Crime and with several international organizations on combating international terrorism, President Rakhmonov has strengthened his international reputation.

In sum, the Tajik leadership was able to use the 'window of opportunity' that opened after September 2001 and uphold the international interest in its country by exploiting issues of major international concern. The Tajik leadership seemed to have learnt the art of diplomacy and the techniques necessary for a small state and weak power to improve its position.

## Implications for Tajikistan's Future Policy

We have concluded that Tajikistan's foreign policy in the years 2002–2004 can be characterized by the official term 'open door policy', including a clear willingness to cooperate with the West, as well as Asian countries, while at the same time 'balancing' Tajikistan's relations with Russia. Although the agreements signed with Russia in October 2004 and the turmoil in Central Asia from the beginning of 2005 (with the Kyrgyz revolution in March 2005 and the events in Andijan in May) may usher in a closer relationship with Russia again, this cannot be taken for granted; nor can it be expected to last. There are several factors that will determine whether this policy will (a) continue and (b) succeed. These are the Russian factor; the US factor; domestic developments in Afghanistan and Uzbekistan; and the internal dynamics in Tajik society, in particular the development of radical Islamism and anti-Americanism. What will happen with Tajik foreign policy if any of these factors diverges seriously from the course of developments of the last four years?

To begin with *the Russian factor*, the most interesting question is of course whether the huge Russian investments in the years to come will bring political influence.

The Russian actors in Tajikistan can be roughly categorized as the Russian government, the military, the energy companies and Russian private business. The Russian military views the greater US/Western security engagement with concern and can be assumed to prefer a reduction of this foreign presence. Russian medium-sized private business is only weakly represented in Tajikistan. In spring 2005 there were about 55 joint Russian–Tajik ventures, most of them run by Tajiks with Russian passports. As Grigorii Rapota, the secretary general of the Eurasian Economic Community, said in 2003 when asked about the Russian reaction to foreign investments in Central Asia, Russia hardly has an economic presence and therefore cannot be said to be squeezed out of this area.

The large Russian economic actors during the years to come will be the state monopoly Unified Energy Systems (RAO UES) and the aluminium oligarch Oleg Deripaska. As it seems, UES will not only take responsibility for Sangtuda-1 but also operate the construction work at Rogun for Deripaska. Other Russian energy companies are not yet active. Lukoil demonstrated its interest in exploiting Tajik gas and oil in 2003, but has so far not followed this up. The director of UES, Anatolii Chubais, has stated clearly that he wants to expand the interests of the company beyond Tajikistan into Afghanistan and even further. In September 2004, one month before the Russian–Tajik agreements of October 2004, he said that UES might enter Afghanistan from Tajikistan and that this would be possible if the projects in Tajikistan materialized. Tajikistan already exports electricity to Afghanistan, but UES will help in expanding the grid.[3]

UES as an actor is described as being very different from the energy companies in the gas and oil sectors. As the American scholar Theresa Sabonis-Helf writes, comparing UES with Gazprom and Lukoil, 'Russian-Joint Stock Company, Unified Energy Systems (RAO-UES), are far more likely to pursue their own market interests, even when those are at odds with Russian state interests'. This is different from most other Russian energy companies, she says, which like 'the gas giant remain very close to the government and are used by the government directly to further foreign policy goals'.[4] This view confirms that UES will be very interested in the export of Tajik electricity to Afghanistan, Pakistan and Iran, and thereby contribute to the new emerging pattern of regional cooperation in the wider region.

The potential for conflicts of interest between the Russian government and UES should not be exaggerated. Rather, President Putin stated in 2001 that the Russian state and private companies, particularly in the energy sector, should promote each other's interests abroad.[5] Nonetheless, both UES and Deripaska are acting as economic units and pursuing their own market interests. It therefore cannot be excluded that the new economic conditions in Tajikistan and Afghanistan, which seem likely to evolve dynamically in the coming years, will be very much in the focus of these large Russian economic actors, and their interests and stakes in exporting from Tajikistan will influence the Russian government. In other words, UES may push the

Russian government to adapt to this new international environment of external powers and companies engaging across borders on former Soviet territory.[6] Russia has lost its previous old-fashioned position as the regional hegemon but may benefit from the new situation if only it enters into economic interaction with other foreign actors. Thus, a larger presence of the Russian energy companies in Tajikistan may not be the sign many Western analysts fear that Russia will be able to use its control of the energy resources in former Soviet republics as a foreign policy tool for projecting political power. Instead, it may be a sign that Russia is in the midst of a long-term process of adapting its external policy to the change in the international environment.

In Dushanbe in summer 2005 there were several foreign observers who were sceptical about the seriousness of Deripaska's intentions to carry through on investment in the Tajik aluminium sector, since his interest was based solidly on his own economic interests. However, since the world price for aluminium has risen drastically since the early 1990s, and there is nothing to point to a fall in the price, his plans are likely to be implemented.

The Russian investments will of course contribute to a larger Russian presence in the sense that there will be more Russians in Tajikistan who are involved in these investments, and the market for Russian television channels, culture and information in Tajikistan will expand; but neither economic nor cultural influence seems likely to be directly transferable into political influence over the Tajik government.

The Russian military presence will remain substantial. These troops remain a guarantor of the agreements signed between Russia and Tajikistan, including agreements in the economic sphere. They are a factor in favour of the status quo in the country and the Rakhmonov regime. Whether the troops would actually intervene in a domestic power struggle in which President Rakhmonov was seriously threatened is a different matter. Within the terms of Russia's obligations under both the Collective Security Treaty and bilateral agreements, Russian troops are allowed to intervene only after a request from the existing regime. President Askar Akaev in Kyrgyzstan never asked for such Russian help during the revolution in Kyrgyzstan in March 2005. Rakhmonov may. Whether Russia would actually intervene is yet another question.

The revolution in Kyrgyzstan in March 2005 had an impact on Russian–Tajik relations. President Rakhmonov's fear of a similar scenario developing in Tajikistan and his desire to ensure the support of Russia in case of that happening explain the meeting between him and Putin that took place on 6 April 2005.[7] Putin and Rakhmonov discussed the situation in Kyrgyzstan and bilateral relations, including military–technical cooperation, economic cooperation, cooperation on the fight against the drug trade, and the CSTO military exercise that was going on.

At the press conference afterwards Putin stated that Russia was ready to bring the situation in Kyrgyzstan back to normal. Significantly, he stressed political measures for doing this. On Russian television the night before the meeting with Putin, Rakhmonov had brought up the role of the CSTO in resolving this kind of crisis in Central Asia;[8] and on 4 April in Dushanbe the head of the CSTO, Nikolai Bordyusha, had stated that article 2 of the CSTO Charter provides a mechanism for stabilizing the situation in member states in the event of unrest or external aggression, and thus could have been applied during the events in Kyrgyzstan. While he said he was in favour of applying the article in the case of Kyrgyzstan, he denied that this would imply the use of military force.[9]

For Rakhmonov this was an important issue. What kind of guarantees could be expected from Russia?

Against the background of Russia's cautious behaviour during the Kyrgyz revolution, the agreement signed between Russia and Uzbekistan when Uzbek President Islam Karimov visited Moscow in June 2005 is also illustrative. Karimov applied for political support after the events in Andijan and received Russian promises to a degree that he had not expected. In exchange Karimov signed a document that states that in the event of a crisis situation in Central Asia Uzbekistan is prepared to open about ten airfields to Russian military aircraft. These airfields are located in Chirchik (on the border with Kazakhstan), Kogaity (in the Surkhandarya region close to Tajikistan), Bukhara, Tuzel (not far from Tashkent), Fergana, Andijan, Nukus and Khanabad. Karimov did not, however, accept the permanent stationing of Russian troops.[10] He did not wish to give up his options for playing both the US and the Russian card.

In theory there is an alternative way for Russia to intervene peacefully in a domestic crisis in Tajikistan. During the revolt in Andijan in the Uzbek Fergana Valley in May 2005, the leaders of the uprising turned to President Putin and asked him to intervene by providing a forum for a dialogue between the opposition and the Uzbek authorities. The Russian government never responded to the request. Neither Russia nor the USA has an interest in a failure of the Uzbek regime. It can therefore not be expected that either of them will actively give support to an opposition until it is obvious that this opposition is already taking power.

Although the Russian influence on Tajik foreign policy making seems to be limited, there is most often a Russian link in the domestic power struggle in Tajikistan, as is illustrated by the negotiations over the aluminium sector, with the links between Deripaska and the mayor of Moscow, Yurii Luzhkov, on the one hand, and the mayor of Dushanbe, Makhmadsaid Ubaidulloyev, and Gaffor Mirzoev, the former head of the Presidential Guard who controlled the aluminium factory at the time, on the other. Had Rakhmonov not eliminated Mirzoev he would have had a powerful adversary to fight, who would have been backed by Russian money and interests. Russia can thus contribute to strengthen or weaken groups and factions in Tajikistan, but the conditions for their interference will be set by the domestic power play inside Tajikistan.

In summer 2005 many of the actors involved, including many representatives of international organizations, feared the implications for the trafficking in drugs from Afghanistan when the Russian border troops leave the Tajik–Afghan border by 2006. Yet, as the UN Office on Drugs and Crime was given greater opportunities to work with the Tajik Anti-Drug Agency and to help in reforming and improving the work of the Tajik border troops, there seemed to be positive prospects for the future. While the Russian and Tajik border troops had previously only confiscated and burned the drugs, the new UN–Tajik cooperation made it possible to do more to set up an effective intelligence organization targeting the drug trade, as well as start the huge task of mapping the organization behind this trade. Not much of this had so far been done. With support from President Rakhmonov this work seemed to be developing successfully.[11]

With regard to *the US factor*, in summer 2005 it remained unclear whether the USA had come to stay or not. Much pointed in that direction, not least the global policy of US President George W. Bush. Yet in 2005 there were hardly any US investments, and trade between Tajikistan and the USA was almost nil. Rather the USA was providing extensive economic development assistance and presenting a high political profile on democracy and human rights issues. Security cooperation between Tajikistan and the USA, as well as the EU, was increasing, yet there were no signs that any of them would be prepared to replace Russia as a security guarantor of Tajikistan.

The USA's policy in Central Asia is a dual one. Its relations with Central Asians governments have developed as relations of strategic partners in a common anti-terrorism endeavour, while at the same time the US administration has wanted to strengthen a process towards democracy in these countries. The US administration thus faces a dilemma in its Central Asia policy. In his 'Greater Middle East Initiative' of February 2004, President Bush called for modernization of the regimes and the reform of governance in all of the Greater Middle East. He called directly for democracy to replace autocracy.[12] So far Tajikistan had not presented great difficulties in this regard, but the events in Andijan illustrated the dilemma for the USA. The question whether the USA could be trusted became an issue, as official representatives on the one hand talked about democratic and human rights while the US administration at the same time ignored violations of these rights, for example, in Uzbekistan. Thus, the USA needed to be much more outspoken with regard to violations in Uzbekistan as the domestic crisis there developed.

The transfer in June 2005, after the events in Andijan, of US military aircraft from the base at Khanabad in Uzbekistan to Manas in Kyrgyzstan and Bagram in Afghanistan seemed to signal a new situation in which the USA was aiming put the Uzbek regime under pressure. It had been reacting for some time to Uzbekistan's restrictions on flight access to Khanabad as a means to get more economic benefit from allowing US aircraft the use of the base.[13] What at first seemed to be a temporary withdrawal of US aircraft from Uzbekistan soon turned out to be more serious when President Karimov requested that the US military leave Uzbekistan within 18 months. For a while it seemed that this could be a chance for Tajikistan to step in as a new host of a US military base. In June 2005 the US embassy in Dushanbe did not exclude the possibility that the Tajik government would be willing to accept a US military base in Tajikistan if the USA were to ask for it.

US criticism of Karimov's handling of the Andijan crisis proved to Karimov that the USA was not a reliable partner for securing the survival of his regime. When official Russian and Chinese statements followed in support of Karimov, against the 'international terrorists' in Andijan and against the US presence in Central Asia, the political situation in the region seemed to be shifting again. Although the geopolitical constellations of the last few years were not reversed, the turn of events illustrated that a 'temporary window of opportunity' may open for Moscow as domestic crises develop in Central Asia and the regimes fear for their survival.

The US withdrawal from Uzbekistan confirmed expectations that a smaller US military presence in the region is to be expected in the future. At the same time the US political presence is a precondition for the regional cooperation that Tajikistan is now developing with Afghanistan and with countries beyond Afghanistan, such as Pakistan, India and even Iran. The US government is actively encouraging regional cooperation between Afghanistan and its neighbours. One interesting and relevant aspect in this is the USA's future relations with Iran. Although the USA is not able to prevent Iran from developing regional cooperation, it would give a substantial push for cooperation if its relations with Iran were normalized. There is a whole region that is now willing to cooperate—Iran, Afghanistan, Tajikistan, Pakistan, China and India. From the Tajik horizon, Tajikistan and Afghanistan together constitute the core of this regional cooperation in the making.

Whether all Tajikistan's projects and plans for regional cooperation will be implemented in future depends on *domestic developments in Afghanistan*. A series of bombings in May 2005 signalled a more tense situation as the parliamentary elections in September were approaching, causing some observers to talk in terms of an 'Iraqization' of the situation in Afghanistan, but there seemed to be slow but gradual movement in the direction of the normalization and stabilization of the country.

The *domestic developments in Uzbekistan* are very different, however, and may become threatening to Tajikistan. Anything connected with a violent transfer of power in Uzbekistan will have negative consequences for Tajikistan and result in further problems on their common border. If there were to be an inflow of refugees from Uzbekistan to Tajikistan, this would seriously complicate the situation for Tajikistan. The Tajik government has tried to reduce its dependence on Uzbekistan by building roads across Kyrgyzstan to connect the north and south of Tajikistan and thereby replace the traditional route across Uzbekistan.

There is also another potential political influence from the events within Uzbekistan. As the Tajik media reported in detail on the events in Andijan in summer 2005, they often reprinted articles by well-known Russian journalists taking a critical stance towards the Uzbek authorities. The Tajik media, whose own freedom of speech was restricted before the Tajik parliamentary elections, willingly engaged in analysis of the reasons behind the Andijan events and questioned the official Uzbek version. Any newspaper article about bloodshed in a neighbouring country reminds the Tajiks of the horror of their own civil war; but at the same time this kind of reporting could work on a different level. Tajik readers drew parallels with conditions in Tajikistan—in the Tajik part of the Fergana Valley above all, but in other places as well.

Where the factor of the *internal dynamics in Tajikistan* is concerned, President Rakhmonov seemed to have secured full control of the political life in the country in good time before the presidential elections that are to take place in late 2006. In 2002, after he had allowed greater freedom to the press and for the activities of political parties and numerous non-governmental organizations (NGOs), and had initiated a cautious reform of governance, he then tightened his grip, reduced the freedom of the media and the political parties, and arrested contenders for political power before the parliamentary elections of February 2005. After that the political opposition could hardly be heard. In this sense the Tajik regime was well prepared when the revolution in Kyrgyzstan and the events in Andijan took place. The opposition in Tajikistan was already silenced. Moreover, the regime could count on the 'civil war syndrome' which had resulted in great fatigue among the population with anything that came close to confrontation and conflict. The Tajiks wanted to live a quite and normal life.

Nevertheless, there are processes going on in Tajik society which may be as difficult to get an overview of as they are to control. In society at large, discontent has become more pronounced. While references to corruption were rare in 2002, by 2004 the government itself was carrying out campaigns against corruption, and in independent public opinion surveys corruption in the authorities was mentioned as one of the country's four worst problems.[14] Criticism of high-up people (including the president) for corruption and theft was frequent. Among the elite, the president's appointment policy, relying on his own kin from the small community of Dangara, was a major source of frustration, and it was a critical question who would articulate this discontent in the future. What forms and direction would it take?

A secular–political opposition could have developed into a constructive opposition if it had been allowed to continue. During the period 2001–2005 several competent leaders of a younger generation emerged from the opposition, for example, Rahmatullo Zoirov and Shokirjon Khakimov from the Social Democratic Party (SDP), and Muhiddin Kabiri from the Islamic Revival Party (IRP). Kabiri became a member of parliament in February 2005, but was as restricted as other opposition leaders in being able to develop a constructive opposition.

A process of 'Tajikization' proceeded in society, encouraged by the nation- and state-building process. The 'Aryan' track was introduced by the regime to consolidate the country around a common national identity and came to be directed against the 'Turkified' people, in particular the Uzbeks. The Uzbeks as a national minority are encountering difficulties. Suspicion of them is increasing as relations between Tajikistan and Uzbekistan become tenser. Still, the ethno-political dimension plays little role—at least so far.

Instead the religious–political factor seems to be growing. Islamic symbols have become expressions of identity. The political struggle over whether girls are to be allowed to wear the hijab at school illustrates this. It is a similar debate to the one that is going on in most European countries today, with the exception that Tajikistan is a genuine Muslim society. Disagreements between different factions within the IRP also reflect increased interest in Islamic symbols. Religion has become a refuge and the mosques a place where oppositional ideas can be expressed more freely. In the many unregistered mosques of different brands of Islam the message varies greatly. The issue of relations between the state and religion is becoming more complex as new aspects emerge, challenging the secular constitution, which prescribes a separation between government and religious affairs.[15]

The Islamization of values in Tajikistan has been going on since the late Soviet period, and the trend is especially strong among young people.[16] This trend runs parallel to a trend of 'ruralization' of society in the sense of a return to the traditional norms and values of the countryside and towards what is defined as the original, Tajik national heritage.[17]

The question whether this ongoing process of an Islamization of values in society at large will result in political radicalization is related, according to many analyses, to (a) how quickly improvements in socio-economic conditions are seen and (b) not least important, how successful the struggle against corruption is. Increasing popular discontent may result in a radicalization of political views decked out in Islamic terms. Radical Islamist groups so far are attracting only a small minority in Tajikistan, but according to most analysts these groups are growing rapidly. The developments in the Uzbek part of the Fergana Valley are a source of inspiration in this regard.

One factor that might trigger a radicalization could be an increase of anti-Americanism. In Tajikistan, as in the rest of Central Asia, there is no tradition of anti-Americanism except for some remnants from Soviet times.[18] However, if a sense of solidarity develops among Tajiks with their Muslim brethren fighting against the USA in other countries, a wave of anti-Americanism could develop in Tajikistan and trigger a process of political radicalization.

There is now a much stronger sense of identity with the Muslim community outside Tajikistan and Uzbekistan than was the case during the Soviet period. People are much more exposed to information about what is going on in the world. There is a growing awareness and knowledge of international affairs, and stronger public concern about what is happening to Muslims in conflict areas around the world. While the Israel–Palestine conflict is still perceived as distant, the developments in Afghanistan, Iran and Iraq are of direct concern.

In the summer of 2004 the chairman of the Tajik IRP, Said Abdullo Nuri, reflected on a growing unease among Muslims about the atrocities perpetrated by US troops in Iraq. The IRP is the only legal Islamic political party in Central Asia. Its legalization was a condition of the General Peace Agreement of 1997 which ended the civil war. As the leader of a small party that is under constant pressure from the state authorities, Nuri is usually very cautious not to provoke the authorities or provide them with a pretext for banning the party. At an international Islamic conference in Iran in the summer of 2004 he called for a joint strategy in responding to US policy towards Muslim countries. He drew the analogy of wolves and tigers appearing in a forest, attacking the first village they found, and eating the sheep. Could we, he asked rhetorically, insist in such a situation that we live on the other side of the forest and that the wolves are not threatening us? No, we could not, he said: 'Tomorrow it may be our turn'. We would not set the forest on fire, he continued, but we would organize a group to block the way for the wolves. Consequently, Nuri said, Muslims of the world have to unite and work out a joint strategy for analysing the enemy and responding to the new international situation in which, he said, Islam is accused of terrorism.[19]

Nuri's concerns with Muslim brethren abroad have no direct political implications for Tajik politics. Nuri is a moderate Islamist and respects the Tajik constitution of a secular state. He is also a proponent of Tajikistan as a nation state, which can be partly explained by the focus on nation- and state-building that has characterized the political debate in all the states on former Soviet territory, including Central Asia. A 'secular nation-state mindset' is a constraint on radical Islamism. In Tajikistan, identity with the larger international Muslim community does not automatically translate into political stands in domestic politics, but the political potential of identification with the larger international Islamic community has not yet been put to the test.

In general, the public response in Tajikistan to the United States' engagement after September 2001 has been positive. The Central Asian countries had no previous direct experience of US policy; their views on it were not coloured by the Israel–Palestine question. The US invasion of Afghanistan in October 2001 put an end to the Taliban regime and thereby reduced the external threat, which the Tajiks welcome. Great expectations ensued that the US engagement in Central Asia would boost economic development in the region. Independent public opinion surveys in Tajikistan during the period 2003–2005 showed that the image of the United States and its influence on Tajikistan remained generally positive,[20] and many respondents stated that they approved of measures taken by the United States in the fight against international terrorism.[21]

At the same time, however, the polls showed that public opinion was changing and support for the USA is falling. In May 2005, 54.7 per cent of those surveyed by the Sharq institute were of the opinion that the United States had had a positive (strongly or mostly positive) influence on Tajikistan.[22] Twelve months earlier (in May 2004) the figure had been 57.4 per cent. These figures were fairly high but meant a reduction from the 69.2 per cent who in December 2003 considered that the USA had had a positive impact on Tajikistan.[23] Similarly, in May 2005, 40.6 per cent of respondents approved of 'the measures taken by the United States in the campaign against international terrorism'. This has to be compared with the corresponding figure of 43.8 per cent in 2004 and 71.5 per cent 2003. Moreover, in 2003, as many as 43.6 per cent had said they trusted the United States' leadership in the international anti-terrorist campaign, while in 2004 only 25.8 per cent did so. Support for the US engagement in Tajikistan therefore remained substantial, but was changing.

It seems reasonable to believe that the more negative views on the US international anti-terrorist policy were connected first of all with US policy in Iraq. The news of US brutality in Iraq that broke in spring

2004, symbolized by the scandal at the Abu Ghraib jail, had an impact on public opinion in Tajikistan. In December 2003, 23.1 per cent of Tajiks surveyed still approved of the US-led military invasion of Iraq, but in May 2004 this figure was down to 11.2 per cent, and in 2005 to 12.2 per cent. Moreover, the percentage of respondents who believed that life in Iraq and in the Middle East region had improved after the overthrow of Saddam Hussein had fallen in the 2004 survey. If we compare views on Afghanistan, there is a similar trend. In 2003, 68.8 per cent of respondents approved of the United States using military force in Afghanistan; in 2004 this figure was down to 48.0 per cent. The way the Tajiks viewed the case of Afghanistan was thus very different from the way they viewed the case of Iraq. Nevertheless, in 2004 many more people had become sceptical about the ways in which life had changed in Afghanistan since the fall of the Taliban and did not believe that any improvement had taken place. The more critical attitude towards US policy was also reflected in shifts in views of Tajikistan's participation in the US-led international anti-terrorist campaign. In 2003, as many as 71.7 per cent of those surveyed approved of their government's participation, while in 2004 only 45.1 per cent did so.

There is a gap in the making between a growing sense among the population of belonging to the cultural–religious world of Islam and the Western-oriented foreign policy of the Central Asian governments. This gap may take political form the day the ground for pragmatic evaluations of the United States' policy and presence disappears, when the USA is considered to be acting only in its own interests and not in the interests of Tajikistan, and when Islamic solidarity comes to be equated with political solidarity with Muslims fighting in other parts of the world. In such a perspective it would not take long before the issue of the Israel–Palestine conflict also infected Central Asia.

There are a few, although not many, signs of a process of 'Middle Easternization' in Tajikistan,[24] such as statements by religious and political leaders that 'the Jews' are behind movements and measures directed against Islam.[25] Thus, even the otherwise sound and intelligent Akhbar Turajonzoda in an article in the newspaper *Tojikiston* claimed that Zionists were behind Hizb-ut-Tahrir in order to disgrace Islam.[26]

The more involved the United States becomes in activities in Tajikistan, the more it will be held responsible for policy failures in these countries. There is thus a dynamic at work here, which works to the disadvantage of the United States. If the United States fails in Afghanistan and Iraq and, on top of that, fails to fulfil hopes of economic improvement and democratic reform in Central Asia, anti-Americanism may spread rapidly in Central Asia.

In most countries the general public has no say in foreign policy making, and more negative attitudes towards the United States among the population of Tajikistan and Uzbekistan may be considered less important than they might be elsewhere as long as the governments remain willing to continue their cooperation with the United States. However, a rise of anti-Americanism among the general population may pave the way for radical Islamism in society. A change of attitude towards the United States may resemble the process that took place in the Middle East after the end of World War II, as described by the American scholar Rashid Khalidi:

> As a result of these and many other episodes, and as [US] power in the world and in the Middle East expanded during and after the Cold War, in the eyes of many in the region [the Middle East] the United States has gradually changed over the past few decades. It went from being considered a benevolent, disinterested outsider to something quite different: a power with a massive presence in the Middle East, a broad range of interests there, and objectives not always compatible with those of the people of the region.[27]

So far, Tajikistan is far from the scenario described by Khalidi. It is not difficult to paint different kinds of worst-case scenarios for Central Asia and Tajikistan, but the potential for crises, conflict and violence is often exaggerated.

Given the many factors of insecurity, it is difficult to predict future developments in Tajikistan. A most crucial factor obviously remains the regime's capacity to fight corruption successfully by reforming—or be overturned. Sad to say, there is nothing to indicate that a serious anti-corruption campaign, including reforms of governance, will take place soon in Tajikistan. The government fears any measures that could undermine the domestic power constellations, but most observers believe that the current president will stay at power for many years to come and the authoritarian trend will increase.

Interestingly for this discussion of Tajik foreign policy, it seems that any government that comes to power in Tajikistan will try to use the new opportunities for regional cooperation. In spite of all the difficulties, the country is now developing stakes and interests in a peaceful development in Afghanistan, which will be the principal precondition for Tajikistan's realizing its dreams of and hopes for an economically sounder future. The analysis of the region thus concludes that Tajikistan will continue to do its best to open up for further cooperation towards countries to the south, and above all Afghanistan.

What do these new opportunities to the south and the obvious interest shown by Tajikistan in developing cooperation with southern states mean for its long-term foreign policy orientation? What long-term orientation is in the making?

The present choice in favour of Western partners for cooperation seems to be a pragmatic choice that is helping Tajikistan to reach out to the world and develop. This policy will most probably continue, but it may not be the orientation that is closest to the heart of the Tajiks. Opinion polls reflect a divided public opinion with regard to the impact of US culture on Tajikistan.[28] An orientation towards Russia will remain, although it is inevitable that this direction will no longer be a priority for Tajikistan. The ongoing Islamization of values in society points in the direction of more cooperation and exchange with the Muslim world, including the Arab world. Most Muslim and Arab regimes are, however, politically conservative. Pan-Islamism is not an evolving trend in Tajikistan. The Iranian/Persian orientation is strong and may strengthen due to the new emphasis on Tajikistan's relations to the south, and to the prospects for exports to and economic cooperation with Afghanistan, Iran and Pakistan. An article in the Tajik paper *Asia Plus* in June 2005 openly discussed whether in future a bloc of the 'Iranian countries—Iran, Afghanistan and Tajikistan' would arise. The author presented the relations between these countries as a 'rhombus' over time in the sense that that they were once connected, then diverged and followed different paths, but in future, hopefully, will come together again.[29] He also pointed out the different constellations of the great powers in these states, and the confrontation in relations between the USA and Iran, as obstacles to such a development. Here we should also point out the Tajik sensitivity about anything reminiscent of Iranian great-power ambitions, since historically the peoples living in what is today Tajikistan had to defend themselves against Iranian conquerors.

Although the population has no say over foreign policy making, opinion poll figures give the general picture of the context in which foreign policy making takes place. In a public opinion poll carried out in January 2005, people were asked what countries they considered themselves closest to with regard to ethnic, religious and cultural affinities. Seventy-four per cent mentioned Uzbekistan, 68 per cent Iran, 43 per cent Afghanistan, 18 per cent Kyrgyzstan, 11 per cent Russia, and 8 per cent Kazakhstan. On the question which countries they felt most sympathy with, 51 per cent answered Russia, 26 per cent Iran, 25 per cent India, 19 per cent Germany, 18 per cent Japan, 14 per cent the USA, 12 per cent France and 10 per cent China.[30] In this context Tajikistan's orientation towards Russia as well as the United States is more a pragmatic choice of which big power can be instrumental for Tajikistan's own national purposes.

Public opinion polls in Tajikistan thus show that the Uzbeks are regarded as the people who are culturally closest to the Tajiks. The relations between the Tajik and Uzbek governments are at present bad, and the Central Asian orientation is not a first choice of policy option, in spite of official statements. Even so, in future the Central Asian orientation will most probably strengthen in Tajik policy. However, it is very likely to go hand in hand with an orientation towards Afghanistan, Iran and to some extent also India and Pakistan. A stronger Tajik emphasis on relations with these latter countries is in line with the present trend of Tajikistan's national self-identification as a country that belongs to a national–cultural sphere of Iranian languages and cultures.

The development of Tajikistan's foreign policy between 2001 and 2005 reflects not only the great changes in the region but also the way in which a small state such as Tajikistan was able to use the window of opportunity provided by the international situation and thereby try to find its own way in international politics. These moments are rare, and they are seldom the focus of international political studies. Instead, studies in international politics most often pay attention to the problems of big powers or to situations of 'business as usual' when the influence of small powers is very restricted. More case studies of the foreign policy of small states in situations of drastic change of the international environment will increase the understanding of when, how and why small states will change their foreign policy.

Trying to look into the future, it cannot be excluded that Tajikistan may turn to Russia for assistance if a post-Soviet 'velvet revolution' scenario comes closer and the Tajik regime fears for its political survival. In a long-term perspective, however, Tajikistan's choice of a pragmatic 'open door policy' after September 2001 is the policy any Tajik government will pursue when it is allowed to find its own way. Moreover, this endeavour of the small power in turn contributes to change the regional system.

# NOTES

## Chapter 1

### INTRODUCTION

[1] Aloviddin Bakhovadin and Khursed Dodikhudoev, 'Tajikistan's geopolitical landmarks', *Central Asia and the Caucasus* 1/31 (2005), p. 124.

[2] Olav Knudsen, 'Analysing small-state security', in Werner Bauwens, Armand Clesse and Olav Knudsen (eds), *Small States and the Security Challenge in the New Europe* (London and Washington, DC: Brassey's, 1996), p. 5.

[3] Robert L. Rothstein, *Alliances and Small Powers* (New York and London: Columbia University Press, 1968), p. 23.

[4] Rothstein, *Alliances and Small Powers*, p. 37.

[5] Stephen M. Walt, *The Origins of Alliances* (Ithaca, N.Y. and London: Cornell University Press, 1987), pp. 18–19. The concepts come from Kenneth Waltz, *Theory of International Politics* (Reading, Mass.: Addison-Wesley, 1979).

[6] Walt, *The Origins of Alliances*, p. 18.

[7] Walt, *The Origins of Alliances*, p. 53.

[8] Walt, *The Origins of Alliances*, p. 18.

[9] Walt, *The Origins of Alliances*, pp. 21–22. Walt writes (p. 22) that it is important also to consider other factors 'that will affect the level of threat that states may pose: aggregate power, geographic proximity, offensive power, and aggressive intentions'.

[10] Roy Allison, 'Regionalism, regional structures and security management in Central Asia', *International Affairs* (London) 80/3 (May 2004), p. 469.

[11] K. J. Holsti, *International Politics: A Framework for Analysis* (Englewood Cliffs, N.J.: Prentice Hall International, Inc., 1982), p. 171.

[12] Charles Hermann, 'Changing courses: when governments choose to redirect foreign policy', *International Studies Quarterly* 34/1 (1990), pp. 5–6.

[13] Compare K. J. Holsti: 'By orientation [foreign policy orientation] we mean a state's general attitudes and commitments toward the external environment, its fundamental strategy for accomplishing its domestic and external objectives and aspirations and for copying with persisting threats'. *International Politics: A Framework for Analysis*, p. 109.

[14] Alexei Malashenko, 'Islam in Central Asia', in Roy Allison and Lena Jonson (eds), *Central Asian Security: The New International Context* (London and

Washington, DC: Royal Institute of International Affairs and Brookings Institution Press, 2001), p. 62.

[15] Holsti gives the following sets of variables for foreign policy change: external factors (military threats, non-military threats, structure of previous relationship); domestic factors (internal threats, economic conditions, political factionalization); and background historical and cultural factors (attitudes to foreigners, colonial experience). As intervening variables Holsti adds policy makers' perceptions and calculations, the policy-making process, personality factors and elite attitudes. K. J. Holsti, *Why Nations Realign: Foreign Policy Restructuring in the Postwar World* (London: George Allen and Unwin, 1982). In a previous study (Lena Jonson, *Vladimir Putin and Central Asia: The Shaping of Russian Foreign Policy* (London and New York: I. B. Tauris, 2004), p. 14), the present author includes the following domestic factors: the economic situation, the domestic security situation, the foreign policy-making process, official perceptions and ideological concepts, and elite attitudes.

[16] Harald Muller and Thomas Risse-Kappen, 'From the outside in and from the inside out: international relations, domestic politics, and foreign policy', in David Skidmore and Valerie M. Hudson (eds), *The Limits of State Autonomy: Societal Groups and Foreign Policy Formulation* (Boulder, Colo., San Francisco, Calif. and Oxford: Westview Press, 1993), p. 31.

[17] Barry Buzan, *People, States and Fear.* 2nd edn (New York and London: Harvester Wheatsheaf, 1991), p. 90; Barry Buzan and Ole Waever, *Regions and Powers: The Structure of International Security* (Cambridge: Cambridge University Press, 2003); and Barry Buzan, Ole Waever and Jaap de Wilde, *Security: A New Framework for Analysis* (Boulder, Colo.: Lynne Rienner, 1998).

[18] Jonson and Allison, 'Internal and external dynamics', in Allison and Jonson (eds), *Central Asian Security: The New International Context*, p. 10.

[19] Buzan, *People, States and Fear.*

[20] Stephen G. Walker, *Role Theory and Foreign Policy Analysis* (Durham, N.C.: Duke University Press, 1987), p. 282.

[21] Valerie M. Hudson, Susan M. Sims and John C. Thomas, 'The domestic political context of foreign policy making', in Skidmore and Hudson (eds), *The Limits of State Autonomy*, p. 54.

[22] Muller and Risse-Kappen, 'From the outside in and from the inside out', p. 34. The authors refer to Peter Katzenstein, 'International relations and domestic structures: foreign economic policies of advanced industrialized states', *International Organization* 30/1 (1976), pp. 1–45; and Stephen Krasner, *Defending the National Interest: Raw Materials Investments and US Foreign Policy* (Princeton, N.J.: Princeton University Press, 1978).

[23] David Skidmore and Valerie M. Hudson, 'Establishing the limits of state autonomy: contending approaches to the study of state–society relations and foreign policy-making', in Skidmore and Hudson (eds), *The Limits of State Autonomy*, p. 10.

[24] Hudson, Sims and Thomas describe the relationship between domestic political conflict and foreign policy behaviour as a two-step process: the influence of the two major factors—'regime strengths and weaknesses' and

'opposition group characteristics and activity'—on 'regime choice of response' is considered a first step, while the influence of the 'regime choice of response' on 'foreign policy effects of response' is considered a second step. Valerie M. Hudson, Susan M. Sims and John C. Thomas, 'The domestic political context of foreign policy making', in Skidmore and Hudson (eds), *The Limits of State Autonomy*, p. 56.

25 On the impact of the drug trade on conflicts in society, see Svante E. Cornell, 'The interaction of narcotics and conflict', *Journal of Peace Research* 42/6 (2005), pp. 751–60.


## Chapter 2

BACK TO THE FUTURE?

1 Graham E. Fuller, 'The impact of Central Asia on the "New Middle East"', in David Menashri (ed.), *Central Asia Meets the Middle East* (London and Portland, Or.: Frank Cass, 1998), p. 212.

2 Emomali Rakhmonov, *The Tajiks in the Mirror of History*, Vol. 1. *From the Aryans to the Samanids* (London: River Editions Ltd, Great Britain, no date), p. 93.

3 Yurii Yakubshokh, 'Omuzishi ttarikhamon az nigokhi hav', *Chumkhuriyat* 61 (1999), pp. 61–62. Quoted by Rakhmonov, *The Tajiks in the Mirror of History*, Vol. I, p. 65.

4 *Istoriya tadzhikskogo naroda, Tom I* (eds B. G. Gafurov and B. A. Litvinskii); and *Tom II* (eds B. G. Gafurov and A. M. Belenitskii (Moskva: Izdatelstvo vostochnoi literatury, 1964 and 1965). See also B. G. Gafurov, *Tadzhiki: Drevneishaya, drevnyaya i srednevekovaya istoriya, kniga I i II* (Dushanbe: Irfon, 1989); and B. A. Litvinskii and V. A. Ranov (eds), *Istoriya tadzhikskogo naroda, Tom 1: Drevneishaya i drevnaya istoriya* (Dushanbe: Akademiya nauk Respubliki Tadzhikistan, 1998). Already in 1910 A. Shishov had described the Tajiks in his ethnographic and anthropological study: A. Shishov, *Tadzhiki: Etnograficheskoe i antropologicheskoe issledovanie* (Tashkent, 1910). See also Rakhim Masov, *Istoriya topornogo razdeleniya* (Dushanbe: 'Irfon', 1991); Rakhim Masov, *Tadzhiki: vytesnenie i assimilatsiya* (Dushanbe, 2003); Sharif Shukorov, *Tadzhiki: Opyt natsional'nogo avtoportreta* (Dushanbe, 1993); Numon Negmatov, *Tadzhikskii fenomen: teoriya i istoriya* (Dushanbe, 1997); Abdugani Mamadazimov, *Novyi Tadzhikistan: Voprosy stanovleniya suvereniteta* (Dushanbe: Donish, 1996); and Abdugani Mamadazimov, *Politicheskaya istoriya tadzhikskogo naroda* (Dushanbe, 2000).

5 Rakhmonov, *The Tajiks in the Mirror of History*, Vol. I, p. 88.

6 Edward Allworth, *The Modern Uzbeks: From the Fourteenth Century to the Present. A Cultural History* (Stanford, Calif.: Stanford University, Hoover Institution Press, 1990). Allworth writes on the creation of an Uzbek nationhood separated from a Tajik.

7 Pulat Shozimov, 'Cultural heritage and the identity issue', *Central Asia and the Caucasus* 30/6 (2004); and Saodat Olimova, 'Political parties in Tajikistan: Facts, figures, analysis' (manuscript prepared by the Sharq independent research

institute for IFES (the International Foundation for Election Systems), Dushanbe, 2005).

[8] V. Barthold, *Turkestan Down to the Mongol Invasion* (London: Oxford University Press, 1928), p. 65.

[9] The upper course of the Pyandzh flows through what were once called the provinces of Wakhan, Shughnan and Karran (probably Roshan and Darwaz of today: Barthold, *Turkestan Down to the Mongol Invasion*, p. 65). The trade route to Tibet ran through Wakhan and Shughnan, and Marco Polo passed there on his way to Kashgar. The Vakhsh rises in the Alai mountains of present-day Kyrgyzstan, taking on the name Surhab when it enters Tajikistan, to become the Vakhsh further downstream. Another tributary of the Amudarya, to the west of the Vakhsh, is the River Kafarnihan. To the east of Vakhsh is the Kyzylsu. The River Gunt is a tributary at the upper part of the Pyandzh close to present-day town of Khorog in the autonomous region of Gorno-Badakhshan in eastern Tajikistan. Other tributaries along the Pyandzh in present-day Gorno-Badakhshan are the Vanj, the Yazgulem, the Bartang and the Shahdara.

[10] To the west of Tajikistan runs the Zerafshan River, which like the Amudarya originates in the Pamir mountains in eastern Tajikistan. The Zerafshan ('the gold-strewing' in Persian), like the Amudarya and the Syrdarya, was a centre of gravity for the different cultures of the area. Bukhara, Samarkand and excavations of Tajik towns like Penjikent in the west of modern Tajikistan, outside Khujand in the north, and in towns in the south along the Amudarya and the Pyandzh are evidence of this.

[11] Svat Soucek, *A History of Inner Asia* (Cambridge: Cambridge University Press, 2000), p. 15.

[12] Tajikistan is crossed by high mountains. Along an east–west axis, from north to south, the mountain ranges that cross the country are the Turkistan range, the Zerafshan range, the Hissar range, and in eastern Tajikistan (present-day Gorno-Badakhshan) the Vanj, Yazgulem, Dushan, Shugnan and Shakhdar ranges. On the other side of the Amudarya rises the Hindu Kush range in Afghanistan.

[13] Soucek, *A History of Inner Asia*, p. 5.

[14] B. N. Vainberg and B. Ya. Stavinskii, *Istoriya i kultura Srednei Azii v drevnosti* (Moscow, 1964), pp. 15–17, quoted by Rakhmonov, *The Tajiks in the Mirror of History*, *Vol. I*, p. 32.

[15] Mamadazimov, *Politicheskaya istoriya tadzhikskogo naroda*, p. 50. Ancient Bactria consisted of the provinces of Khutalon, Kabodiyon, Hissar, Termez, Vashgird, Badakhshan, Sogdiana, Samarkand, Bukhara and Merv, and the borderlands of Tus, Nishapur and Sarakhs.

[16] Rakhmonov, *The Tajiks in the Mirror of History*, *Vol. I*, p. 56

[17] Rakhmonov, *The Tajiks in the Mirror of History*, *Vol. I*, p. 72; and B. Gafurov, *Tadzhiki: Istoriya tadzhikskogo naroda, Tom 1. S drevneiskhikh vremen do V v.n.e.* (Moscow: Izd. Vostochnoi literatury, 1965).

[18] Tajik official historiography writes 'East Iranian'.

[19] The term 'Tukharistan' was later used by the Arabs to embrace all the provinces on both shores of the Amudarya which were economically dependent on Balkh. Barthold, *Turkestan Down to the Mongol Invasion*, p. 68.

[20] Soucek, *A History of Inner Asia*, p. 5.

[21] Rakhmonov, *The Tajiks in the Mirror of History, Vol. I*, p. 41.

[22] Rakhmonov, *The Tajiks in the Mirror of History, Vol. I*, p. 72; and Gafurov, *Tadzhiki: Istoriya tadzhikskogo naroda, Tom 1* (1965), p. 68.

[23] On the Vakhsh, at the confluence with the Pyandzh, there is a temple devoted to Okhsho, the deity of the rivers Vakhsh and Amu, in accordance with the role of water and rivers in the Zoroastrian belief. Rakhmonov, *The Tajiks in the Mirror of History, Vol. I*, p. 72; and *Istoriya tadzhikskogo naroda, Tom I* (eds Gafurov and Litvinskii), p. 28.

[24] Gafurov, *Tadzhiki, kniga I*, pp. 98–99.

[25] Frank Holt, *Alexander the Great and Bactria: The Formation of a Greek Frontier in Central Asia* (Leiden: E. J. Brill, 1988), p. 42.

[26] Soucek, *A History of Inner Asia*, p. 48.

[27] Holt, *Alexander the Great and Bactria*, p. 32.

[28] Holt, *Alexander the Great and Bactria*, p. 29.

[29] Holt, *Alexander the Great and Bactria*, pp. 29–30.

[30] Bessus established himself as King Artaxerxes. H. Sidky, *The Greek Kingdom of Bactria: From Alexander to Eucratides the Great* (Lanham, Md., New York and Oxford: University Press of America, 2000), pp. 27–28.

[31] Sidky, *The Greek Kingdom of Bactria*, p. 40. Although Bessus had some 8,000 Bactrians under arms and support of his Scythian allies, he did not have the support of his people. He was defeated, and Alexander appointed a Persian, Artabazus, as his own satrap in Bactria. Holt, *Alexander the Great and Bactria*, p. 49.

[32] Holt, *Alexander the Great and Bactria*, p. 53.

[33] Holt, *Alexander the Great and Bactria*, p. 56.

[34] On Spitamen and the resistance by the Sogdians see Gafurov, *Tadzhiki: Drevneishaya, drevnyaya i srednevekovaya istoriya, kniga I* (Dushanbe, 1989), pp. 120–26.

[35] Holt, *Alexander the Great and Bactria*, pp. 59 and 64.

[36] Holt, *Alexander the Great and Bactria*, p. 68. According to Gafurov, Alexander distributed the property and belongings of the rebels to those who had helped him against the rebels or abstained from participating in the revolts. Gafurov, *Tadzhiki, kniga I*, p. 123. He also encouraged his commanders to marry into the local aristocracy, and set an example himself: Alexander captured the family of Prince Oxyartes, brother of Darius, thus winning him over, and married Oxyartes' daughter, Roxane. He had Seleucus, one of his commanders, marry the daughter of Spitamen in 324 BC. She later became the empress of the Seleucid dynasty. Sidky, *The Greek Kingdom of Bactria*, p. 76.

[37] See Sidky, *The Greek Kingdom of Bactria*, p. 9. Cleitus, one of Alexander's commanders, described the situation as follows after being appointed satrap for Bactria-Sogdiana: 'You assign me the region of Sogdiana, rebellious and not merely resolute, but actually impossible to subdue. I am thrown to wild beasts'. Quoted by Holt, *Alexander the Great and Bactria*, p. 82. Alexander had Cleitus murdered before the latter took up his new duties.

[38] Sidky, *The Greek Kingdom of Bactria*, p. 129.

[39] Sidky, *The Greek Kingdom of Bactria*, p. 134. Sidky (p. 135) writes that the road from India went through the Khyber Pass into the Kabul Valley. From there access to Bactria was possible via the Bamiyan or Panjshir valleys.

[40] Sidky, *The Greek Kingdom of Bactria*, p. 133.

[41] Sidky, *The Greek Kingdom of Bactria*, pp. 140–41.

[42] Gafurov, *Tadzhiki, kniga I*, p. 155.

[43] Sidky, *The Greek Kingdom of Bactria*, p. 145.

[44] Edgar Knobloch, *Monuments of Central Asia: A Guide to the Archeology, Art and Architecture of Turkestan* (London and New York: I. B. Tauris, 2001), p. 116.

[45] Gafurov, *Tadzhiki, kniga I*, p. 149.

[46] Holt, *Alexander the Great and Bactria*, p. 5.

[47] Gafurov, *Tadzhiki, kniga I*, p. 146.

[48] Sidky, *The Greek Kingdom of Bactria*, p. 82.

[49] Sidky, *The Greek Kingdom of Bactria*, p. 221.

[50] Quoted by Sidky, *The Greek Kingdom of Bactria*, p. 226.

[51] Gafurov, *Tadzhiki, kniga I*, p. 189. The capital became Purushapura (present-day Peshawar).

[52] H. A. R. Gibb, *The Arab Conquests in Central Asia* (London: Royal Asiatic Society, 1923), p. 2.

[53] *Central Asia in the Kushan Period. Proceedings of the International Conference*, Vols I and II (Moscow: Izdatel'stvo 'Nauka', 1975).

[54] Gafurov, *Tadzhiki, kniga I*, pp. 198–99.

[55] V. Dubovitskii, 'Kak "lechili" tadzhikskogo Buddu', *Asia-Plus* 22 (29 May 2003), p. 6. Today the Sleeping Buddha can be seen at the Museum of Antiquity in Dushanbe.

[56] Soucek, *A History of Inner Asia*, p. 56.

[57] Barthold, *Turkestan Down to the Mongol Invasion*, p. 182.

[58] Gafurov, *Tadzhiki: Drevneishaya, drevnyaya i srednevekovaya istoriya, kniga I* (Dushanbe, 1989), pp. 365–72.

[59] '[T]he khaganate ...never raised above the fragile and ephemeral existence characteristic of most nomadic empires' (Soucek, *A History of Inner Asia*, p. 46). The Turks' empire lasted from 522 to 744 AD.

[60] Tukharistan included the fiefdoms of Termez, Chaganian (the north-east of the Sukhandarinskii Valley and the west of the Hissar Valley), Shuman (east and central parts of the Hissar Valley and probably down to the Kafarnihan), Kabodiyon, Vakhsh, Khutalon (east of the Vakhsh around Kulyab), and the Pamir. Gafurov, *Tadzhiki: Drevneishaya, drevnyaya i srednevekovaya istoriya, kniga I* (Dushanbe, 1989), p. 284.

[61] Soucek, *A History of Inner Asia*, p. 10.

[62] Gafurov, *Tadzhiki: Drevneishaya, drevnyaya i srednevekovaya istoriya, kniga II*, p. 12.

[63] Barthold, *Turkestan Down to the Mongol Invasion*, p. 185; and Philip K. Hitti, *History of the Arabs: From the Earliest Times to the Present* (London: Macmillan, 1951), pp. 208–10.

[64] Gibb, *The Arab Conquests in Central Asia*, pp. 89–90. He began regulating relations between the representatives of Arab power and the local population. He created a strict tax regime and released converts from taxes. 'I am concerned about the Muslims, defend them, and transfer their burden on to the infidels.' *Istoriya tadzhikskogo naroda, Tom II* (eds Gafurov and Belenitskii), *kniga 1*, pp. 110–11 and footnote 80.

[65] Gibb, *The Arab Conquests in Central Asia*, p. 92.

[66] *Istoriya tadzhikskogo naroda, Tom II* (eds Gafurov and Belenitskii), *kniga 1*, p. 113.

[67] Barthold, *Turkestan Down to the Mongol Invasion*, p. 195.

[68] Rakhmonov, *The Tajiks in the Mirror of History, Vol. I*, p. 93.

[69] *Istoriya tadzhikskogo naroda, Tom II* (eds Gafurov and Belenitskii), *kniga 1*, p. 121. *Rabats* were stations for cavalry sections whose duty it was to defend the frontier from enemy attacks (resembling to some extent the Russian Cossack organization). Barthold, *Turkestan Down to the Mongol Invasion*, p. 189.

[70] *Istoriya tadzhikskogo naroda, Tom II* (eds Gafurov and Belenitskii), *kniga 1*, p. 124.

[71] Barthold, *Turkestan Down to the Mongol Invasion*, p. 198.

[72] Rakhmonov, *The Tajiks in the Mirror of History, Vol. I*, p. 6.

[73] The Samanid Empire also included to the north Khwarazm and Taraz, to the south Seistan and Ghazna, to the east the western Pamir, and to the west Kumiz and Rei. Gafurov, *Tadzhiki, kniga I*, p. 137.

[74] Barthold writes, 'to those who were dissatisfied with their condition there remained one alternative, that of joining the "Warriors for the Faith", and setting out for some locality where war with the infidel and the heretic was being carried on. The guild of warriors for the Faith … possessed, like all Eastern guilds, a corporate organization. The leaders of similar volunteer troops not infrequently attained considerable fame and enjoyed official recognition; as they were not tied to their native country, the volunteers, especially those from Transoxania, offered their services wherever a holy war was in progress and wherever booty might be expected. Rulers, of course, could not always avail themselves of these services without some danger to themselves. In all probability it is the volunteers that are referred to in the characteristic tirade by Maqdisi against the inhabitants of Binkath [present-day Tashkent], as constituting at once "a support and a source of anxiety" to the Samanid administration' (Barthold, *Turkestan Down to the Mongol Invasion*, p. 215).

[75] Soucek, *A History of Inner Asia*, p. 70.

[76] Barthold, *Turkestan Down to the Mongol Invasion*, p. 226.

[77] Soucek, *A History of Inner Asia*, pp. 72–73.

[78] When Firdawsi completed his epic poem *Shahname*, describing the heroic struggle of the Iranian peoples against foreign conquerors, the Samanid Empire was coming to an end. Firdawsi dedicated the poem to the Turkic Gaznavid, but the Sultan perceived it as anti-Turkic and anti-Arab, and punished the author. Mamadazimov, *Novyi Tadzhikistan*, pp. 25–26.

[79] Barthold, *Turkestan Down to the Mongol Invasion*, p. 254.

[80] Soucek, *A History of Inner Asia*, p. 46.

[81] Barthold, *Turkestan Down to the Mongol Invasion*, p. 268.

[82] Stephen Tanner, *Afghanistan: A Military History from Alexander the Great to the Fall of the Taliban* (Karachi: Oxford University Press, 2003).

[83] Barthold, *Turkestan Down to the Mongol Invasion*, pp. 271–72.

[84] Soucek, *A History of Inner Asia*, p. 87.

[85] Soucek, *A History of Inner Asia*, p. 84.

[86] Soucek, *A History of Inner Asia*, p. 104.

[87] Soucek, *A History of Inner Asia*, p. 117.

[88] Soucek, *A History of Inner Asia*, p. 126.

[89] Soucek, *A History of Inner Asia*, p. 126.

[90] V. V. Barthold, *Four Studies on the History of Central Asia, Vol. II. Ulugh Beg* (Leiden: E. J. Brill, 1958).

[91] Soucek, *A History of Inner Asia*, p. 135.

[92] Soucek, *A History of Inner Asia*, p. 149.

[93] Soucek, *A History of Inner Asia*, p. 151.

[94] Soucek, *A History of Inner Asia*, p. 180.

[95] Khaidarso Pirumshoev, *Rossiisko-sredneaziatskie otnosheniya XV—serediny XIX vekov v Russkoi istoriografii* (Dushanbe: Akademiya nauk Respubliki Tadzhikistan/Izdatel'stvo Maolif, 2000), p. 140.

[96] Eugene Scuyler, *Turkestan: Notes of a Journey in Russian Turkistan, Khokand, Bukhara and Kuldja* (London, 1876), quoted in Richard Pierce, *Russian Central Asia 1867–1917: A Study in Colonial Rule* (Berkeley, Calif. and Los Angeles, Calif.: University of California Press, 1960), p. 25.

[97] N. A. Khalfin, *Politika Rossii v Srednei Azii (1857–1868)* (Moscow: Izdatel'stvo vostochnoi literatury, 1960), p. 232.

[98] A. V. Ignatiev et al. (eds), *Istoriya vneshnei politiki Rossii: V toraya polovina XIX veka* (Moscow: Mezhdunarodnye otnosheniya, 1997), p. 109.

[99] Hélène Carrère d'Encausse, *Islam and the Russian Empire: Reform and Revolution in Central Asia* (London: I. B. Tauris, 1988), p. 38.

[100] Namoz Khotamov, *Sverzhenie emirskogo rezhima v Bukhare* (Dushanbe: Akademiya nauk Respubliki Tadzhikistan, 1997), p. 12.

[101] Becker, Seymour, *Russia's Protectorates in Central Asia: Bukhara and Khiva, 1865–1924* (Cambridge, Mass.: Harvard University Press, 1968), p. 90.

[102] Becker, *Russia's Protectorates in Central Asia*, p. 92.

[103] Carrère d'Encausse, *Islam and the Russian Empire*, p. 38.

[104] Khotamov, *Sverzhenie emirskogo rezhima v Bukhare*, p. 16.

[105] Becker, *Russia's Protectorates in Central Asia*, pp. 152–53.

[106] Becker, *Russia's Protectorates in Central Asia*, p. 157.

[107] Soucek, *A History of Inner Asia*, p. 199.

[108] Becker, *Russia's Protectorates in Central Asia*, p. 173.

[109] Khotamov, *Sverzhenie emirskogo rezhima v Bukhare*.

[110] On Ahmad Donish, see Muhammadsharif Himmatzoda, 'Rol' prosvetitelei Srednei Azii v dukhovnom probuzhdenii narodov regiona', in *Musul'manskie lidery: sotsial'naya rol' i avtoritet* (Dushanbe: Nauchno-issledovatelskii Tsentr Sharq i Fond im. Fridrikha Eberta, 2003), pp. 34–39.

[111] Alexandre Bennigsen and S. Enders Wimbush, *Muslims of the Soviet Empire* (Bloomington, Ind.: Indiana University Press, 1986). On the Jadidis see also Shoshana Keller, *To Moscow, Not Mecca: The Soviet Campaign Against Islam in Central Asia 1917–1941* (New York: Praeger, 2001; and Carrère d'Encausse, *Islam and the Russian Empire*.

[112] Keller, *To Moscow, Not Mecca*, p. 47.

[113] Alexandre Bennigsen, Paul B. Henze, George K. Tanham and S. Enders Wimbush, *Soviet Strategy and Islam* (London: Macmillan, 1989), p. 14.

[114] S. M. Akimbekov, *Afganskii uzel i problemy bezopasnosti Tsentral'noi Azii* (Almaty: Kontinent, 2003), p. 44.

[115] In 2000 the monument to Firdawsi was moved to the outskirts of Dushanbe and was replaced with the huge golden monument to Ismoil Somoni

of the Samanid Empire Pulat Shozimov, 'Tajikistan: cultural heritage and the identity issue', *Central Asia and the Caucasus* (Umeå), 6 (2005), p. 146.

[116] Rakhmonov, *The Tajiks in the Mirror of History, Vol. I*, p. 24.

[117] Rakhmonov, *The Tajiks in the Mirror of History, Vol. I*, p. 104.

[118] Rakhmonov, *The Tajiks in the Mirror of History, Vol. I*, p. 89.

## Chapter 3

### THE FIRST TEN YEARS OF INDEPENDENCE

[1] Rafis Abazov, 'Independent Tajikistan: ten lost years', in Sally N. Cummings (ed.), *Oil, Transition and Security in Central Asia* (London and New York: Routledge Curzon, 2003), p. 59.

[2] 'Uvazhaemu R. Nabievu: Rezolyutsiya uchastnikov mitingov na ploshchadi Shakhidon goroda Dushanbe ot 29 marta 1992', repr. in *Tadzhikistan v ogne* (Dushanbe: Irfon, 1993), pp. 156–58.

[3] Rakhmonov came to power above all thanks to the support of Sangak Safarov, a commander of the People's Front and a former jailbird. He was appointed president against the background of Safarali Kenjaev being physically removed from the Congress in order to prevent him from taking power.

[4] Shirin Akiner, *Tajikistan: Disintegration or Reconciliation?* (London: Royal Institute of International Affairs, 2001), p. 39.

[5] Mohammad-Reza Djalili, Frederic Grare and Shirin Akiner (eds), *Tajikistan: The Trials of Independence* (Richmond: Curzon Press, 1998); Shirin Akiner, *Tajikistan: Disintegration or Reconciliation?*; Monica Whitlock, *Beyond the Oxus: The Central Asians* (London: John Murray, 2002); Sergei Gretsky, 'Civil war in Tajikistan: causes, developments, and prospects for peace', in Roald Sagdeev and Susan Eisenhower (eds), *Central Asia: Conflict, Resolution, and Change* (Chevy Chase, Md.: CPSS, 1995); Muriel Atkin, 'Tajikistan: ancient heritage, new politics', in Ian Bremmer and Ray Taras (eds), *Nation and Politics in the Soviet Successor States* (Cambridge: Cambridge University Press, 1993); V. I. Bushkov and D. V. Mikulskii, *Anatomiya grazhdanskoi voiny v Tadzhikistane (etno-sotsial'nye protsessy i politicheskaya bor'ba, 1992–1995* (Moscow, 1995); Aziz Niyazi, 'Tajikistan', in Mohiaddin Mesbahi (ed.), *Central Asia and the Caucasus after the Soviet Union* (Gainsville, Fl.: University Press of Florida, 1996); A. I. Kuzmin, 'Tadzhikistan: Prichiny i uroki grazhdanskoi voiny', in *Postsovetskaya Tsentral'naya Aziya: Poteri i obreteniya* (Moscow: 'Vostochnaya literatura', RAN, 1998); Mark Khrustalev, *Grazhdanskaya voina v Tadzhikistane: istoki i perspektivy* (Moscow: TsMI, MGIMO, no. 11, 1997); I. Neumann and S. Solodovnik, 'The case of Tajikistan', in Lena Jonson and Clive Archer (eds), *Peacekeeping and the Role of Russia in Eurasia* (Boulder, Colo.: Westview Press, 1996); Olivier Roy, *The Civil War in Tajikistan: Causes and Implications* (Washington DC: United States Institute of Peace, 1993); and Olivier Roy, *The New Central Asia: The Creation of Nations* (New York: New York University Press, 2000).

[6] Djalili, Grare and Akiner (eds), *Tajikistan: The Trials of Independence*, p. 247.

[7] Payam Foroughi, 'Hope and despair: an assessment of returnee households in Khatlon region of Tajikistan', UNHCR, Dushanbe, 1998.

[8] Payam Foroughi, 'Tajikistan: nationalism, ethnicity, conflict, and socio-economic disparities. Sources and solutions', *Journal of Muslim Minority Affairs* 22/1 (2002); and V. I. Bushkov and D. V. Mikulskii, *Istoriya grazhdanskoi voiny v Tadzhikistane* (Moscow: Institut etnologii i antropologii, RAN, 1996).

[9] Shireen T. Hunter, *Islam in Russia: The Politics of Identity and Security* (Armonk and London: M. E. Sharpe, 2004), p. 322. See also Karen Dawisha and Hélène Carrère d'Encausse, 'Islam in the foreign policy of the Soviet Union: a double-edged sword', in Adeed Dawisha (ed.), *Islam in Foreign Policy* (Cambridge: Cambridge University Press, 1983).

[10] Sultan Khamadov (the independent Tajik journalist with experience from the Tajik opposition and Afghanistan), 'Mezhdunarodnyi kontekst: afganskii faktor', in *Religioznyi ekstremizm v Tsentral'noi Azii: Problemy i perspektivy. Materialy konferentsii, Dushanbe, 25 aprelya 2002* (Dushanbe: OSCE Mission to Tajikistan, 2002), pp. 140–41.

[11] Aleksei Malashenko, 'Islam and politics in Central Asian States', in Lena Jonson and Murad Esenov (eds), *Political Islam and Conflicts in Russia and Central Asia* (Stockholm: Swedish Institute of International Affairs, 1999).

[12] The government side was called the *yurchiki*.

[13] Lena Jonson, *The Tajik War: A Challenge to Russian Policy*, Discussion Paper 74 (London: Royal Institute of International Affairs, 1998); and Dov Lynch, *Russian Peacekeeping Strategies* (London: Palgrave Macmillan, 2001).

[14] Kamoludin Abdullaev and Catherine Barnes (eds), *Politics of Compromise: The Tajikistan Peace Process* (London: Accord Conciliation Resources, 2001, issue 10, 2001); and Iji Tetsuro, 'Cooperation, coordination, and complementarity in international peacekeeping: the Tajikistan experience', *International Peacekeeping* 12/2 (June 2005).

[15] Rahmatullo Zoir [Zoirov] and Scott Newton, 'Constitutional and legal reform', in Abdullaev and Barnes (eds), *Politics of Compromise*, p. 56.

[16] Arne Seifert, 'OSCE longterm mission to Tajikistan', in *OSCE Yearbook 1998: Yearbook of the Organization on Security and Cooperation in Europe* (Baden-Baden: Nomos Verlagsgesellschaft, 1999).

[17] Shahram Akbarzadeh, 'Abdullajanov and the "third force"', in Abdullaev and Barnes (eds), *Politics of Compromise*.

[18] Foroughi, 'Tajikistan: nationalism, ethnicity, conflict, and socio-economic disparities, p. 59, note 55.

[19] While the leadership of the UTO lived outside Tajikistan, many members of the Democratic Party remained in the country. Among them were Oinihol Bobonazarova and Asliddin Sohibnazarov.

[20] Rashid G. Abdullo, 'Implementation of the 1997 General Agreement: successes, dilemmas and changes', in Abdullaev and Barnes (eds), *Politics of Compromise*, pp. 30–32.

[21] Said Abdullo Nuri, chairman of the IRP, at a press conference, Asia-Plus, 5 April 2002; and Zoir and Newton, 'Constitutional and legislative reform'.

[22] *Country Profile 2004 Tajikistan* (London: Economist Intelligence Unit, 2004), p. 24.

[23] Z. A. Dadabaeva, *Tadzhikistan: mezhdunarodnye otnosheniya v period transformatsii obshchestva* (Dushanbe: Akademiya nauk Respubiki Tadzhikistan, 2000), pp. 61–65.

[24] The 201st MRD is manned by contract servicemen and consists of three infantry regiments, one artillery regiment, one air defence regiment, plus separate battalions—tank, infantry, medical, engineers, and communications— and several life-support formations. It has aircraft at its disposal, namely Mi-8 and Mi-24 combat helicopters. Interfax 19 and 25 September 2001.

[25] Of the contract servicemen 71 per cent and of warrant officers 17 per cent were Tajik citizens. The Russian troops were to be financed by the Tajiks and Russians on a 50 : 50 basis but Russia has paid the lion's share over the years. Aleksandr Markin (commander of the Russian border troops), 'Chem otvetit na rezkuyu narkoekspansiyu na Pyandzhe?', *Nezavisimaya gazeta* 10 November 2003.

[26] Zafar Saidov, *Vneshnyaya politika prezidenta Rakhmonova* (Dushanbe: Izdatelstvo 'Avasto', 2000), p. 68.

[27] Saidov, *Vneshnyaya politika prezidenta Rakhmonova*, pp. 46–58.

[28] Pauline Jones Luong and Erika Weinthal, 'New friends, new fears in Central Asia', *Foreign Affairs* 81/2 (March/April 2002). See also 'Central Asia: developments and the administration's policy: a testimony of Elisabeth Jones', 29 October 2003, pp. 5–6, http://usinfo.state.gov.dhr/Archive/2003/Nov/04-122493.html.

[29] Dadabaeva, *Tadzhikistan*, p. 66.


## Chapter 4

### BIG-POWER ENGAGEMENT AND TAJIK POLICY

[1] William Tow, *Subregional Security Cooperation in the Third World* (Boulder, Colo. and London: Lynne Rienner, 1990), pp. 4–5, referred to in Roy Allison, 'Regionalism, regional structures and security management in Central Asia', *International Affairs* 80/3 (May 2004), p. 463.

[2] Deputy Foreign Minister Abdunabi Sattorzoda in interview with the author, Dushanbe, June 2005.

[3] *Jamestown Monitor* 170 (18 September 2001).

[4] *Jamestown Monitor* 170 (18 September 2001).

[5] According to an official at the US embassy in Dushanbe, 2002. President Rakhmonov told US Secretary of State Colin Powell that Tajikistan would cooperate with the USA to fight terrorism. BBC Monitoring, *Inside Central Asia* 395 (1–7 October 2001).

[6] Lena Jonson, *Vladimir Putin and Central Asia: The Shaping of Russian Foreign Policy* (London and New York: I. B. Tauris, 2004), pp. 83–86.

[7] Vladimir Mukhin, 'SshA ishchut voennye bazy v SNG: Uzbekistan, Tadzhikistan i severnyi Afganistan mogut stat' zalozhnikami antiterroristicheskoi operatsii', *Nezavismaya gazeta* 15 September 2001.

[8] ORT Vremya programme, 14 September 2001/ITAR-TASS, 14 September 2001; and *Jamestown Monitor* 170 (18 September 2001).

[9] DPA, 18 October 2001; and *Jamestown Monitor* 204 (6 November 2001).

[10] Interfax, 31 October 2001.

[11] *Jamestown Monitor* 204 (6 November 2001).

[12] Raffi Khatchadourian, 'US eyes bases in Tajikistan', *Eurasia Insight* 6 November 2001.

[13] Secretary of the Tajik Security Council Amirkul Azimov and head of the Foreign Ministry Igor Sattarov, in an interview with Viktoriya Panfilova, *Nezavisimaya gazeta,* 11 October 2001.

[14] According to US Ambassador Richard Hoagland, the main reason why no US military base was built in Tajikistan was that the USA found it did not need more bases in the region. Interview with the author, Dushanbe, June 2005.

[15] Asia-Plus, 24 September 2002.

[16] *Jamestown Monitor* 225 (7 December 2001).

[17] It was a result of 'the favourable and specific conditions which came into being, which stimulated and speeded up a rapprochement between Russia and the West'. U. Saidaliev, 'Amerikanskii faktor vo vnutripoliticheskikh protsessakh Tsentral'noi Azii', in *Problema bezopasnosti v geopoliticheskom komplekse Tsentral'noi Azii: Materialy mezhdunarodnoi nauchnoi konferentsii (g. Dushanbe, 16–17 iyunya 2003 goda)* (Dushanbe, 2004).

[18] BBC Monitoring, *Inside Central Asia* 414 (18–24 February 2002).

[19] Zafar Saidov, *Politika otkrytykh dverei* (Dushanbe: 'Sharki Ozod', 2003), p. 211.

[20] Saidov, *Politika otkrytykh dverei*, p. 213.

[21] Saidov, *Politika otkrytykh dverei*, p. 3.

[22] Author's interview with Deputy Foreign Minister Abdunabi Sattorzoda, Dushanbe, June 2004.

[23] Interview with Professor Guzel Maitdinova, Dushanbe, June 2005.

[24] Jonson, *Vladimir Putin and Central Asia: The Shaping of Russian Foreign Policy*, pp. 93–112.

[25] BBC Monitoring, *Inside Central Asia* 424 (29 April–5 May 2002).

[26] BBC Monitoring, *Inside Central Asia* 454 (25 November–1 December 2002).

[27] They also became the physical target of Russian skinheads and increasing xenophobia in Russia. A large number of Tajiks died in Russia, many of them as a result of violence and murder at the hands of Russians. In Ekaterinburg in the Russian Urals anti-Tajik demonstrations took place in 2003 and 2004, organized by a group called City without Drugs and led by a State Duma deputy, blaming the Tajiks for the widespread use of drugs in the city. Radio Free Europe/Radio Liberty (RFE/RL), *RFE/RL Central Asia Report* 4/23 (15 June 2004).

[28] Sukhrob Sharipov in Asia-Plus, *Tajik Press Review*, 18–25 April 2003.

[29] Jonson, *Vladimir Putin and Central Asia: The Shaping of Russian Foreign Policy.*

[30] Jonson, *Vladimir Putin and Central Asia: The Shaping of Russian Foreign Policy*, pp. 63–82.

[31] BBC Monitoring, *Inside Central Asia*, 20 April 2003.

[32] ITAR-TASS, 8 August 2003.

[33] Varorud news agency 30 April 2003. The Tajik media also reported that, in talks on regulating the status of the Russian Okno radar station in Tajikistan, built in Soviet times, the Tajik side wanted Russia to write off Tajikistan's debt and relieve the situation of Tajiks in Russia as a kind of compensation. See below in this chapter.

[34] Interfax, 24 July 2003.

[35] Russian deputy defence minister and commander-in-chief of the Russian ground forces, General Nikolai Kormiltsev, in ITAR-TASS, 8 August 2003/BBC Monitoring, *Inside Central Asia*, 10 August 2003.

[36] Okno is an optical-electronic complex sited in Nurek. This system for detecting high-orbit space targets has a considerably longer range than traditional radar systems and greater accuracy in measuring the coordinates of space targets in geostationary and high elliptical orbits. It is capable of detecting a target at a distance of up to 40,000 km. The choice of Tajikistan, with its mountainous territory, as the location for the Okno station was no accident: high up in the Tajik mountains—2,200 metres above sea level—there is the greatest frequency of clear nights and the atmosphere is very stable and clear. No regions on Russian territory offer these unique conditions. Viktoriya Panfilova, [Tajikistan is leaving Russia for NATO], *Nezavisimaya gazeta*, 19 March 2004, p. 5.

[37] ITAR-TASS, 8 August 2003/BBC Monitoring, *Inside Central Asia*, 10 August 2003.

[38] Russian NTV, 26 April 2003/BBC Monitoring, *Inside Central Asia*, 27 April 2003.

[39] Asia-Plus, 28 April 2003.

[40] *RFE/RL Central Asia Report* 3/34 (10 October 2003).

[41] Iran Mashhad Radio, 18 September/BBC Monitoring, *Inside Central Asia*, 21 September 2003.

[42] Interfax, 25 September 2003.

[43] Interfax, 26 September 2003.

[44] Igor Plugatarev, 'Dushanbe vygonyaet rossiiskykh pogranichnikov', *Nezavisimaya gazeta*, 25 September 2003.

[45] Aleksandr Markin (commander of the Russian border troops in Tajikistan), 'Chem otvetit na rezkuyu narkoekspantsiyu na Pyandzhe?', *Nezavisimaya gazeta*, 10 November 2003.

[46] Vladimir Mukhin, [Russia and Tajikistan have different points of view regarding the future of guarding the Afghan border], *Nezavisimaya gazeta*, 12 December 2003.

[47] Yurii Zemmel, Nigora Bukhari-zade and Darya Bryantseva, 'Kto luchshe zashchitit tadzhikskuyu granitsu?', Avesta News Agency, http://www.avesta.tj/?c=58&a=1600.

[48] [Cooperation alternatives], *Narodnaya gazeta* (Dushanbe), 3 December 2003, p. 2. *Narodnaya gazeta* was established in 1925 in the Russian language and published jointly by the parliament and the government.

[49] Muhammadali Zokirov, 'Bezotvetnaya lyubov ili brak po raschetu?', Asia-Plus, 22 January 2004.

[50] He made this statement on 17 February. *RFE/RL Central Asia Report* 8 (25 February 2004).

[51] ITAR-TASS, 30 April 2004; *Eurasian Daily Monitor* 1/2 (4 May 2004); and *RFE/RL Central Asia Report* 4/19 (11 May 2004).

[52] Interview with Vyacheslav Trubnikov, Vladimir Skvosyrev, 'Est' predel ustupkam Moskvy', *Nezavisimaya gazeta*, 12 May 2004.

[53] Compare Saolhiddin Fathulloyev, *Tojikistan* (Dushanbe), 29 April 2004.

[54] Interfax, 14 May 2004.

[55] Interview with Tajik Foreign Minister Talbak Nazarov in Viktoriya Panfilova, 'Sozdaetsya atmosfera neterpimosti', *Nezavisimaya gazeta*, 18 May 2004.

[56] RFE *Central Asia Report* 4/21 (31 May 2004).

[57] Prikhodko stated that the agreement gave Russia the right to receive 'free of charge and in perpetuity' the use of territory for a military base, that the centre at Nurek was to be Russian property, that the border handover was to be postponed until 2006, and that a new Russian operational group was to be created to assist the Tajik border troops at the border. *RFE/RL Central Asia Report* 4/22 (8 June 2004).

[58] US Department of State, 'US government assistance to and cooperative activities with Eurasia: fiscal year 2002', released by the Bureau of European and Eurasian Affairs January 2003; 'Country assessment Tajikistan', http://www.state.gov/p/eur/rls/rpt/23626.htm; and (for fiscal year 2001) http://www.state.gov/documents/organization/17714.pdf. See also S. Neil MacFarlane, 'The United States and regionalism in Central Asia', *International Affairs* 80/3 (May 2004), pp. 447–61.

[59] For example, a joint Tajik–French tactical military exercise was carried out in May 2004 and involved a Tajik mountain airborne company and a mountain platoon of the French army in a scenario of rescuing a military transport aircraft crashing in an area controlled by terrorists. Asia-Plus, 6 May/BBC Monitoring, 6 May 2004. France contributed to the preparation of military specialists and helped in the de-mining of Tajik territory and in repairing the landing strips of the Dushanbe airport. Avesta news agency, 3 September 2004.

[60] US Department of State, 'FY 2000 US assistance to the NIS', http://www.state.gov/p/eur/rls/rpt/c10250.htm.

[61] US Department of State, 'FY 2001 US assistance to Eurasia' and 'FY 202 US assistance to Eurasia', http://www.state.gov/p/eur/rls/rpt/c10250.htm.

[62] BBC Monitoring, *Inside Central Asia*, 30 March 2003.

[63] BBC Monitoring, *Inside Central Asia*, 28 September 2003.

[64] Asia-Plus, 25 September/BBC Monitoring, *Inside Central Asia*, 28 September 2003; and *RFE/RL Newsline*, 25 September 2003.

[65] European Union, 'Strategy paper 2002–2006' and 'Indicative programme 2002–2004' for Central Asia,
http://www.europa.eu.int/comm/external_relations/cceca/rsp2/02_06_eng .pdf.

[66] Vladimir Mukhin, [Russia and Tajikistan have different viewpoints regarding the future of guarding the Afghan border], *Nezavisimaya gazeta*, 3 December 2004.

[67] Russia invested 8,452,600 USD, and the UK 14,507,600 USD. *Ezhegodnik Respubliki Tadzhikistan 2003* (Dushanbe: Gosudarstvennyi komitet statistiki Respubliki Tadzhikistan, 2003), p. 186.

[68] There were also Cabool Textiles (production of textiles) and some joint companies. Irina Dubovitskaya, 'Vremya ne zhdet', *Biznes i politika* (Dushanbe), 3 (2004), p. 2.

[69] Total FDI in 2003 amounted to 31,649,700 USD. Of this 10,950,000 USD was from Russia and 20,699,700 USD from the 'far abroad' (10,178,100 USD of it from Cyprus). *Vneshneekonomicheskaya deyatelnost' respubliki Tadzhikistan:*

*Statisticheskii sbornik* (Dushanbe: Gosudarstvennyi Komitet Statistiki Respubliki Tadzhikistan, 2004), p. 380.

[70] Foreign investment of less than 500,000 USD are free of tax on the profit during the first two years; investments of between 500,000 USD and 2 million USD are exempt from tax for the first three years; and investments of more than 5 million USD are exempt for the first five years. Dubovitskaya, 'Vremya ne zhdet', p. 2.

[71] Author's interview with Rashid Abdullo, Dushanbe, June 2005.

[72] Construction work on Sangtuda had started in 1989.

[73] R. Ghani (political scientist), in *Biznes i politika*, 18 March 2002. The Russian ambassador to Tajikistan, Maxim Peshkov, in June reaffirmed the Russian plans for cooperation with Tajikistan, mentioning the construction of the Sangtuda hydroelectric power station and the transmission of electricity produced by the Dushanbe thermal-electric power station to Afghanistan. 'Both projects are very beneficial. Russia has technical and personnel opportunities for implementing them, but it does not always have financial opportunities.' Work had to be done to drum up foreign investment, Peshkov stated.

[74] BBC Monitoring, *Inside Central Asia* 450 (28 October–3 November 2002). The first stage was to consist of the construction of a 150–160-metre-high dam and the commissioning of two units, and the second stage the construction of another 335-metre-high dam and the commissioning of four units. The Tajik–Russian agreement was estimated to be worth 100 million USD. Tajik Radio, 30 October 2002/BBC Monitoring, *Inside Central Asia* 450 (28 October–3 November 2002). In September 2004 the Russian energy minister stated that Russia's participation in the financing of Rogun would be decided after Sangtuda had been completed (Avesta, 25 September 2004).

[75] Asia-Plus, 13 March 2003.

[76] Asia-Plus, 28 April 2003.

[77] Total estimated resources are about 1,000 billion cubic metres. Interfax/BBC Monitoring, *Inside Central Asia*, 18 May 2003.

[78] Marika S. Karayanni, 'Russia's foreign policy for Central Asia passes through energy agreements', *Central Asia and the Caucasus* 4 (2003), pp. 93–94.

[79] Avesta, 16 November 2004.

[80] Saidov, *Politika otkrytykh dverei*, p. 215.

[81] Author's interview with Abdurahim Muhidov from the US Agency for International Development (USAID), Dushanbe, June 2005.

[82] ITAR-TASS news agency, Moscow, 17 March 2004, 0857 GMT (in Russian)/BBC Monitoring, 17 March 2004.

[83] Tajik Radio first programme, 17 March 2004/BBC Monitoring, 17 March 2004.

[84] 'ES ezhegodno budet vydelyat' Tadzhikistanu 6 mln Evro', Asia-Plus, 25 October 2004.

[85] The Avesta News Agency lists the documents signed on 16 October 2004:

• an agreement on long-term cooperation between the government of Tajikistan and OAO 'Russkii alyuminii' (signed by Oleg Deripaska and the Tajik minister of economy and trade, Kh. Soliev);

• an agreement between the Russian Anti-Drug Agency and the Tajik Anti-Drug Agency (V. Cherkesov and R. Nazarov);

• an agreement between the Russian and Tajik governments on labour work and defence of the rights of Russian citizens in Tajikistan and Tajik citizens in Russia (the director of the Russian Federal Migration Agency M. Chernenko and Tajik Labour Minister M. Ilolov);

• an agreement between the Russian and Tajik governments in the field of information (foreign ministers Sergei Lavrov and T. Nazarov);

• an agreement between the Russian and Tajik governments on the Russian participation in the construction of the Sangtuda hydro-energy complex (signed by energy ministers V. Khristenko and Dzh. Nurmakhamadov);

• an appendix to an agreement between the governments on the regulation of Tajikistan's debt to Russia by transferring to Russia the Nurek optical-electronic complex and investments corresponding to the remaining debt in the construction of the Sangtuda hydro-energy complex (finance ministers A. Kudrin and S. Nadzhmuddinov);

• an agreement between the two governments on the composition and organizational structure of the Russian military base in Tajikistan (ministers of defence Sergei Ivanov and Sherali Khairullaev);

• an agreement between the two governments on the transfer of movable property located at military units before 25 May 1993 to temporary use by the Russian military base (defence ministers Ivanov and Khairullaev);

• an agreement between the governments on the transfer to Russian ownership of the Okno space monitoring complex (ministers of defence S. Ivanov and Sh. Khairullaev);

• a protocol on the exchange of official documents about the ratification of the treaty on the status and conditions of the Russian military base in Tajikistan from 16 April 1999;

• an agreement between Russia and Tajikistan on the transfer of movable property for temporary use of the Russian military base;

• an agreement between Russia and Tajikistan on cooperation on border issues; and

• an agreement between Russia and Tajikistan on the order of transfer of the different sections of the Tajik–Afghan border to Tajikistan. Avesta, 16 October 2004.

[86] Chubais    in    an    interview    in    *Izvestiya*,    22    April    2005, http://www.izvestia.ru/economic/article1645573.

[87] According to Dmitrii Skryabin, analyst of the investment company Finam. See 'Iran predlagaet za kontrol'nyi paket aktsii tadzhikskoi elektrostantsii bol'she, chem Rossiya', Fergana.ru web site, 14 September 2004, http://www.news.fergana.ru/detail.pgp?id=345356177628.14,1328,15928756.

[88] 'Iran predlagaet za kontrolnyi paket aktsii tadzhikskoi elektrostantsii bol'she, chem. Rossiya'.

[89] 'Iran pomozhet Tadzhikistanu probit tonnel pod Anzobskim perevalom: Itogi vizita Khotami v Dushanbe', Asia-Plus, 14 September 2004.

[90] Interfax, 16 October 2004. When the documents were signed between the companies in mid-February 2005, the foundation capital was 100 million USD. The Russian share was 75 per cent and the Tajik share 25 per cent. Russia will bear all the costs of constructing Sangtuda-1. Sangtuda is the third-largest power

station complex in Tajikistan after Nurek and Rogun (the latter of which is not completed). *Avesta*, 16 February 2005.

[91] 'Energy divorce? Russia and Iran decided to build different hydro-energy stations', *Avesta*, 12 January 2005.

[92] The aluminium factory at Turzunzade is the third-largest in terms of capacity on CIS territory, with a production capacity of 600,000 tonnes a year. It will be privatized during the years 2005–2007. RusAl showed its interest early. *Avesta*, 8 December 2004.

[93] RusAl was to build a second aluminium factory in Tajikistan, with a capacity of 200,000 tonnes a year, within seven years. It was also to reconstruct the two sections of the existing factory and increase its capacity to 100,000 tonnes a year. 'Pravitel'stvo RT nameremo rassmotret' vopros opredeleniya mesta raspolozheniya alyuminuevogo zavoda v Khatlone', *Avesta*, 25 January 2005.

[94] *Avesta*, 23 February 2005.

[95] Maksim Glikin, 'Putin priglasil tadzhikov v Rossiyu', *Nezavisimaya gazeta*, 14 May 2004.

[96] Vladimir Mukhin, 'Podvodnye kamni na puti rossiisko-tadzhikskogo sblizheniya', Fergana.ru web site, 22 October 2004.

[97] *Avesta*, 1 February 2005.

[98] Interfax, 16 October 2004.

[99] Albert Valentinov, 'Iz Tadzhikistana v Rossiyu nachala postupat' elektroenergiya', *Rossiyskaya gazeta*, 17 September 2004.

[100] *Avesta*, 27 November 2004.

[101] According to the Russian Defence Ministry, the Russian air force unit in Tajikistan was to include up to 20 war planes and helicopters (attack planes and fighters, and Mi-24 and Mi-8 fire-support helicopter gunships, to be deployed at the Aini airfield 20 km from Dushanbe). 'Russia to deploy up to 20 aircraft in Tajikistan', Interfax, 20 October 2004.

[102] Defence Minister Sergei Ivanov on 5 April: Interfax/BBC Monitoring, *Inside Central Asia*, 10 April 2005. Ivanov stated that in two to three years Russia would invest 1.124 billion roubles (RUR) in the base, including 250 million in 2005. Asia-Plus, 6 April 2005.

[103] Nuriddin Karshiboev, Viktoriya Panfilova and Igor Plugatarev, 'V Tadzhikistane poyavilas voennaya baza RF', *Nezavisimaya gazeta*, 18 October 2004.

[104] Asia-Plus, 18 March 2005.

[105] ITAR-TASS, 4 January 2005.

[106] *Avesta*, 8 December 2004.

[107] The operation included operational units located at the Pyandzh and Moskovskii border stations in Tajikistan; at Batken, Khaidarskii and Osh in Kyrgyzstan and Uzbekistan; at Aktau, Beineusk, Sarygashkii and Tarazskom in Kazakhstan; and at Astrakhan, Kupinsk and Rubtsovsk in Russia. *Nezavisimoe voennoe obozrenie*, 11–17 March 2005. On the SCO and the RATS see below in this chapter.

[108] Major-General Saidamir Sukhurov, Asia-Plus, 15 March 2005.

[109] See Putin's statement at the press conference in Dushanbe on 16 October 2004, *Avesta*, 16 October 2004.

[110] 'USA, EU to help Tajik troops protect borders', BBC Monitoring, *Inside Central Asia*, 13 June 2004.

[111] Interfax, 29 July 2004.

[112] Avesta, 28 July 2004.

[113] BBC Monitoring, *Inside Central Asia*, 18 July 2004.

[114] *RFE/RL Newsline*, 21 October 2004.

[115] 'NATO leader makes historic visit to Central Asia', *Eurasia Daily Monitor* 1/112 (2004).

[116] Asia-Plus, 21 October 2004.

[117] Asia-Plus, 21 October 2004.

[118] Interfax, 17 November 2004.

[119] On Lance Smith's visit see Avesta, 10 November 2004. Whitcombe announced that Tajikistan had received a large consignment of technical equipment from the US administration. BBC Monitoring, *Inside Central Asia*, 19 December 2004.

[120] Avesta, 31 March 2005; and Asia-Plus, 1 April 2005.

[121] 'Voprosy regional'noi bezopasnosti obsudili predstaviteli spetssluzhb Tsentr Azii', Avesta, 28 January 2005.

[122] 'Zavtra v Dushanbe otkroetsya stol po sodeistviyu mezhdunarodnogo soobshchestva RT v upravlenii granitsei', Asia-Plus, 14 February 2005.

[123] As announced in early 2005, the total aid from the EU was to amount to 10.5 million USD and the USA was to contribute 9.5 million USD. Interfax, 16 February 2005.

[124] Ambassador Alan Waddams in 'Evrokommissiya vnesla predlozheniya po stroitelstvu akademii pogranvoisk Tsentral'noi Azii', Asia-Plus, 17 February 2005.

[125] Interfax, 6 April 2005.

[126] Asia-Plus, 17 February 2005.

[127] 'Delovye vozmozhnosti Tadzhikistana obsudyat tadzhikskie i amerikanskie biznesmeny', Asia-Plus, 4 February 2005.

[128] 'Amerikanskie biznesmeny gotovy investirovat' v Tadzhikistan', Avesta, 19 October 2004.

[129] Among the parties from the USA were the Department of Trade's BISNIS, the State Department, the Overseas Private Investment Corporation and the Agency on Trade and Development. 'Delovye vozmozhnosti Tadzhikistana obsudyat tadzhikskie i amerikanskie biznesmeny', Asia-Plus, 4 February 2005.

[130] Interview with US Ambassador Richard Hoagland, Dushanbe, June 2005.

[131] Roy Allison, 'Structures and frameworks for security policy cooperation in Central Asia', in Roy Allison and Lena Jonson (eds), *Central Asian Security in a New International Context* (London and Washington, DC: Royal Institute of International Affairs and Brookings Institution Press, 2001), p. 234.

[132] *Mezhdunarodny portret: Kitaiskaya narodnaya respublika*, vypusk 4 (Dushanbe: Upravlenie informatsii MID Respubliki Tadzhikistana, 2004), p. 68. On 17 September 2001 China announced free technical aid to Tajikistan worth 8 million yuan (CNY). Previously Tajikistan had received free aid worth 5 million CNY. Interfax, 11 September 2001.

[133] 'V Dushanbe pribudet zamestitel' ministra kommertsii KNR', Avesta 21 February 2005.

[134] During the first year (it was open from May to November), 167 people and 233 tonnes of freight used the new road. Twenty-nine vehicles travelled from China to Tajikistan, and 26 from Tajikistan to China. The Tajik vehicles carried only ten tonnes of freight; the rest was Chinese (Avesta, 25 May 2005).

[135] *Mezhdunarodny portret: Kitaiskaya Narodnaya Respublika*, p. 69.

[136] Zafar Abdullaev, 'Tadzhikistan prorubil "okno v Aziyu"', Avesta, http://www.avesta.tj/?c=42&a=1598.

[137] BBC Monitoring, *Inside Central Asia*, 20 June 2004.

[138] Avesta, 22 February and 29 March 2005.

[139] Asia-Plus, 22 February 2005; and 'V Dushanbe pribudet zamestitel' ministra kommertsii KNR', Avesta, 21 February 2005.

[140] They also discussed Chinese support for the reconstruction of the transformator factory in Kurgan-Tyube and the irrigation of cotton fields in northern Tajikistan. 'Itak i podvedem itogi...' *Biznes i politika* 1/2004 (29 December 2003).

[141] The bilateral second trade/economic commission discussed Chinese participation in the consortium for the construction of Sangtuda. CentrAsia web site 20 August 2004. China also showed interest in investing in smaller power stations and the gas exploitation at Sargazon, Rengan and Sarikamysh. Avesta, 22 February 2005, http://www.CentrAsia.Ru/newsA.php4?st=1092950340.

[142] Cooperation Agreement among SCO Members on Fighting Against Narcotics, Mental Drugs, and Their Precursors, signed at the Tashkent summit meeting in June 2004. BBC Monitoring, *Inside Central Asia*, 20 June 2004.

[143] Stephen Blank, 'China's military footprint in Central Asia', *Central Asia–Caucasus Analyst*, 25 August 2004.

[144] BBC Monitoring, *Inside Central Asia*, 20 June 2004.

[145] 'Kitai smozhet lovit' terroristov pryamo v Dushanbe', Avesta, 28 October 2004; and Hsinhua, 27 October 2004/BBC Monitoring, *Inside Central Asia*, 31 October 2004.

[146] Avesta, 27 December 2004.

[147] During the Soviet era, workshops for the maintenance of MiG aircraft were located there. During the civil war (1992–97) the entire infrastructure of the airfield became defunct.

[148] *Biznes i politika* 1/2004 (29 December 2003), pp. 2, 3.

[149] 'Itak podvedem itogi ... ', *Biznes i politika* 1/2004 (29 December 2003), pp. 2–3.

[150] Timur Onica, 'Indian prime minister visits Tajikistan', *Tajikistan Daily News*, 18 November 2003, http://www.eurasianet.org/resource/tajikistan/hypermail/200311/0019.shtml.

[151] 'Tadzhikistan i Pakistan budut sotrudnichat' v bor'be s terrorizmom i drugimi prestupleniyami', Asia-Plus, 10 February 2005.

[152] Asia-Plus, 13 May 2004.

[153] Avesta, 30 March 2005.

[154] Asia-Plus, 31 March 2005. The capacity was to be 750 kWatt-hour.

[155] Associated Press of Pakistan news agency, Islamabad, 13 May 2004, 1136 GMT (in English)/BBC Monitoring, 13 May 2004.

[156] *Ezhegodnik Respubliki Tadzhikistan 2003*, pp. 258–60.

[157] The ECO was created by Iran, Pakistan and Turkey. In 1992 Afghanistan, Azerbaijan, Kazakhstan, Kyrgyzstan, Tajikistan, Turkmenistan and Uzbekistan joined.

[158] Power stations in northern Aini, southern Darband, and eastern Rasht, Fayzobod and Jirgatol districts. BBC Monitoring, *Inside Central Asia*, 20 June 2004.

[159] A 660 MWt hydropower plant on the Vakhsh River in Sangtuda to the south of Dushanbe.

[160] Tajik Television first channel, Dushanbe, 19 December 2003, 1400 GMT (in Russian)/*Tajikistan Daily Digest*, 7 January 2004.

[161] The capacity of Sangtuda-2 is 220 MW but can increase to 260 MW. The project will cost 160–180 million USD, which Iran will invest. Avesta, 12 January 2005.

[162] Tajiks would thereby not have to cross Uzbek territory to travel between Khujand and Dushanbe. Asia-Plus, 4 September 2003.

[163] Kambiz Arman, 'Investing in tunnel, Iran nurtures ambitions in Tajikistan', *Eurasia Insight*, 8 January 2003.

[164] ITAR-TASS, 3 March 2004.

[165] Avesta, 15 February 2005.


## Chapter 5

### AFGHANISTAN, UZBEKISTAN AND TAJIK POLICY

[1] The common history is reflected in the fact that 'Kabul was primarily a Tajik town until Timur, the son of Ahmad Shah Durrani, moved his court to Kabul in 1776 and declared it to be the Pushtoon capital. In Kabul the Tajiks are still dominant and well-represented in the upper-middle class.' Library of Congress, 'Afghanistan', Library of Congress Country Studies, http://lcweb2.loc.gov/cgi-bin/query/r?frd/cstdy:@field(DOCID+af0038).

[2] Between 1.5 and 2 million Uzbeks (about 9 per cent of Afghanistan's population) live in the central part of northern Afghanistan along the border with Uzbekistan, and up to 500,000 Turkmen live along the border with Turkmenistan.

[3] Martin Ewans, *Afghanistan: A Short History of Its People and Politics* (New York: Perennial, 2002), p. 9.

[4] The Turkmen–Afghan border stretches 854 km, while the Uzbek–Afghan border is only 156 km long.

[5] Alexandre Bennigsen, Paul B. Henze, George K. Tanham and S. Enders Wimbush, *Soviet Strategy and Islam* (London: Macmillan, 1989), p. 14.

[6] Vyacheslav Belokrenitsky, 'Russian–Afghan relations', in Gennady Chufrin (ed.), *Russia and Asia: The Emerging Security Agenda* (Oxford: Oxford University Press for the Stockholm International Peace Research Institute (SIPRI), 1999), p. 199.

[7] Amin Saikal, 'Russia and Central Asia', in Amin Saikal and William Maley (eds), *Russia in Search of its Future* (Cambridge: Cambridge University Press, 1995), p. 145.

[8] A. D. Davydov (ed.), *Afganistan: Problemy voiny i mira* (Moscow: Institut Vostokovedeniya RAN, 1996), p. 144.

[9] Lena Jonson, *The Tajik War: A Challenge to Russian Policy*, Discussion Paper 74 (London: Royal Institute of International Affairs, 1998), pp. 37–38.

[10] Rabbani and his Tajik-dominated government mediated two important meetings between Tajik President Rakhmonov and the UTO leader, Said Abdullo Nuri.

[11] Jonson, *The Tajik War*, p. 12.

[12] Lena Jonson, *Vladimir Putin and Central Asia: The Shaping of Russian Foreign Policy* (London and New York: I. B. Tauris, 2004).

[13] *Sotsial'no-politicheskaya situatsiya v post-sovetskom mire* 10/54 (October 1996), p. 38.

[14] Yurii Golotyuk, 'Rossiya poka ne usilivaet svoi kontingent v Tadzhikistane', *Segodnya*, 15 October 1996.

[15] *Krasnaya zvezda*, 1 November 1996, p. 1.

[16] Vladimir Mukhin (Professor of the Russian Academy of Military Sciences), 'Extension of the zone of Taleban's influence may significantly infringe upon Russia's interests in Central Asia', *Former Soviet Union 15 Nations: Policy and Security* August 1998, pp. 18–23.

[17] S. M. Akimbekov, *Afganskii uzel i problemy bezopasnosti Tsentral'noi Azii* (Almaty: Kontinent, 2003), p. 295.

[18] Akimbekov, *Afganskii uzel i problemy bezopasnosti Tsentral'noi Azii*, p. 297.

[19] William Maley, *The Afghanistan Wars* (Hampshire and New York: Palgrave Macmillan, 2002), p. 248.

[20] Lena Jonson, *Vladimir Putin and Central Asia*.

[21] *Nezavisimaya gazeta*, 5 August 2000.

[22] Sultan Akimbekov, 'The conflict in Afghanistan: conditions, problems, and prospects', in Boris Rumer (ed.), *Central Asia: A Gathering Storm?* (New York and London: M. E. Sharpe, 2002), p. 101.

[23] Roy Allison, 'Structures and frameworks for security policy cooperation in Central Asia', in Roy Allison and Lena Jonson (eds), *Central Asian Security: The New International Context* (Washington, DC and London: Brookings Institution and Royal Institute of International Affairs, 2001), p. 225.

[24] Akimbekov, *Afganskii uzel i problemy bezopasnosti Tsentral'noi Azii*, p. 340.

[25] BBC Monitoring, *Inside Central Asia* 392 (10–16 September 2001), p. 2.

[26] Vladimir Mukhin, 'Vashington i Moskva uzhe planiruet poslevoennoe ustroistvo mira', *Nezavisimaya gazeta*, 21 September 2001. See also BBC Monitoring, *Inside Central Asia* 393 (17–23 September 2001). Kvashnin and Fahim also met on 18 October. BBC Monitoring, *Inside Central Asia*, 15–21 October 2001.

[27] Vladimir Georgiev, 'Uzbekistan prodal'sya Vashingtonu za 8 mld. dollarov', *Nezavisimaya gazeta*, 19 October 2001, p. 1. The military complained that the US Air Force only bombed those targets which would benefit Dostum and his troops, not the Tajik troops.

[28] 'War in Afghanistan', *Strategic Survey 2001/2002* (London: International Institute for Strategic Studies, 2002), p. 236.

[29] 'War in Afghanistan', *Strategic Survey 2001/2002*, p. 243.

[30] Aleksandr Umnov, 'Rossiya i Pakistan na afganskom pole', *Nezavisimaya gazeta*, 17 October 2001, p. 6.

[31] Interfax, 3 November 2001.

[32] The Hazaras are mostly Shia Muslims.

[33] Charles Fairbanks, 'Being there', *The National Interest* 68 (2002).

[34] Kathy Gannon, 'Afghanistan unbound', *Foreign Affairs* May/June 2004.

[35] S. Frederick Starr, 'US Afghanistan policy: it's working', Central Asia–Caucasus Institute, Johns Hopkins University, October 2004, p. 5.

[36] A. Jamali, 'Karzai's new cabinet and the challenges ahead', *Eurasia Daily Monitor* 2/4 (6 January 2005).

[37] Camelia Entekhabi-Fard, 'Afghan government attention turns to upcoming parliamentary election', *Eurasia Insight,* 7 January 2005.

[38] 'Afghan president appoints Dostum chief of staff', Radio Free Europe/Radio Liberty (RFE/RL), *RFE/RL Newsline,* 1 March 2005.

[39] *Tajik Press Review,* 7–14 February 2002.

[40] Asia-Plus, 4 September 2002.

[41] Barnett R. Rubin and Andrea Armstrong, 'Regional issues in the reconstruction of Afghanistan', *World Policy Journal* 20/1 (spring 2003).

[42] Asia-Plus, 4 September 2002. Tajikistan exports 45 million kWh of electricity a year to Afghanistan along this line.

[43] Voice of the Islamic Republic of Iran (Mashhad), 16 March 2004, 1330 GMT (in Dari)/BBC Monitoring Service, 17 March 2004.

[44] Tajikistan stated in 2004 that it was ready to construct two more transmission lines to Kabul, Imamsokhiba and Faizabad and to the border with Pakistan if the construction could be financed. These investments must wait until the Rogun and Sangtuda hydro-power stations have been constructed. '"Nedostupnyi" Afganistan', Asia-Plus, 23 September 2004.

[45] Akhmed Rashid, 'The Great Trade Game', *Far Eastern Economic Review* 30 January 2003.

[46] Interview with the Afghan ambassador to Tajikistan, Makhmuddovud Pansheri, in '"Nedostupnyi" Afganistan', Asia-Plus, 23 September 2004; and Ambassador Pansheri in conversation with the author in Dushanbe, June 2004.

[47] 'Prigranichnaya torgovlya na trekh KPP mezhdu RT i Afganistanom nachnetsya v kontse noyabrya', Asia-Plus, 10 November 2004.

[48] On 4 May 2004 Russian Foreign Ministry spokesman Aleksandr Yakovenko stated that Russia was ready to participate actively in the development of oil and gas fields in northern Afghanistan. Interfax, 4 May 2004. The director of the Russian electricity monopoly UES, Anatolii Chubais, declared in September 2004 that UES may enter the energy system in Afghanistan through Tajikistan. Centran.ru web site, 29 September 2004, http://www.centran.ru/cgi-bin/index.pl?text_id=17186&all=yes.

[49] '"Nedostupnyi" Afganistan', Asia-Plus 23 September 2004.

[50] 'Tadzhikistan aktiviziruet sotrudnichestvo so stranami regiona v oblasti transporta', Avesta, 24 August 2004.

[51] Timofei Zhukov and Andrei Kudryashov, 'Uzbekistan na dengi SshA postroit zheleznuyu dorogu iz Termeza v Mazari-Sharif', 11 October 2004, http://www.fergana.ru/detail.php?id=942519777540.44,1424,15694748.

[52] Afghanistan Television, 15 September, 1430 GMT (in Dari)/BBC Monitoring Service, 15 September 2004.

[53] Interfax, 18 October 2004.

[54] Anita Sengupta, *The Formation of the Uzbek Nation State: A Study in Transition* (Lanham, Md., Boulder, Colo., New York, Toronto and Oxford: Lexington Books, 2003), chapter 2.

[55] Aloviddin Bakhovadin and Khursed Dodikhudoev, 'Tajikistan's geopolitical landmarks', *Central Asia and the Caucasus* 1/31 (2005), p. 126.

[56] Rakhim Masov, *Istoriya topornogo razdeleniya* (Dushanbe: Irfon, 1991), p. 23.

[57] Sengupta, *The Formation of the Uzbek Nation State*, p. 43.

[58] Edward A. Allworth, *The Modern Uzbeks: From the Fourteenth Century to the Present. A Cultural History* (Stanford, Calif.: Stanford University, Hoover Institution Press, 1990), p. 181.

[59] Allworth, *The Modern Uzbeks*, pp. 193–200.

[60] Segupta, *The Formation of the Uzbek Nation State*, pp. 90–92.

[61] Allworth, *The Modern Uzbeks*, p. 199.

[62] Allworth, *The Modern Uzbeks*, p. 207.

[63] Segupta, *The Formation of the Uzbek Nation State*, p. 98.

[64] Masov, *Istoriya topornogo razdeleniya*, p. 34.

[65] Masov, *Istoriya topornogo razdeleniya*, p. 34.

[66] Chairman Nusratullo Maksum (Lutfullaev). Quoted by Masov, *Istoriya topornogo razdeleniya*, pp. 50–51. Sokh is today an Uzbek exclave on Kyrgyz territory but with a mainly Tajik population.

[67] Allworth, *The Modern Uzbeks*, p. 208.

[68] Masov, *Istoriya topornogo razdeleniya*, p. 62; also included were the Matchinskii, Shakhristanskii, Falgarskii, Kshtutskii, Margiyano-Farabskii and other districts. M. Asimov (ed.), *Tadzhikskaya Sovetskaya Sotsialisticheskaya Respublika* (Dushanbe: Glavnaya nauchnaya redaktsiya Tadzhikskoi sovetskoi entsiklopedii, 1984), p. 105.

[69] Masov, *Istoriya topornogo razdeleniya*, p. 90.

[70] Neil Melvin, *Uzbekistan: Transition to Authoritarianism on the Silk Road* (Amsterdam: Harwood Academic Publishers, 2000), p. 49.

[71] See Masov, *Istoriya topornogo razdeleniya*; Sengupta, *The Formation of the Uzbek Nation State*; and Allworth, *The Modern Uzbeks*.

[72] See Khaknazar Nazarov, *K istorii proiskhozhdeniya i rasseleniya plemen i narodov Tsentral'noi Azii* (Dushanbe, 2004); and Masov, *Istoriya topornogo razdeleniya*.

[73] Melvin, *Uzbekistan: Transition to Authoritarianism on the Silk Road*, p. 50.

[74] Melvin, *Uzbekistan: Transition to Authoritarianism on the Silk Road*, p. 50; and Richard Foltz, 'Uzbekistan's Tajiks: A case of repressed identity', *Central Asia Monitor* 6 (1996), pp. 17–26.

[75] See Jonson, *The Tajik War*, pp. 35–36.

[76] *Sotsial'no-politicheskaya situatsiya v post-sovetskom mire* 9/53 (September 1996), p. 34.

[77] 'Sovmestnoe zayavlenie prezidentov RF i Respubliki Uzbekistan', *Diplomaticheskii vestnik* 6 (June 1998), pp. 30–31.

[78] Melvin, *Uzbekistan: Transition to Authoritarianism on the Silk Road*, p. 55.

[79] *RFE/RL Newsline* 2/84, Part 1 (4 May 1998), quoted by Melvin, *Uzbekistan: Transition to Authoritarianism on the Silk Road*, p. 56.

[80] Melvin, *Uzbekistan: Transition to Authoritarianism on the Silk Road*, pp. 56–57.

[81] Gulfira Gayeva and Yuri Chubchenko, 'Russia names its principal ally in Central Asia', *Kommersant Daily*, 26 February 1999, p. 3/*Former Soviet Union 15 Nations: Policy and Security* February 1999, p. 85.

[82] Ahmed Rashid, *Jihad: The Rise of Militant Islam in Central Asia* (New Haven, Conn. and London: Yale University Press, 2002), p. 162.

[83] BBC Monitoring, *Inside Central Asia* 294 (27 September–3 October 1999).

[84] Ferghana Valley Working Group, *Calming the Ferghana Valley: Development and Dialogue in the Heart of Central Asia. Report of the Ferghana Valley Working Group* (New York: Century Foundation Press, 1999), p. 38.

[85] Khulkar Yusupov, 'Vyidet li iz transportnogo tupika Ferganskaya dolina?', *Varorud* (Khujand), 27 May 2004.

[86] Author's interview with an Uzbek journalist, Andijan, November 2004.

[87] Yusupov, 'Vyidet li iz transportnogo tupika Ferganskaya dolina?'.

[88] The Uzbek authorities reconstructed the road through the Kuraminskii range (the Kamchik Pass, 2,267 metres above sea level) with Japanese funding.

[89] The Anzob tunnel is under construction and will be completed only in 2006.

[90] Travelling from Sogd in Tajikistan to Russia they have to cross 12 km of Uzbek territory in the Uzbek exclave of Sokh in Kyrgyzstan. In order to cross these 12 km an Uzbek visa is needed.
In December 2002 Uzbek officials began closing border crossing posts along the frontiers with Kyrgyzstan, Tajikistan, Turkmenistan and Kazakhstan as part of the government's efforts to make the Uzbek currency convertible. In early 2003 the border with Kyrgyzstan was practically sealed in order to stop Uzbek shoppers from taking hard currency out of the country, and tensions between the two states increased. Yusupov, 'Vyidet li iz transportnogo tupika Ferganskaya dolina?'.

[91] 'Uzbek border row introduces new element of tension in Central Asia', Eurasianet, 27 January 2003,
http://www.eurasianet.org/departments/business/articles/eav012703.shtml.

[92] In summer 2004 the Tajik paper *Odamu olam* [The Man and the World] published an open letter to President Rakhmonov asking him to resolve the question of joining territories of the Uzbek Surkhandarya region up with Tajikistan. The authors referred to an article published in the newspaper *Turkestanskie vedomosti* which stated that before incorporation into the USSR the Hissar state consisted of ten fiefdoms—Guzar, Sherabad, Baisun, Deanu, Yurchi, Khisor, Balzhuvan, Kulyab, Kurgan-Tyube and Kabadien. After the formation of the USSR the Samarkand, Bukhara, Surkhandarya and Kashkadarinskii regions joined Uzbekistan. The authors called as a first step for the Baisuntskii district to be transferred to Tajikistan. 'Umedoman az shumost', *Odamu olam* 2004, quoted by Sukhrob Ubaidulloyev, '"Medbezhya usluga" baisuntsam ne nuzhna', centrasia.ru web site, 10 August 2004, http://www.CentrAsia.Ru/newsA.php4?st=1092083460.

[93] Tajikistan has unofficial claims on Kyrgyzstan—specifically to the Batken region—demanding land corridors to the Tajik exclaves of Varukh and Qalacha close to the Tajik city of Isfara.

[94] Stuart Horsman, 'Water in Central Asia: regional cooperation or conflict?', in Allison and Jonson (eds), *Central Asian Security: The New International Context*.

[95] 'Hanging separately', *The Economist*, 26 July 2003.

[96] BBC Monitoring, *Inside Central Asia* 394 (24–30 September 2001).

[97] According to the Tajik Ministry of the Economy and Trade, the volume of exports and imports fell because of the introduction by Kazakhstan and Uzbekistan of restrictions on the movement of Tajik traffic through their territory. *Biznes i politika*, 15 March 2002.

[98] BBC Monitoring, *Inside Central Asia* 394 (24–30 September 2001).

[99] Chairman of the State Border Protection Committee of Tajikistan Saidanvar Kamolov, Dushanbe, 2002. As reported, most of those killed were from the Asht, Shahriston, Isfara and Penjikent districts of Sogd province.

[100] Asia-Plus, 13 February 2002.

[101] Iskandar Asadullaev, 'O kornyakh terrorizma', *Biznes i politika*, 1 March 2002, pp. 1–2.

[102] Asia-Plus, 31 July 2002.

[103] BBC Monitoring, *Inside Central Asia* 446 (30 September–6 October 2002, online version).

[104] Asia-Plus, 27 August 2002.

[105] BBC Monitoring, *Inside Central Asia*, 27 June 2004.

[106] An Uzbek visa could be applied for only at the Uzbek embassy in Dushanbe. 'Teper grazhdanam RT poezdom v Rossiyu bez transitnoi vizy RU ne popast'', Asia-Plus, 26 October 2004.

[107] Of Tajikistan's total exports of electricity in 2003, of 1 billion kWh, 550 million went to Uzbekistan, 108 million to Kyrgyzstan, 170 million to Kazakhstan, and 188 million to Russia. Asia-Plus, 15 December 2003.

[108] Asia-Plus, 15 December 2003.

[109] Asia-Plus, 15 December 2003.

[110] ITAR-TASS, 21 February 2004.

[111] Albert Valentinov, *Rossiiskaya gazeta*, 17 September 2003. The members of Eurasian Economic Community were the six countries which were also members of the Collective Security Treaty Organization.

[112] Avesta, 23 September 2004. Anatolii Chubais, director of RAO UES, stated: 'We have so far not received electricity from Tajikistan but this is not because of our Tajik partners. There is a problem with the transit across the territory of Tajikistan's neighbours, which has not yet been solved'. 'Uzbekistan otkazal Tadzhikistanu v tranzite elektroenergii cherez svoyu territoriyu', Fergana.ru web site, 21 September 2004,
http://www.fergana.ru/detail.php?id=258184583807.66,2132,8493089&code _phrase=%D2%E0%E4%E6%E8%EA%E8%F1%F2%E0%ED.

[113] Avesta, 23 February 2005.

[114] 'Viktoriya Panfilova, 'Rossiya mozhet poteryat' milliony dollarov', *Nezavisimaya gazeta*, 22 September 2004, p. 5.

[115] 'Uzbek–Tajik–Asian Bank agreement to help implement power supply project', BBC Monitoring, 17 March 2004.

[116] Tajik Television first channel, Dushanbe, 22 March 2004, 1530 GMT (in Tajik)/BBC Monitoring, 23 March 2004.

[117] 'Tajik road builders complete alternative north–south route', *Tajikistan Daily Digest*, 9 December 2003.

[118] Igor Rotar, 'Uzbekistan: varying availability of adult religious education', F18News, 23 November 2004, http://www.forum18.org/Archive.

[119] S. Neil MacFarlane, 'The United States and regionalism in Central Asia', *International Affairs* 80/3 (May 2004), pp. 447–61.

## Chapter 6

### EFFORTS TO STRENGTHEN THE REGIME

[1] Interview with the author in Dushanbe, June 2005.

[2] Martha Brill Olcott, 'Shifting sands in Central Asia?', *Helsinki Monitor* 1 (2003).

[3] These appointments are to be confirmed by the local parliaments but in reality the parliaments always accept the president's candidates. The level of local government (*jamoat*) falls outside the state system, and the chairman of the city council is elected by the local councils (*mahalla*) but confirmed by the *hukumat* on the higher administrative level. The members of the 356 *jamoats* are paid by the state but not considered part of the state structures. A *jamoat* normally covers between two and five villages, and consists of about 25 *mahalla* leaders (a *mahalla* is the council for one village or one street in the city).

[4] Kathleen Collins, 'Clans, pacts, and politics in Central Asia', *Journal of Democracy* 13/3 (2002), pp. 137–52.

[5] Hermine De Soto, Sabine Beddies and Svetlana Sharipova, 'Social dimensions of regional differences in Tajikistan' (draft Concept Paper), Social Development Unit, ECSS, World Bank, 6 April 2004.

[6] Saodat Olimova, 'Vospriyatie yavleniya "regionalizm" osnovnymi politicheskimi salami v Tadzhikistane', in Luigi Martino (ed), *Tadzhikistan: optimizatsiya otnoshenii mezhdu tsentrom i regionam: vyzovy i vozmozhnosti* (Geneva: CIMERA, January 2004), pp. 104–105.

[7] Olimova, 'Vospriyatie yavleniya "regionalizm" osnovnymi politicheskimi salami v Tadzhikistane'.

[8] These appointments are to be confirmed by the parliament. It is also worth noting that the president appoints all members of the Central Election Committee, to be confirmed by the lower chamber.

[9] His call was made on 31 March. *Narodnaya gazeta* (the official newspaper of the Tajik government) 23–24 (2002). At the same time he stated that the threat to domestic stability comes from the underdeveloped state of the economy and the difficult socio-economic conditions in which the majority of the population live.

[10] Asia-Plus, 10 September 2001.

[11] Author's interview in Dushanbe, June 2004. See also T. Kasimova, 'Tadzhikistan: aresty islamistov na fone "verkhuechnogo skandala"', 26 August 2004, http://www.centrasia.ru/news.php4?CR=4.

[12] BBC Monitoring, *Inside Central Asia* 434 (8–14 July 2002).

[13] Asia-Plus, 12 July 2002.

[14] BBC Monitoring, *Inside Central Asia* 436 (22–28 July 2002).

[15] BBC Monitoring, *Inside Central Asia* 434 (8–14 July 2002). The Wahhabites are a reformist Saudi Arabian sect of which the origins are in the 18th century.

[16] *Eurasia Insight*, 29 August 2002, http://www.eurasianet.com.

[17] BBC Monitoring, *Inside Central Asia* 436 (22–28 July 2002).

[18] On Hizb-ut-Tahrir see also chapter 7.

[19] BBC Monitoring, *Inside Central Asia* 437 (29 July–4 August 2002).

[20] See also the reporting by the Forum 18 web site (Oslo), http://www.forum18org/Archive.php?article_id=118.

[21] *Ozodi va inkishof* 17 May 2002. The author, Zarif Gulomov, was introduced to the readers as a lawyer and a member of the Union of Journalists working in the presidential apparatus.

[22] The deputy chairman of the ruling party PDP commented that it would be premature to discuss the issue of extending the mandate of the president; he did not, however, rule out the question altogether.

[23] Radio Free Europe/Radio Liberty (RFE/RL), *Central Asia Report* 3/22 (26 June 2003).

[24] *RFE/RL Central Asia Report* 3/21 (20 June 2003). See also Kambiz Arman, 'Islamic party reduces tension in Tajikistan by moderating stance on upcoming referendum', *Eurasia Insight*, 12 June 2003.

[25] *RFE/RL Central Asia Report* 4/3 (19 January 2004).

[26] International Crisis Group (ICG), 'Tajikistan's politics: confrontation or consolidation?', ICG, Dushanbe and Brussels, 19 May 2004.

[27] Said Abdullo Nuri, Interview in *Kyrgyzstan segodnya* 9/17 (2004), http://www.CentrAsia.ru/newsA.php4?st=1094791020.

[28] Marash Mamadshoev, 'Padenie Shevardnadze: Revolyutsiya "roz" ili revolyutsiya rozog?', Asia-Plus, 48 (27 November 2003).

[29] *RFE/RL Central Asia Report* 3/40 (28 November 2003).

[30] 'Gruzinskie sobytiya vesma vstrevozhili prezidenta Tadzhikistana Rakhmonova', *Kommersant (Mezhdunarodnyi otdel)*, 2 December 2003.

[31] Reported by the Russian newspaper *Kommersant*.

[32] Salamsho Muhabbatov (nickname General Salam) led an armed group in Vanj in Gorno-Badakshan, and was appointed UTO commander there in 1994. In contrast to Iskandarov he was not politically active. In late spring 2004 he was appointed head of the Tajik tourism agency, Tadzhikturizm.

[33] 'Prezident Tadzhikistana amnistiruet osuzhdennykh soratnikov G. Mirzoeva i Ya. Salimova', Centrasia, 13 August 2004, http://www.centrasia.ru&news.php4?st=1092406260 (source: Reuter).

[34] Lidia Isamova and Zafar Abdullaev, 'Tajikistan: out with the Old Guard', http://www.iwpr.net/index.pl?archive/rca/rca_200401_262_3_eng.txt.

[35] 'M. Iskandarov: Vazhen otkrytyi sud nad Mirzoevym (intervyu)', Centrasia 31 August 2004 http://www.centrasia.ru&news.php4?st=1093923360 (source: *Vremya novostei* 156 (31 August 2004).

[36] Two other issues were whether the numerous road posts of the traffic police (GAI), which Iskandarov claimed hindered the traffic and took bribes, would be removed, and guarantees for the independent press.

[37] In the Majlisi Milli, a clear majority of those elected or appointed hold high posts in the regional *hukumat* (government) and its administration. As state

officials they report to the president. It should also be mentioned that the president appoints all chairmen of the regional and district *hukumats*. Previous presidents also have the right to have a seat in the chamber (at present there is only one former president). Thus, in 2002 over 80 per cent of the deputies of the upper chamber were employees of the local executive branch constitute.

[38] Lena Jonson, 'The OSCE Long-Term Mission to Tajikistan', in *OSCE Yearbook 2002* (Baden-Baden: Nomos Verlagsgesellschaft, 2002).

[39] Shukur Sultanov, 'Politicheskie partii i vlast', *Varorud* 29/117 (21 June 2004).

[40] Umed Babakhanov and Zebo Tajibayeva, 'Swan, crayfish and pike', Asia-Plus, 13 May 2004.

[41] BBC Monitoring, *Inside Central Asia*, 11 July 2004.

[42] BBC Monitoring, *Inside Central Asia*, 18 July 2004.

[43] It was reduced for the registration of candidates for the party list and for the candidates for the single-member electoral districts. The deposit was to be returned to parties which passed the 5 per cent threshold.

[44] Interview with the author in Dushanbe, June 2004.

[45] 'V Dushanbe gotovyatsya k vyboram', *Centrasia*, 6 September 2004, http://www.centrasia.ru&newsa.php4st=1094437080.

[46] He was arrested in dramatic circumstances by security personnel who threw him to the floor, handcuffed him and put a sack over his head. T. Dikaev, 'Tyazhkaya dolya tadzhikskikh generalov: Mirzoevu odeli na golovu pylnyi meshok', *Centrasia*, 30 August 2004, http://www.centrasia.ru&newsa.php4st=1093830540 (source TRIBUNE-uz).

[47] 'Arrest of Tajikistan's drug tsar stirs political tension in Dushanbe', *Eurasia Insight*, 9 August 2004, http://www.eurasianet.org.

[48] *Vremya novostei* 141 (10 August 2004), http://www.CentrAsia.Ru/newsA.php4?st=109210896.

[49] Hikmatullo Saifullozoda of the IRP, in BBC Monitoring, *Inside Central Asia*, 8 August 2004.

[50] Arkadii Dubnov, 'V Tadzhikistane v eti dni proizkhodyat sobytiya, kotorye mogut vzorvat stabilnost'', obretennuyu stranoi', *Vremya novostei*, 29 January 2004, p. 5.

[51] 'M. Iskandarov: Vazhen otkrytyi sud nad Mirzoevym (intervyu)'.

[52] Rakhmonov at the 80th anniversary of the Tajik Office of Prosecutors on 24 December 2004. BBC Monitoring, *Inside Central Asia*, 2 January 2005.

[53] BBC Monitoring, *Inside Central Asia*, 12 December 2004. He was accused of terrorism, banditry and attempted murder. Avesta, 11 December 2004.

[54] According to the prosecutor-general. Avesta, 13 December 2004.

[55] 'M. Iskandarov budet isklyuchen iz partiinogo spiska', Asia-Plus, 12 January 2005.

[56] 'Reuter: Soratnika prezidenta Tadzhikistana obvinyayut v ubiistve', 7 August 2004, http://www.CentrAsia.Ru/newsA.php4?st=1091868060.

[57] Marat Mamadshoev, 'A Q&A with Ghaffor Mirzoev', Asia-Plus, 10 July 2003.

[58] In January 2005, among others, the deputy prime minister, the commander of the internal troops, the first deputy head of the Anti-Drug Agency, the deputy interior minister and the head of the traffic police were moved. The

official reason announced was usually bad performance, misconduct, or even illegal activities. It is difficult to tell how far this was true or whether it was only a pretext for getting rid of opponents or rivals. BBC Monitoring, *Inside Central Asia*, 9 January 2005.

⁵⁹ 'Novaya era v kadrovoi politike?', Avesta, 7 1 (4–9 January 2005).

⁶⁰ Koimdodov was one of the most experienced politicians from the 1992 session of the Supreme Soviet, when Rakhmonov was appointed head of state. In 1992–2000 he was deputy chairman of the parliament. In 2000 he became deputy prime minister with responsibility for agriculture. He represented the interests of Gorno-Badakhshan in the government. 'Novaya era v kadrovoi politike?', Avesta, 7 1 (4–9 January 2005).

⁶¹ *RFE/RL Newsline* 234 (15 December 2003). The new appointee is Makhmadnazar Salikhov, formerly chairman of Tajikistan's Justice Council. He served as head of the presidential administration in 1998–2000.

⁶² Two other people who had not come under persecution but were expected to should be mentioned here—Sukhrob Kasymov and Mirzo Ziyo. Kasymov was a former commander of the People's Front and the head of a Special Forces brigade of the Interior Ministry. Without any military training (he had trained in Moscow to be a educationalist working with children), Kasymov had studied the martial arts and set up a karate school. In 1992 when the civil war erupted he sided with the authorities, organized a volunteer detachment of 55 men in Dushanbe, and became a commander of an OMON (special forces) detachment (which was later transformed). Kasymov's troops were a well-trained and disciplined force loyal to Rakhmonov. It was used for mountain warfare in fighting with the opposition before the 1997 General Peace Agreement, and against warlords like the Sanginov brothers in 2001. In December 2003 Kasymov's brigade included four battalions, five companies, a helicopter detachment, and some special units at a base 80 km from Dushanbe. Kasymov has always been considered independent-minded and not always predictable. For several years there were rumours that the president would soon clamp down on him, but nothing of the kind happened, and in the meantime Kasymov maintained control of his territory in Varzob, which in the post-war period he developed into an area for luxury villas and recreation on the outskirts of Dushanbe.

Mirzo Ziyo was a former UTO commander who had become a minister for emergency situations in Rakhmonov's government. He was in charge of the paramilitary troops of the ministry, which were not included in the Tajik military forces. They were regarded as a professional force consisting mainly of former fighters of the opposition who were integrated after the General Peace Agreement. During the civil war Ziyo had Juma Namangani among his men, and his enemies never forgave him for this. His contacts with people who became leaders of the IMU helped him to broker a deal in 1999 and 2000 and have IMU fighters leave Tajik territory for Afghanistan. He was well integrated in society, and no longer took part in politics, yet he could not be sure that his position was unassailable.

⁶³ The Taraqqiyot Party had repeatedly been denied registration. It was led by Sulton Kuvvatov and was founded in May 2001 on the basis of the so-called Tehran faction of the Democratic Party of Tajikistan. Kuvvatov was a former

close associate of Rakhmonov and had been chairman of the Tax Committee before 1996. He was denied registration as a candidate for the presidency in 1999, and in the 2000 parliamentary elections his victory in one constituency was annulled. For three years he had tried without result to register the party. In March 2003 the three deputy chairmen of the party went on hunger strike. They published the text of an open letter to Rakhmonov, the prosecutor general, the justice minister, and the UN and OSCE missions. Kuvvatov stated that he would use all legitimate means to fight this tyranny. 'We will find an adequate answer if weapons are used against us', he is reported to have said (Arkadii Dubnov, [President of Tajikistan personally decides which party should be granted registration and which denied], *Vremya Novostei* (Moscow), 18 March 2004, p. 6). In the late summer of 2004 the Taraqqiyot Party's situation deteriorated. In early August Kuvvatov warned publicly that he intended to take Taraqqiyot's case to the International Court of Justice. In response, on 25 August the state authorities searched the party's offices for documents, and two days later took a deputy chairman for interrogation. T. Diakev, 'Put' v Gaagu: cherez podval MB Tadzhikistana? Priklyucheniya lidera partii "Tarrakiet" S. Kuvvatova', 13 September 2004, http://www.Centrasia.ru.

64 Avesta, 7 1 (4–9 January 2005).

65 ITAR-TASS, 3 December 2003/BBC Monitoring, 3 December 2003. In 2003, 421 companies were privatized, which was 269 more than in 2002. From the beginning of privatization in 1991 up to May 2004, 7,501 companies had been sold, most of which were small. In 2004, 110 medium-sized and large companies were to be privatized. 'Po itogam privatizatsii v 2003 godu v Tadzhikistane byl prodan 421 objekt, chto na 269 bol'she, chem. v 2002', Asia-Plus web site, http://www.asiaplus.tajik.net/nr/m/2.htm.

66 The transmission of power will be performed by the National Power Lines of Tajikistan open joint-stock company, which will combine all the high-voltage lines and substations. ITAR-TASS, Moscow, 3 December 2003, 1002 GMT (in Russian)/BBC Monitoring, 3 December 2003.

67 Avesta, 8 December 2004. It was rumoured that Ubaidulloyev, the mayor of Dushanbe, was helping Russian aluminium oligarch Oleg Deripaska to get control over part of the Tajik aluminium factory. Ubaidulloyev had long been regarded as a major challenger to Rakhmonov, and many believed that he had secret plans to stand in the presidential elections. An attempt was made on his life in 2000, which injured him, but he continued his work as previously. He was firmly in the saddle and had close contacts with Russia. On the investments in aluminium by Deripaska and RusAl, see chapter 4.

68 *Tajikistan: Country Report, March 2004* (London: Economist Intelligence Unit, 2004), p. 13.

69 Rakhmonov dismissed the management of the aluminium factory and the Tajik company Anzol. Following an announcement by the Tajik prosecutor-general that legal procedures were to start against these people for financial misconduct, they fled the country.

70 The chairman of the Central Election Committee in Asia-Plus, 2 March 2005.

71 *Izvestiya*, 6 April 2005.

[72] As reported by a senior European diplomat and based on published statements in Tajik news agencies. On 2 June 2005 the events in Andijan were discussed at a meeting of the Shanghai Cooperation Organization (of the secretaries of the member states' national security councils) in Astana.

## Chapter 7

### THE DYNAMICS OF THE DOMESTIC SCENE

[1] *Tajikistan: Country Report 2005* (London: Economist Intelligence Unit, 2005), p. 10.

[2] International Monetary Fund, *Republic of Tajikistan: Poverty Reduction Strategy Paper Progress Report*, IMF Country Report 04/280 (August 2004), p. 8, http://www.imf.org/external/pubs/ft/scr/2004/cr04280.pdf.

[3] Saodat Olimova, 'Political parties in Tajikistan: facts, figures, analysis' (manuscript prepared by the Sharq independent research institute for IFES (formerly the International Foundation for Election Systems), Dushanbe 2005).

[4] Olimova, 'Political parties in Tajikistan: facts, figures, analysis'.

[5] Olimova, 'Political parties in Tajikistan: facts, figures, analysis'.

[6] Nauchno-Issledovatelskii Tsentr Sharq, *Opros obshchestvennogo mneniya v Tadzhikistane (3–16 maya 2004 g.)* (Dushanbe: Nauchno-Issledovatelskii Tsentr Sharq, 2004).

[7] Quoted by Olimova, 'Political parties in Tajikistan: facts, figures, analysis'.

[8] Olimova, 'Political parties in Tajikistan: facts, figures, analysis'.

[9] Saodat Olimova, 'Political Islam and conflict in Tajikistan', in Lena Jonson and Murad Esenov (eds), *Political Islam and Conflicts in Russia and Central Asia* (Stockholm: Swedish Institute of International Afffairs, 1999); and Shirin Akiner, *Tajikistan: Disintegration or Reconciliation?* (London: Royal Institute of International Affairs, 2001).

[10] Saodat Olimova, 'Dukhovnye lidery v sovremennom musul'manskom obshchestve Tsentral'noi Azii: Opyt Tadzhikistana', in *Musul'manskie lidery: sotsial'naya rol' i avtoritet* (Dushanbe: Nauchno-issledovatelskii Tsentr Sharq i Fond im. Fridrikha Eberta, 2003), p. 31.

[11] Olimova, 'Political parties in Tajikistan: facts, figures, analysis'.

[12] 'Nasha partiya ne yavlyaetsya religioznoi', Interview with Kabiri in *Varorud* 49/85 (10 December 2003).

[13] Sulton Khamadov, interviewed in Marat Mamadshoyev, 'Tajikistan's media market: struggle starts?', Asia-Plus, 29 January 2004, http://www.asiaplus.tajik.net/anal2004.htm#.

[14] Interview with Iskandarov, Asia-Plus, 29 April 2004.

[15] Umed Babakhanov and Zebo Tajibayeva, 'Swan, crayfish and pike', Asia-Plus, 13 May 2004.

[16] Avesta, 19 December 2004.

[17] Avesta, 12 January 2005.

[18] Asia-Plus, 7 March 2005.

[19] Asia-Plus, 3 May 2005.

20 Avesta, 1 March 2005.

21 BBC Monitoring, *Inside Central Asia* 27 (March 2005).

22 Avesta, 28 March 2005.

23 Olimova, 'Political Islam and conflict in Tajikistan', p. 125.

24 Bakhtiyor Babajanov, 'Dukchi Ishan und der Aufstand von Andizan 1898', in Anke von Kugelgen, Michael Kemper and Allen J. Frank, *Muslim Culture in Russia and Central Asia from the 18th to the Early 20th Centuries, Vol. 2* (Berlin: Klaus Schwarz Verlag, 1998), pp. 167–91; Hélène Carrère d'Encausse, *Islam and the Russian Empire: Reform and Revolution in Central Asia* (London: I. B. Tauris, 1988), pp. 168–69; Richard Pierce, *Russian Central Asia 1867–1917: A Study in Colonial Rule* (Berkeley, Calif. and Los Angeles, Calif.: University of California Press, 1960), pp. 226–32; and Shoshana Keller, *To Moscow, Not Mecca: The Soviet Campaign Against Islam in Central Asia, 1917–1941* (Westport, Conn. and London: Praeger, 2001), p. 17.

25 Keller, *To Moscow, Not Mecca*, p. 62.

26 Keller, *To Moscow, Not Mecca*, pp. 189–93.

27 Waqf is property given as endowments to mosques, schools, hospitals and so on.

28 Keller, *To Moscow, Not Mecca*, pp. 247–48.

29 Carrère d'Encausse, *Islam and the Russian Empire: Reform and Revolution in Central Asia*.

30 Among those eliminated were Abdurrauf Fitrat (killed 1938), Munzim Fayzullo Khjayev (1938) and Abduqadir Muhiddinov (1938). Interview with Abdullo Hakim Rahnamo by Jean-François Mayer, Religioscope, 25 April 2004, http://www.religion.info.

31 Interview with Abdullo Hakim Rahnamo by Jean-François Mayer.

32 Aleksei Malashenko, 'Islam and politics in Central Asian states', in Jonson and Esenov (eds), *Political Islam and Conflicts in Russia and Central Asia*.

33 Muzaffar Olimov and Saidanvar Shokhumorov, 'Mukhammadzhan Khindustani: zhizn' i deyatelnost'', in *Musul'manskie lidery: sotsial'naya rol' i avtoritet*, pp. 83–101.

34 Olimova, 'Dukhovnye lidery v sovremennom musul'manskom obshchestve Tsentral'noi Azii: Opyt Tadzhikistana', p. 17.

35 Ashirbek Muminov, 'Traditsionnye i sovremennye religiozno-teologicheskie shkoly v Tsentral'noi Azii', *Tsentral'naya Aziya i Kavkaz* 4/5 (1999); and Bakhtiar Babadzhanov, 'Islam in Uzbekistan: from the struggle for "religious purity" to political activism', in Boris Rumer (ed.), *Central Asia: A Gathering Storm?* (New York and London: M. E. Sharpe, 2002), p. 303.

36 The Wahhabites are a reformist Saudi Arabian sect of which the origins are in the 18th century.

37 Babadzhanov, 'Islam in Uzbekistan', p. 311.

38 Its three main functions are to control the activities of religious organizations, to coordinate the work of all the state authorities involved in controlling religious activities, and to inform ministries and the state institutions about developments in the field. Under the committee there is a Coordinating Consultative Council of 38 leading representatives of the different religious communities active in Tajikistan. The purpose of the council, which was

founded in April 2001, was to encourage religious tolerance between different confessions.

[39] Said Akhmedov (chairman of the State Committee on Religious Affairs), *Biznes i politika*, 27 September 2001.

[40] To register a *pyatikratnyi* mosque there has to be a request from at least ten people, while a Friday mosque can be registered as a *jomea* only in areas where at least 15,000 people live. There is no charge for registering mosques. In November 2003 it was reported that a draft of a new law on religion was under preparation, which might increase the number of requests from believers required for registering a *pyatikratnyi* mosque from ten to 70. See Igor Rotar, 'Tajikistan: religious freedom survey, November 2003', F18News, 20 November 2003, http://www.forum18.org/Archive.php?article_id=190.

[41] Ghclib Goibov, 'Stroitel'stvo svetskogo kharaktera obshchestva i ustanovlenie otnosheniya religioznoi terpimosti v Tadzhikistane', in Organization for Security and. Co-operation in Europe (OSCE), Mission to Tajikistan, *Religioznyi ekstremizm v Tsentral'noi Azii: Problemy i perspektivy. Materialy konferentsii, Dushanbe, 25 aprelya 2002* (Dushanbe: OSCE Mission to Tajikistan, 2002).

[42] 'Speech to the intelligentsia' of 20 March 2002.

[43] For example, in Leninskii district south of Dushanbe the number of mosques was reduced from *c.* 225 to 156. Where previously there had been one mosque for each of 13 villages in Faizabad, there were now three for all 13.

[44] According to Said Akhmedov, chairman of the State Committee on Religious Affairs, 'a total of some 250 mosques and 20 religious schools would undergo appraisal. Imams (pontiffs), khatibs (preachers), muezzins (who call the people to prayer) and lecturers will sit examinations on the canons of Islam, rituals, teaching methods and other subjects. The appraisal will be conducted by the Council of Ulemas (religious scholars) jointly with the Committee on Religious Affairs'. Asia-Plus, 6 August 2002/BBC Monitoring, *Inside Central Asia* 438 (August 2002).

[45] Interview by the author, Dushanbe, February 2002. During the three first months of 2005 the authorities discovered 26 non-registered mosques. Avesta, 26 April 2005. By April 2005 there were altogether 228 Friday mosques, 2,860 *pyatikratnye*, 18 madrasas, and one Islamic university in the country. Avesta, 26 April 2005.

[46] Hizb-ut-Tahrir was severely criticized by the IRP. Hodji Akhbar Turajonzoda, a former leader of the Islamic flank of the UTO and currently first deputy prime minister of Tajikistan, published a lengthy article in early summer 2004 which was followed up by interviews later during the year. He argued that Hizb-ut-Tahrir was no Islamic party and that its interpretations of religious affairs are far from the Koran, and criticized its political programme and approach. Akhbar Turajonzoda, 'Dukhovnoe nevezhestvo naseleniya sposobstvuet rosru ekstremizma v respublikakh Srednei Azii', *Nezavisimaya gazeta*/Asia-Plus, 4 August 2004.

[47] Nadezhda Kerovkova, 'Spiski terroristov', *Smysl*, 28 February 2003, pp. 34–35.

[48] See e.g. three Hizb-ut-Tahrir documents, 'The American campaign to suppress Islam'; 'Dangerous concepts to attack Islam and consolidate Western

culture'; and 'The system of Islam' on the web site of Hizb-ut-Tahrir, http://www.hizb-ut-tahrir.org.

[49] Compare the organizational structures of the Bolshevik Party in Tsarist Russia, as well as the Front National de Libération (FNL) in Algeria against French colonial rule.

[50] Suha Taji-Farouki, *A Fundamental Quest: Hizb-al-Tahrir and the search for the Islamic Caliphate* (London: Grey Seal, 1996), pp. 76–113.

[51] Kurbonali Mukhabbatov, 'Religiozno-oppozitsionnye gruppy v Tadzhikistane: Hizb-ut-Tahrir', in Organization for Security and Co-operation in Europe (OSCE), Mission to Tajikistan, *Religioznyi ekstremizm v Tsentral'noi Azii: Problemy i perspektivy*. They were mainly sentenced under the articles in the Criminal Law that cover attempts to seize power by force, overthrow of the constitutional system, and stirring up national and religious dissent.

[52] BBC Monitoring, *Inside Central Asia* 443 (9–15 September 2002). According to the prosecutor of the Sogd region, Kurbonali Mukhabbatov, up to April 2002, 108 members had been sentenced in the northern Sogd region alone. Mukhabbatov, 'Religiozno-oppozitsionnye gruppy v Tadzhikistane: Hizb-ut-Tahrir'.

[53] According to the Tajik Interior Ministry, over 100 alleged members of the organization were arrested in 2004, and 50 had been jailed. BBC Monitoring, *Inside Central Asia*, 9 January 2005.

[54] One leader, an imam, was arrested for the murder of a local businessman, and another member for the murder of a head of the Baptist community in the Isfara district. T. Kasimova, 'Tadzhikistan: aresty islamistov na fone "verkhushechnogo skandala". Politicheskaya pereorientatsiya soprovozhdaetsya gromkimi sudebnymi protsessami', 26 August 2004,
http://www.centrasia.ru/news.php4?CR=4.

[55] Turajonzoda, 'Dukhovnoe nevezhestvo naseleniya sposobstvuet rostu ekstremizma v respublikakh Srednei Azii'.

[56] Interview with Rahnamo Rakhmullo, Dushanbe, June 2004.

[57] Martha Brill Olcott, 'Common legacies and conflicts', in Roy Allison and Lena Jonson (eds), *Central Asian Security: The New International Context* (London and Washington, DC: Royal Institute of International Affairs and Brookings Institution Press, 2001), p. 38.

[58] Emomali Rakhmonov, *The Tajiks in the Mirror of History, Vol. 1. From the Aryans to the Samanids* (London: River Editions Ltd, Great Britain, no year), p. 101.

[59] Rakhmonov, *The Tajiks in the Mirror of History*, p. 41. See chapter 2. It is, however, also stressed that the Avesta is the 'spiritual product of a people that used to be an integral part of a single Indo-European nation' (p. 34).

[60] Saodat Olimova, 'Vospriyatie yavleniya "regionalizm" osnovnymi politicheskimi i sotsial'nymi silami v Tadzhikistane', in Luigi de Martino (ed.), *Tadzhikistan: optimizatsiya otnoshenii mezhdu tsentrom i regionami. Vyzovy i vozmozhnosti* (Geneva: CIMERA, January 2004), pp. 104–105.

[61] Rakhmonov, *The Tajiks in the Mirror of History*, p. 31.

[62] Rakhmonov, *The Tajiks in the Mirror of History*, p. 31.

[63] See for example Rakhim Masov, *Istoriya topornogo razdeleniya* (Dushanbe: 'Irfon', 1991); Rakhim Masov, *'Kriticheskaya' lozh' po zakazu* (Dushanbe, 2001);

Rakhim Masov, *Tadzhiki: vytesnenie i assimilatsiya* (Dushanbe, 2003); Khaknazar Nazarov, *K istorii proiskhozhdeniya i rasseleniya plemen i narodov Tsentral'noi Azii* (Dushanbe, 2004); and Sokhib Tabarov, *Spor 'derevenskogo intelligenta' s 'gorodskim intelligentom'* (Dushanbe, 2004).

[64] Masov, *Tadzhiki: vytesnenie i assimilatsiya.*

[65] Nazarov, *K istorii proiskhozhdeniya i rasseleniya plemen i narodov Tsentral'noi Azii*, p. 4.

[66] Article in the Tajik republican paper *Odamu olam (Chelovek i mir)* as reported by S. Ubaidulloyev, "'Medvedya usluga" baisuntsam ne nuzhna: Ob uzbeksko-tadzhikskom spore', 10 August 2004, http://www.centrasia.ru/news.php4?CR=4.

[67] In addition to Bukhara and Samarkand in Uzbekistan, which are historically and culturally Tajik cities with a mainly Tajik population, there are Tajiks all over the Samarkand region and in the Surkhandarya and Karshi regions in southern Uzbekistan.

[68] *Ezhegodnik Respubliki Tadzhikistana 2003* (Dushanbe: Gosudarstvennyi Komitet Statistiki Respubliki Tadzhikistan, 2003), p. 151.

[69] *Regiony Respubliki Tadzhikistana: Statisticheskii sbornik* (Dushanbe: Gosudarstvennyi Komitet Statistiki Respubliki Tadzhikistan, 2004), pp. 63–67.

[70] These are people's self-estimations. The figure for those who are competent in Russian was even lower, at 21.2 per cent. *Ezhegodnik Respubliki Tadzhikistan* (2003), p. 153.

[71] BBC Monitoring, *Inside Central Asia* 406 (17 December 2001–1 January 2002).

[72] Ghayur Qahhorov in *Biznes i politika* 6 (2002).

[73] BBC Monitoring, *Inside Central Asia*, 20 March 2004.

[74] See for example the Ministry of Communication as reported in Avesta, 27 October 2004.

[75] Asia-Plus, 30 September 2004.

[76] Saodat Olimova, 'Natsiona'lnye gosudarstva i etnicheskie territorii', in Martha Brill Olcott and Alexei Malashenko (eds), *Mnogomernye granitsy Tsentral'noi Azii* (Moscow: Carnegie Centre, 2000), electronic version, http://pubs.carnegie.ru/books/2000/04am.

[77] For example, in 2001 books in Tajik were removed from libraries and schools in Bukhara and Samarkand. *Europa World Yearbook 2003, Vol. II* (London and New York: Europa, 2003).

[78] 'Tajiks demonstrate in two cities against Uzbek policy', Tajikistan's *Daily News*, 24 November 2003, Eurasianet, http://www.eurasianet.org/resource/tajikistan/hypermail/200311/0022.shtml; and 'Inter-ethnic tension threatens fragile Tajik–Uzbek relations', *Eurasia Insight*, 14 February 2003, http://www.eurasianet.org.

## Chapter 8

### CONCLUSIONS

[1] Author's interview with Deputy Foreign Minister Abdunabi Sattorzoda in Dushanbe, June 2005.

[2] Maria Papadakis and Harvey Starr, 'Opportunity, willingness, and small states: the relationship between environment and foreign policy', in Charles F. Hermann, Charles W. Kegley and James N. Rosenau (eds), *New Directions in the Study of Foreign Policy* (Boston, Mass.: George Allen and Unwin, 1987), p. 426.

[3] 'RAO UES mozhet voiti v energosistemu Afganistana cherez Tadzhikistan', 29 September 2004, http://www.centran.ru/cgi-bin/index.pl?text_id=17186&all=yes.

[4] Theresa Sabonis-Helf, 'Power, influence and stability: the Unified Energy Systems of Russia (RAO UES) in the southern tier "'near abroad"', Paper prepared for the 2004 Central Eurasian Studies Society Fifth Annual Conference, Bloomington, Ind., 16–17 October 2004.

[5] 'Vstrecha prezidenta Rossiiskoi Federatsii s rukovodyashchim sostavom diplomaticheskoi sluzhby MID Rossii', *Diplomaticheskii vestnik* 2 (2001), p. 11.

[6] For more on this, see Lena Jonson, *Vladimir Putin and Central Asia: The Shaping of Russian Foreign Policy* (London and New York: I. B. Tauris, 2004).

[7] *Izvestiya*, 7 April 2005.

[8] BBC Monitoring, *Inside Central Asia* 10 April 2005.

[9] Avesta, 4 April 2005; and Radio Free Europe/Radio Liberty, *RFE/RL Newsline* 9/63 (5 April 2005), Part I.

[10] Viktoriya Panfilova and Vladimir Mukhin, 'Menyayu Vashington na Moskvu: Islam Karimov peresmotrel strategichskie prioritety', *Nezavisimaya gazeta*, 30 June 2005, p. 5; and Vladimir Mukhin, 'Karimov razzhilsya vertoletami i vodometami', *Nezavisimaya gazeta*, 5 July 2005.

[11] Interview in Dushanbe, June 2005.

[12] *Strategic Survey 2003/2004* (International Institute for Strategic Studies), London, 2004.

[13] Author's interview with the US ambassador in Dushanbe, June 2005.

[14] Nauchno-Issledovatelskii Tsentr Sharq, *Opros obshchestvennogo mneniya v Tadzhikistane (20 sentyabrya–3 oktyabrya 2004 g.)* (Dushanbe: Nauchno-Issledovatelskii tsentr Sharq, 2004), table 7b.

[15] See the volumes published from the Islam–Secular Power Dialogue Project initiated by Arne Seifert, discussing these relations. Anna Kreikemeyer and Arne C. Seifert (eds), *Zur Vereinbarkeit von politischem Islam und Sicherheit im OSZE-Raum: Dokumente eines islamisch-säkularen Dialogs in Tadschikistan* (Baden-Baden: Nomos Verlagsgesellschaft, 2002/2003).

[16] Research carried out by the Sharq Independent Research Institute (Dushanbe). See Saodat Olimova, 'Ob obshchestvennom vospriyatii umerennogo i radikal'nogo islama', in A. Seifert and Anna Kreikemeier (eds), *O sovmestimosti politicheskogo islama i bezopasnosti prostranstve OBSE* (Dushanbe: Sharki Ozod, 2003).

[17] Saodat Olimova, 'Political Islam and conflict in Central Asia', in Lena Jonson and Murad Esenov (eds), *Political Islam and Conflicts in Russia and Central Asia* (Stockholm: Swedish Institute of International Affairs, 1999).

[18] Michael Rywkin, 'Central Asia in the forefront of attention', *American Foreign Policy Interests* 24 (2002), p. 35.

[19] Said Abdullo Nuri, 'Nuzhna edinaya strategiya posledovatelei Islama', *Nachyot* (newspaper of the Tajik Islamic Revival Party) June 2004.

[20] Surveys are carried out regularly by the Sharq Independent Research Institute (Dushanbe), led by Prof. Muzaffar Olimov and Dr Saodat Olimova. See Nauchno-Issledovatelskii Tsentr Sharq, *Opros obshchestvennogo mneniya v Tadzhikistane (4–17 Dekabr 2003 g.)* (Dushanbe: Nauchno-Issledovatelskii Tsentr Sharq, 2003; *Opros obshchestvennogo mneniya v Tadzhikistane (3–16 maya 2004 g.)* (Dushanbe: Nauchno-Issledovatelskii Tsentr Sharq, 2004); and *Opros obshchestvennogo mneniya v Tadzhikistane (mai 2005 g.)* (Dushanbe: Nauchno-Issledovatelskii Tsentr Sharq, 2005).

[21] Nauchno-Issledovatelskii Tsentr Sharq, *Opros obshchestvennogo mneniya v Tadzhikistane (3–16 maya 2004 g.)*, p. 10.

[22] Nauchno-Issledovatelskii Tsentr Sharq, *Opros obshchestvennogo mneniya v Tadzhikistane (mai 2005 g.)*.

[23] All figures are from the opinion surveys carried out by the Sharq Independent Research Institute as mentioned above, *Opros obshchestvennogo mneniya v Tadzhikistane*.

[24] Lena Jonson, 'Central Asia and the "Greater Middle East"', in Bo Hult, Tomas Ries, Jan Mörtberg and Johanna Sandefelt (eds), *Strategic Yearbook 2005: The Wider Middle East* (Stockholm: Swedish National War College, 2005).

[25] See Muhabbat Jurayeva, 'The fundamental nature of Hezb-e Tahrir', *Sughd* 1 September 2004, p. 2/BBC Monitoring Service 15 September 2004. See also Hodji Akhbar Turajondoza, 'Dukhovnoe nevezhestvo naseleniya sposobstvuet rostu ekstremizma v respublikakh Srednei Azii', *Nezavisimaya gazeta*/Asia-Plus, 4 September 2004.

[26] Hodji Akhbar Turajondoza, 'Hizb-ut-Tahrir in the name of Islam—against Islam', *Tojikiston* (Dushanbe), 8 May 2004. See also reporting in BBC Monitoring Service, 9 May 2004 ('Top Tajik official says Hezb-e Tahrir created to disrepute Islam').

[27] Rashid Khalidi, *Resurrecting Empire: Western Footprints and America's Perilous Path in the Middle East* (Boston, Mass.: Beacon Press, 2004), p. 35.

[28] Nauchno-Issledovatelskii Tsentr Sharq, *Opros obshchestvennogo mneniya v Tadzhikistane (3–16 maya 2004 g.)*.

[29] Fakhriddin Kholbek, 'Persidskii romb: Vozmozhen li v blizhaishem budushchem soyuz trekh iranskikh gosudarstv—Irana, Afghanistana i Tadzhikistana?', *Asia-Plus* 23 (9 June 2005), p. 7.

[30] ROMIR Monitoring, reported by Asia-Plus, 28 January 2005.

# BIBLIOGRAPHY AND FURTHER READING

## Political and International Relations Theory

Bauwens, Werner, Armand Clesse and Olav Knudsen (eds), *Small States and the Security Challenge in the New Europe* (London and Washington, DC: Brassey's, 1996)

Buzan, Barry, *People, States and Fear.* 2nd edn (New York and London: Harvester Wheatsheaf, 1991)

— and Ole Waever, *Regions and Powers: The Structure of International Security* (Cambridge: Cambridge University Press, 2003)

—, Ole Waever and Jaap de Wilde, *Security: A New Framework for Analysis* (Boulder, Colo.: Lynne Rienner, 1998)

Hermann, Charles, 'Changing courses: when governments choose to redirect foreign policy', *International Studies Quarterly* 34/1 (1990)

—, Charles W. Kegley and James N. Rosenau (eds), *New Directions in the Study of Foreign Policy* (Boston, Mass.: George Allen and Unwin, 1987)

Holsti, K. J., *International Politics: A Framework for Analysis* (Englewood Cliffs, N.J.: Prentice/Hall International, Inc., 1982)

—, *Why Nations Realign: Foreign Policy Restructuring in the Postwar World* (London: George Allen and Unwin, 1982)

Hudson, Valerie M., Susan M. Sims and John C. Thomas, 'The domestic political context of foreign policy making', in David Skidmore and Valerie M. Hudson (eds), *The Limits of State Autonomy: Societal Groups and Foreign Policy Formulation* (Boulder, Colo., San Francisco, Calif. and Oxford: Westview Press, 1993)

Knudsen, Olav, 'Analysing small-state security', in Werner Bauwens, Armand Clesse and Olav Knudsen (eds), *Small States and the Security Challenge in the New Europe* (London and Washington, DC: Brassey's, 1996)

Muller, Harald and Thomas Risse-Kappen, 'From the outside in and from the inside out: international relations, domestic politics, and foreign policy', in David Skidmore and Valerie M. Hudson (eds), *The*

*Limits of State Autonomy: Societal Groups and Foreign Policy Formulation* (Boulder, Colo., San Francisco, Calif. and Oxford: Westview Press, 1993)

Rothstein, Robert L., *Alliances and Small Powers* (New York and London: Columbia University Press, 1968)

Skidmore, David and Valerie M. Hudson, 'Establishing the limits of state autonomy: contending approaches to the study of state–society relations and foreign policy-making', in David Skidmore and Valerie M. Hudson (eds), *The Limits of State Autonomy: Societal Groups and Foreign Policy Formulation* (Boulder, Colo., San Francisco, Calif. and Oxford: Westview Press, 1993)

Walker, Stephen G., *Role Theory and Foreign Policy Analysis* (Durham, N.C.: Duke University Press, 1987)

Walt, Stephen M., *The Origins of Alliances* (Ithaca, N.Y. and London: Cornell University Press, 1987)

Waltz, Kenneth, *Theory of International Politics* (Reading, Mass: Addison-Wesley, 1979)

## Central Asian and Tajik History

Allworth, Edward, *The Modern Uzbeks: From the Fourteenth Century to the Present. A Cultural History* (Stanford, Calif.: Stanford University, Hoover Institution Press, 1990)

Asimov, M. (ed.), *Tadzhikskaya Sovetskaya Sotsialisticheskaya Respublika* (Dushanbe: Glavnaya nauchnaya redaktsiya Tadzhikskoi sovetskoi entsiklopedii, 1984)

Bakhovadin, Aloviddin and Khursed Dodikhudoev, 'Tajikistan's geopolitical landmarks', *Central Asia and the Caucasus* 1/31 (2005)

Barthold, V., *Four Studies on the History of Central Asia, Vol. II: Ulugh Beg* (Leiden: E. J. Brill, 1958)

Barthold, V. V., *Turkestan Down to the Mongol Invasion* (London: Oxford University Press, 1928)

Becker, Seymour, *Russia's Protectorates in Central Asia: Bukhara and Khiva, 1865–1924* (Cambridge, Mass.: Harvard University Press, 1968)

Bennigsen, Alexandre and S. Enders Wimbush, *Muslims of the Soviet Empire* (Bloomington, Ind.: Indiana University Press, 1986)

Bennigsen, Alexandre, Paul B. Henze, George K. Tanham and S. Enders Wimbush, *Soviet Strategy and Islam* (London: Macmillan, 1989)

Carrère d'Encausse, Hélène, *Islam and the Russian Empire: Reform and Revolution in Central Asia* (London: I. B. Tauris, 1988)

*Central Asia in the Kushan Period: Proceedings of the International Conference,* *Vols I and II* (Moscow: Izdatel'stvo 'Nauka', 1975)

Dawisha, Karen and Helène Carrère d'Encausse, 'Islam in the foreign policy of the Soviet Union: a double-edged sword', in Adeed Dawisha (ed.), *Islam in Foreign Policy* (Cambridge: Cambridge University Press, 1983)

Ewans, Martin, *Afghanistan: A Short History of Its People and Politics* (New York: Perennial, 2002)

Gafurov, B., *Tadzhiki: Drevneishaya, drevnyaya i srednevekovaya istoriya, kniga I i II* (Dushanbe: 'Irfon', 1989)

—, *Tadzhiki: Istoriya tadzhikskogo naroda, Tom 1. S drevneiskhikh vremen do V v.n.e.* (Moscow: Izd. Vostochnoi literatury, 1965)

Gibb, H. A. R., *The Arab Conquests in Central Asia* (London: Royal Asiatic Society, 1923)

Hitti, Philip K., *History of the Arabs: From the Earliest Times to the Present* (London: Macmillan, 1951)

Holt, Frank, *Alexander the Great and Bactria: The Formation of a Greek Frontier in Central Asia* (Leiden: E. J. Brill, 1988)

Ignatiev, A. V. et al. (eds), *Istoriya vneshnei politiki Rossii: Vtoraya polovina XIX veka* (Moscow: Mezhdunarodnye otnosheniya, 1997)

*Istoriya tadzhikskogo naroda, Tom I* (eds B. G. Gafurov and B. A. Litvinskii); and *Tom II* (eds B. G. Gafurov and A. M. Belenitskii (Moskva: Izdatel'stvo vostochnoi literatury, 1964 and 1965)

Keller, Shoshana, *To Moscow, Not Mecca: The Soviet Campaign Against Islam in Central Asia, 1917–1941* (Westport, Conn. and London: Praeger, 2001)

Khalfin, N. A., *Politika Rossii v Srednei Azii (1857–1868)* (Moscow: Izdatel'stvo vostochnoi literatury, 1960)

Khotamov, Namoz, *Sverzhenie emirskogo rezhima v Bukhare* (Dushanbe: Akademiya nauk Respubliki Tadzhikistan, 1997)

von Kugelgen, Anke, Michael Kemper and Allen J. Frank, *Muslim Culture in Russia and Central Asia from the 18th to the Early 20th Centuries, Vol. 2* (Berlin: Klaus Schwarz Verlag, 1998)

Library of Congress. 'Afghanistan', Library of Congress Country Studies, http://lcweb2.loc.gov/cgi-bin/query/r?frd/cstdy:@field(DOCID+af0038)

Litvinskii, B. A. and V. A. Ranov (eds), *Istoriya tadzhikskogo naroda, Tom 1: Drevneishaya i drevnyaya istoriya* (Dushanbe: Akademiya nauk Respubliki Tadzhikistan, 1998)

Maley, William, *The Afghanistan Wars* (Hampshire and New York: Palgrave Macmillan, 2002)

Mamadazimov, Abdugani, *Novyi Tadzhikistan: Voprosy stanovleniya suvereniteta* (Dushanbe: Donish, 1996)

—, *Politicheskaya istoriya tadzhikskogo naroda* (Dushanbe: 2000)

Masov, Rakhim, *Istoriya topornogo razdeleniya* (Dushanbe: 'Irfon', 1991)

—, *Tadzhiki: vytesnenie i assimilatsiya* (Dushanbe, 2003)

Nazarov, Khaknazar, *K istorii proiskhozhdeniya i rasseleniya plemen i narodov Tsentral'noi Azii* (Dushanbe, 2004)

Negmatov, Numon, *Tadzhikskii fenomen: teoriya i istoriya* (Dushanbe, 1997)

Pierce, Richard, *Russian Central Asia 1867–1917: A Study in Colonial Rule* (Berkeley, Calif. and Los Angeles, Calif.: University of California Press, 1960)

Pirumshoev, Khaidarso, *Rossiisko-sredneaziatskie otnosheniya XV–serediny XIX vekov v Russkoi istoriografii* (Dushanbe: Akademiya nauk Respubliki Tadzhikistan/Izdatel'stvo Maolif, 2000)

Rakhmonov, Emomali, *The Tajiks in the Mirror of History, Vol. 1: From the Aryans to the Samanids* (London: River Editions Ltd, Great Britain, no date)

Shishov, A., *Tadzhiki: Etnograficheskoe i antropologicheskoe issledovanie* (Tashkent, 1910)

Shukorov, Sharif, *Tadzhiki: Opyt natsional'nogo avtoportreta* (Dushanbe, 1993)

Sidky, H., *The Greek Kingdom of Bactria: From Alexander to Eucratides the Great* (Lanham, Md., New York and Oxford: University Press of America, 2000)

Soucek, Svat, *A History of Inner Asia* (Cambridge: Cambridge University Press, 2000)

Vainberg, B. N. and B. Ya. Stavinskii, *Istoriya i kultura Srednei Azii v drevnosti* (Moscow, 1964)

Whitlock, Monica, *Beyond the Oxus: The Central Asians* (London: John Murray, 2002)

## Contemporary Central Asia

Akimbekov, S. M., *Afganskii uzel i problemy bezopasnosti Tsentral'noi Azii* (Almaty: Kontinent, 2003)

Allison, Roy, 'Regionalism, regional structures and security management in Central Asia', *International Affairs* (London) 80/3 (May 2004)

—, 'Structures and frameworks for security policy cooperation in Central Asia', in Roy Allison and Lena Jonson (eds), *Central Asian Security: The New International Context* (London and Washington, DC: Royal

Institute of International Affairs and Brookings Institution Press, 2001)

— and Lena Jonson (eds), *Central Asian Security: The New International Context* (London and Washington, DC: Royal Institute of International Affairs and Brookings Institution Press, 2001)

Babadzhanov, Bakhtiar, 'Islam in Uzbekistan: from the struggle for "religious purity" to political activism', in Boris Rumer (ed.), *Central Asia: A Gathering Storm?* (New York and London: M. E. Sharpe, 2002)

Bremmer, Ian and Ray Taras (eds), *Nation and Politics in the Soviet Successor States* (Cambridge: Cambridge University Press, 1993)

Collins, Kathleen, 'Clans, pacts, and politics in Central Asia', *Journal of Democracy* 13/3 (2002)

Cornell, Svante E., 'The interaction of narcotics and conflict', *Journal of Peace Research* 42/6 (2005)

Cummings, Sally N. (ed.), *Oil, Transition and Security in Central Asia* (London and New York: Routledge Curzon, 2003)

Ferghana Valley Working Group, *Calming the Ferghana Valley: Development and Dialogue in the Heart of Central Asia. Report of the Ferghana Valley Working Group* (New York: Century Foundation Press, 1999)

Foltz, Richard, 'Uzbekistan's Tajiks: a case of repressed identity', *Central Asia Monitor* 6 (1996)

Fuller, Graham E., 'The impact of Central Asia on the "New Middle East"', in David Menashri (ed.), *Central Asia Meets the Middle East* (London and Portland, Or.: Frank Cass, 1998)

Horsman, Stuart, 'Water in Central Asia: regional cooperation or conflict?', in Roy Allison and Lena Jonson (eds), *Central Asian Security: The New International Context* (London and Washington, DC: Royal Institute of International Affairs and Brookings Institution Press, 2001)

Hunter, Shireen T., *Islam in Russia: The Politics of Identity and Security* (Armonk and London: M. E. Sharpe, 2004)

Jonson, Lena, 'Central Asia and the "Greater Middle East"', in Bo Hult, Tomas Ries, Jan Mörtberg and Johanna Sandefelt (eds), *Strategic Yearbook 2005: The Wider Middle East* (Stockholm: Swedish National War College, 2005)

—, *Vladimir Putin and Central Asia: The Shaping of Russian Foreign Policy* (London and New York: I. B. Tauris, 2004)

— and Roy Allison, 'Internal and external dynamics', in Roy Allison and Lena Jonson (eds), *Central Asian Security: The New International Context* (London and Washington, DC: Royal Institute of International Affairs and Brookings Institution Press, 2001)

— and Murad Esenov (eds), *Political Islam and Conflicts in Russia and Central Asia* (Stockholm: Swedish Institute of International Affairs, 1999)

Jones Luong, Pauline and Erika Weinthal, 'New friends, new fears in Central Asia', *Foreign Affairs* 81/2 (March/April 2002)

Karayanni, Marika S., 'Russia's foreign policy for Central Asia passes through energy agreements', *Central Asia and the Caucasus* 4 (2003)

Khamadov, Sultan, 'Mezhdunarodnyi kontekst: afganskii faktor', in Organization for Security and Co-operation in Europe (OSCE), Mission to Tajikistan, *Religioznyi ekstremizm v Tsentral'noi Azii: Materialy konferentsii, Dushanbe, 25 aprelya 2002* (Dushanbe: OSCE Mission to Tajikistan, 2002)

MacFarlane, S. Neil, 'The United States and regionalism in Central Asia', *International Affairs* 80/3 (May 2004), pp. 447–61

Malashenko, Alexei, 'Islam in Central Asia', in Roy Allison and Lena Jonson (eds), *Central Asian Security: The New International Context* (London and Washington, DC: Royal Institute of International Affairs and Brookings Institution Press, 2001)

—, 'Islam and politics in Central Asian States', in Lena Jonson and Murad Esenov (eds), *Political Islam and Conflicts in Russia and Central Asia* (Stockholm: Swedish Institute of International Affairs, 1999)

Melvin, Neil, *Uzbekistan: Transition to Authoritarianism on the Silk Road* (Amsterdam: Harwood Academic Publishers, 2000)

Menashri, David (ed.), *Central Asia Meets the Middle East* (London and Portland, Or.: Frank Cass, 1998)

Mesbahi, Mohiaddin (ed.), *Central Asia and the Caucasus after the Soviet Union* (Gainsville, Fl.: University Press of Florida, 1996)

Muminov, Ashirbek, 'Traditsionnye i sovremennye religiozno-teologicheskie shkoly v Tsentral'noi Azii', *Tsentral'naya Aziya i Kavkaz* 4/5 (1999)

Olcott, Martha Brill, 'Common legacies and conflicts', in Roy Allison and Lena Jonson (eds), *Central Asian Security: The New International Context* (London and Washington, DC: Royal Institute of International Affairs and Brookings Institution Press, 2001)

—, 'Shifting sands in Central Asia?', *Helsinki Monitor* 1 (2003)

— and Alexei Malashenko (eds), *Mnogomernye granitsy Tsentral'noi Azii* (Moscow: Carnegie Centre, 2000), electronic version, http://pubs.carnegie.ru/books/2000/04am

Olimova, Saodat, 'Natsiona'lnye gosudarstva i etnicheskie territorii', in Martha Brill Olcott and Alexei Malashenko (eds), *Mnogomernye granitsy*

*Tsentral'noi Azii* (Moscow: Carnegie Centre, 2000), electronic version, http://pubs.carnegie.ru/books/2000/04am

—, 'Ob obshchestvennom vospriyatii umerennogo i radikal'nogo islama', in A. Seifert and Anna Kreikemeier (eds), *O sovmestimosti politicheskogo islama i bezopasnosti prostranstve OBSE* (Dushanbe: Sharki Ozod, 2003)

Organization for Security and Co-operation in Europe (OSCE), Mission to Tajikistan, *Religioznyi ekstremizm v Tsentral'noi Azii: Problemy i perspektivy. Materialy konferentsii, Dushanbe, 25 aprelya 2002* (Dushanbe: OSCE Mission to Tajikistan, 2002)

*Postsovetskaya Tsentral'naya Aziya: Poteri i obreteniya* (Moscow: 'Vostochnaya literatura', RAN, 1998)

Rashid, Ahmed, *Jihad: The Rise of Militant Islam in Central Asia* (New Haven, Conn. and London: Yale University Press, 2002)

Roy, Olivier, *The New Central Asia: The Creation of Nations* (New York: New York University Press, 2000)

Rumer, Boris (ed.), *Central Asia: A Gathering Storm?* (New York and London: M. E. Sharpe, 2002)

Saikal, Amin, 'Russia and Central Asia', in Amin Saikal and William Maley (eds), *Russia in Search of its Future* (Cambridge: Cambridge University Press, 1995)

Seifert, A. and Anna Kreikemeier (eds), *O sovmestimosti politicheskogo islama i bezopasnosti prostranstve OBSE* (Dushanbe: Sharki Ozod, 2003)

Sengupta, Anita, *The Formation of the Uzbek Nation State: A Study in Transition* (Lanham, Md., Boulder, Colo., New York, Toronto and Oxford: Lexington Books, 2003)

Taji-Farouki, Suha, *A Fundamental Quest: Hizb-al-Tahrir and the Search for the Islamic Caliphate* (London: Grey Seal, 1996)

Whitlock, Monica, *Beyond the Oxus: The Central Asians* (London: John Murray, 2002)

## Contemporary Tajikistan: Politics, Society and Economics

Abazov, Rafis, 'Independent Tajikistan: ten lost years', in Sally N. Cummings (ed.), *Oil, Transition and Security in Central Asia* (London and New York: Routledge Curzon, 2003)

Abdullaev, Kamoludin and Catherine Barnes (eds), *Politics of Compromise: The Tajikistan Peace Process* (London: Accord Conciliation Resources, 2001, Issue 10, 2001)

Abdullo, Rashid G., 'Implementation of the 1997 General Agreement: successes, dilemmas and changes', in Kamoludin Abdullaev and

Catherine Barnes (eds), *Politics of Compromise: The Tajikistan Peace Process* (London: Accord Conciliation Resources, 2001, Issue 10, 2001)

Akbarzadeh, Shahram, 'Abdullajanov and the "third force"', in Kamoludin Abdullaev and Catherine Barnes (eds), *Politics of Compromise: The Tajikistan Peace Process* (London: Accord Conciliation Resources, 2001, Issue 10, 2001).

Akiner, Shirin, *Tajikistan: Disintegration or Reconciliation?* (London: Royal Institute of International Affairs, 2001)

Atkin, Muriel, 'Tajikistan: ancient heritage, new politics', in Ian Bremmer and Ray Taras (eds), *Nation and Politics in the Soviet Successor States* (Cambridge: Cambridge University Press, 1993)

Bakhovadin, Aloviddin and Khursed Dodikhudoev, 'Tajikistan's geopolitical landmarks', *Central Asia and the Caucasus* 1/31 (2005)

Bushkov, V. I. and D. V. Mikulskii, *Anatomiya grazhdanskoi voiny v Tadzhikistane (etno-sotsial'nye protsessy i politicheskaya bor'ba, 1992–1995* (Moscow, 1995)

Bushkov, V. I. and D. V. Mikulskii, *Istoriya grazhdanskoi voiny v Tadzhikistane* (Moscow: Institut etnologii i antropologii, RAN, 1996)

*Country Profile 2004 Tajikistan* (London: Economist Intelligence Unit, 2004)

Dadabaeva, Z. A., *Tadzhikistan: mezhdunarodnye otnosheniya v period transformatsii obshchestva* (Dushanbe: Akademiya nauk Respubliki Tadzhikistan, 2000)

Djalili, Mohammad-Reza, Frederic Grare and Shirin Akiner (eds), *Tajikistan: The Trials of Independence* (Richmond: Curzon Press, 1998)

*Ezhegodnik Respubliki Tadzhikistan 2003* (Dushanbe: Gosudarstvennyi Komitet Statistiki Respubliki Tadzhikistan, 2003)

Foroughi, Payam, 'Hope and despair: an assessment of returnee households in Khatlon region of Tajikistan', UNHCR, Dushanbe, 1998

—, 'Tajikistan: nationalism, ethnicity, conflict, and socio-economic disparities. Sources and solutions', *Journal of Muslim Minority Affairs* 22/1 (2002)

Goibov, Gholib, 'Stroitel'stvo svetskogo kharaktera obshchestva i ustanovlenie otnosheniya religioznoi terpimosti v Tadzhikistane', in Organization for Security and Co-operation in Europe (OSCE), Mission to Tajikistan, *Religioznyi ekstremizm v Tsentral'noi Azii: Problemy i perspektivy. Materialy konferentsii, Dushanbe, 25 aprelya 2002* (Dushanbe: OSCE Mission to Tajikistan, 2002)

Gretsky, Sergei, 'Civil war in Tajikistan: causes, developments, and prospects for peace', in Roald Sagdeev and Susan Eisenhower (eds),

*Central Asia: Conflict, Resolution, and Change* (Chevy Chase, Md.: CPSS, 1995)

International Crisis Group (ICG), 'Tajikistan's politics: confrontation or consolidation?', ICG, Dushanbe and Brussels, 19 May 2004

Jonson, Lena, *The Tajik War: A Challenge to Russian Policy*, Discussion Paper 74 (London: Royal Institute of International Affairs, 1998)

—, 'The OSCE Long-Term Mission to Tajikistan', in *OSCE Yearbook 2002* (Baden-Baden: Nomos Verlagsgesellschaft, 2002

International Monetary Fund, *Republic of Tajikistan: Poverty Reduction Strategy Paper Progress Report*, IMF Country Report 04/280 (August 2004), http://www.imf.org/external/pubs/ft/scr/2004/cr04280.pdf

Khrustalev, Mark, *Grazhdanskaya voina v Tadzhikistane: istoki i perspektivy* (Moscow: TsMI, MGIMO, no. 11, 1997)

Kreikemeyer, Anna and Arne Seifert (eds), *Zur Vereinbarkeit von politischem Islam und Sicherheit im OSZE-Raum: Dokumente eines islamisch-säkularen Dialogs in Tadschikistan* (Baden-Baden: Nomos Verlagsgesellschaft, 2002/2003)

Kuzmin, A. I., 'Tadzhikistan: Prichiny i uroki grazhdanskoi voiny', in *Postsovetskaya Tsentral'naya Aziya: Poteri i obreteniya* (Moscow: 'Vostochnaya literatura', RAN, 1998)

Martino, Luigi (ed.), *Tadzhikistan: optimizatsiya otnoshenii mezhdu tsentrom i regionam: vyzovy i vozmozhnosti* (Geneva: CIMERA, January 2004)

Mukhabbatov, Kurbonali, 'Religiozno-oppozitsionnye gruppy v Tadzhikistane: Hizb-ut-Tahrir', in Organization for Security and Co-operation in Europe (OSCE), Mission to Tajikistan, *Religioznyi ekstremizm v Tsentral'noi Azii: Problemy i perspektivy. Materialy konferentsii, Dushanbe, 25 aprelya 2002* (Dushanbe: OSCE Mission to Tajikistan, 2002)

Nauchno-Issledovatelskii Tsentr Sharq, *Opros obshchestvennogo mneniya v Tadzhikistane (4–17 Dekabr 2003 g.)* (Dushanbe: Nauchno-Issledovatelskii Tsentr Sharq, 2003)

—, *Opros obshchestvennogo mneniya v Tadzhikistane (3–16 maya 2004 g.)* (Dushanbe: Nauchno-Issledovatelskii Tsentr Sharq, 2004)

—, *Opros obshchestvennogo mneniya v Tadzhikistane (20 sentyabrya–3 oktyabrya 2004 g.)* (Dushanbe: Nauchno-Issledovatelskii tsentr Sharq, 2004)

—, *Opros obshchestvennogo mneniya v Tadzhikistane (mai 2005)* (Dushanbe: Nauchno-Issledovatelskii Tsentr Sharq, 2005)

Neumann, I. and S. Solodovnik, 'The case of Tajikistan', in Lena Jonson and Clive Archer (eds), *Peacekeeping and the Role of Russia in Eurasia* (Boulder, Colo.: Westview Press, 1996)

Niyazi, Aziz, 'Tajikistan', in Mohiaddin Mesbahi (ed.), *Central Asia and the Caucasus after the Soviet Union* (Gainsville, Fl.: University Press of Florida, 1996)

Olimova, Saodat, 'Dukhovnye lidery v sovremennom musul'manskom obshchestve Tsentral'noi Azii: Opyt Tadzhikistana', in *Musul'manskie lidery: sotsial'naya rol' i avtoritet* (Dushanbe: Nauchno-issledovatelskii Tsentr Sharq i Fond im. Fridrikha Eberta, 2003)

——, 'Political Islam and conflict in Tajikistan', in Lena Jonson and Murad Esenov (eds), *Political Islam and Conflicts in Russia and Central Asia* (Stockholm: Swedish Institute of International Afffairs, 1999)

——, 'Political parties in Tajikistan: Facts, figures, analysis' (manuscript prepared by the Sharq independent research institute for IFES (formerly the International Foundation for Election Systems), Dushanbe, 2005)

——, 'Vospriyatie yavleniya "regionalizm" osnovnymi politicheskimi salami v Tadzhikistane', in Luigi Martino (ed.), *Tadzhikistan: optimizatsiya otnoshenii mezhdu tsentrom i regionam: vyzovy i vozmozhnosti* (Geneva: CIMERA, January 2004)

*Regiony Respubliki Tadzhikistana: Statisticheskii Sbornik* (Dushanbe: Gosudarstvennyi Komitet Statistiki Respubliki Tadzhikistan, 2004)

Rotar, Igor, 'Tajikistan: religious freedom survey, November 2003', F18News, 20 November 2003, http://www.forum18.org/Archive.php?article_id=190

Roy, Olivier, *The Civil War in Tajikistan: Causes and Implications* (Washington, DC: United States Institute of Peace, 1993)

Sagdeev, Roald and Susan Eisenhower (eds), *Central Asia: Conflict, Resolution, and Change* (Chevy Chase, Md.: CPSS, 1995)

Saidov, Zafar, *Politika otkrytykh dverei* (Dushanbe: 'Sharki Ozod', 2003)

——, *Vneshnyaya politika prezidenta Rakhmonova* (Dushanbe: Izdatel'stvo 'Avasto', 2000)

Seifert, Arne, 'OSCE longterm mission to Tajikistan', in *OSCE Yearbook 1998: Yearbook of the Organization on Security and Cooperation in Europe* (Baden-Baden: Nomos Verlagsgesellschaft, 1999)

Shozimov, Pulat, 'Tajikistan: cultural heritage and the identity issue', *Central Asia and the Caucasus* (Umeå), 6 (2005)

de Soto, Hermine, Sabine Beddies and Svetlana Sharipova, 'Social dimensions of regional differences in Tajikistan' (draft Concept Paper), Social Development Unit, ECSS, World Bank, 6 April 2004

Tetsuro, Iji, 'Cooperation, coordination, and complementarity in international peacekeeping: the Tajikistan experience', *International Peacekeeping* 12/2 (June 2005)

US Department of State, 'Country assessment Tajikistan', http://www.state.gov/p/eur/rls/rpt/23626.htm

*Tajikistan: Country Report, March 2004* (London: Economist Intelligence Unit, 2004)

*Tajikistan: Country Report 2005* (London: Economist Intelligence Unit, 2005)

*Vneshneekonomicheskaya deyatelnost' respubliki Tadzhikistan: Statisticheskii sbornik* (Dushanbe: Gosudarstvennyi Komitet Statistiki Respubliki Tadzhikistan, 2004)

Zoir [Zoirov], Rahmatullo and Scott Newton, 'Constitutional and legal reform', in Kamoludin Abdullaev and Catherine Barnes (eds), *Politics of Compromise: The Tajikistan Peace Process* (London: Accord Conciliation Resources, 2001, Issue 10, 2001)

## News Agencies and Web Sites Most Frequently Consulted

Asia-Plus (Dushanbe)

Avesta (Dushanbe)

BBC Monitoring, *Inside Central Asia*

*Biznes i politika* (Dushanbe)

Centrasia .... http://www.CentrAsia.Ru

*Eurasia Insight*

*Interfax*

*Jamestown Monitor*

Radio Free Europe/Liberty (RFE/RFL), *RFE/RL Newsline* and *Central Asia Report*

# INDEX